THE LAND OF CHARITY

THE LAND OF CHARITY

A DISCRIPTIVE ACCOUNT OF

TRAVANCORE AND ITS PEOPLE

WITH ESPECIAL REFERENCE TO MISSIONARY LABOUR

BY THE

REV. SAMUEL MATEER, F. L.S.

OF THE LONDON MISSIONARY SOCIETY

GYAN

Published by

Gyan Publishing House
5, Ansari Road
Daryaganj, New Delhi-110002
Phone: 011-47034999, 9811692060
E-mail: books@gyanbooks.com

Distribution Network
gyanbooks.com
India, USA, Canada, UK, Australia, France

ISBN : 978-81-212-3677-5 (PB)
First Published, 1871

2nd Impression 2020

Printed at: Gyan Press, Delhi.

The book at your disposal is the edition of an old book originally published long back. The Text quality of this book may not be at par as compared to our other books but many readers approached us to reprint this important book so that it could satiate their hunger. We request all the readers of this book to help us to improve its quality by providing the necessary text of those pages which are not properly visible. Your valuable support in this case will be highly appreciated and acknowledged and our future readers will be benefitted immensely.

"THE LAND OF CHARITY:"

A DESCRIPTIVE ACCOUNT OF

TRAVANCORE AND ITS PEOPLE.

WITH ESPECIAL REFERENCE TO MISSIONARY LABOUR

BY THE

REV. SAMUEL MATEER, F.L.S.,

OF THE LONDON MISSIONARY SOCIETY.

VIEW OF SEA-COAST FROM MUTTAM.

LONDON
JOHN SNOW AND CO.,
2, IVY LANE, PATERNOSTER ROW.
1871.

DEVIL DANCER, WITH INSTRUMENTS AND OFFERINGS.

PREFACE.

A POPULAR, comprehensive work upon Travancore and Missionary operations in that territory, for the use of missionaries and students and the friends of missions at home, has long been felt to be a desideratum. During a residence of over nine years in India wholly occupied in vernacular labours amongst the natives, and constantly enjoying as close familiar intercourse with them as is possible for a European, the writer continued, both as a matter of duty and of pleasure, to collect information of all kinds about the country and people, and several years ago sketched out the plan of this work.

Having conceived, however, a high ideal of the excellence, both in substance and style, which ought to characterize a work produced by a competent and graphic pen on a subject so extensive and so interesting in every aspect, he waited for other and abler hands to undertake the duty, and repeatedly expressed his surprise that this had not been done.

In his frequent tours during the last two years in Great Britain and Ireland, lecturing and preaching on behalf of the London Missionary Society, receiving everywhere the kindest hospitality, and enjoying Christian intercourse with many friends of the Society, he has had special opportunities of learning what kind of information is wanted by the supporters of our Indian missions; and this he has attempted to supply in the present volume. Nearly the whole of the multitudinous questions which are naturally put to an Indian missionary are here answered. Ministers and other friends at home ask their missionaries to give them *facts*. Here is what might be called a Handbook of Travancore—a compendium of facts grouped, classified, and arranged for convenient reference.

Works on India are sometimes full of misstatements and error, generally arising, in such cases, from insufficient acquaintance with the native languages and customs. Throughout this work we have aimed at special accuracy in every assertion that has been made, and at giving a fair, unvarnished statement of both sides of every question. Intelligent readers can thus form their own conclusions. These facts can also be adduced and enlarged upon by preachers and public lecturers. They will be found, we think, powerfully to illustrate the moral guilt and spiritual wretchedness of the heathen, their urgent need of the Gospel of Christ, the converting and renewing power of Divine grace, and the bright prospects already opening up of the complete and final triumph of Christian truth in India.

The circumstances of the *young*, and of general readers who may not have had time or opportunity for studying many works on India, have been borne in mind; and the attempt has been made to explain everything very simply and clearly, without taking for granted the possession of much special knowledge on the part of our readers. In order to bring the matter at our disposal within as small a compass as possible, and to furnish a cheap illustrated volume for wide popular distribution and perusal, suitable for placing in Sunday school and Congregational libraries, &c., we have condensed our remarks, and for the most part omitted practical observations and the discussion of principles which otherwise would have found place in such a work, but would have made it much larger and more expensive.

Where Indian customs appear to throw light, either directly or indirectly, upon Holy Scripture, the passages have been suggested for comparison, examination, and inquiry.

In the statistical chapters and in the history of our Mission I have, where necessary, freely compiled from the annual Reports of the various missionaries (including my own); the Selections from the Government records of Travancore; and the Dewān's Reports of the Administration, with copies of which I have been favoured by that statesman. Other works, a list of which is subjoined, have also been consulted and used to a greater or less extent. Still it would only appear pedantic and cumbersome to give formal references to volume and page of each minor quotation or allusion.

My best thanks are due to the Rev. R. Robinson, Home Secretary, London Missionary Society, for the use of a number of woodcuts; and to the Rev. C. C. Fenn, M.A., Secretary, Church Missionary Society, for the use of two engravings for the illustration of this volume.

It is, of course, possible that, notwithstanding all the care that has been taken, errors may have crept in. Should a second edition be required, we shall be happy to avail ourselves of any further information, corrections, or suggestions which may tend to render the book more complete or useful.

Indian words, some of them rather formidable in length and appearance, must of necessity occur. To assist our readers in their pronunciation, please observe that—

â is pronounced like *a* in father.
î „ „ „ *ee*, or like *i* in pique.
ai or *ei* „ „ *eye*, or English *i*.
u generally „ „ *oo* in food.
e „ „ „ *a* in fate.
a often „ „ *u* in drum, or *a* in avoid.

If such terms are otherwise pronounced like English words, a sufficiently accurate approximation to the true pronunciation will be made.

May that one true and living God, whose kingdom and the saving knowledge of whose Son we humbly seek to extend, grant that this little work may be of some service in exciting, reviving, and nourishing a more intelligent and prayerful interest in the great work of Christian missions! S. M.

LONDON, *29th November*, 1870.

PRINCIPAL WORKS REFERRED TO.

Madras Journal of Literature and Science.
Fra Bartolomeo's Voyage to the East Indies. London, 1800.
The Tinnevelly Shânars ... ... *Caldwell.* London, 1850.
Comparative Grammar of the Drâvidian Languages ... ... *Caldwell.* London, 1856.
Missionary Life and Labours of Xavier ... *Venn.* London, 1862.
The Land of the Permauls, or Cochin ... *Day.* Madras, 1863.
The Useful Plants of India ... ... *Drury.* Trevandrum, 1858.
Popular Description of the Palmyra Palm... *Ferguson.* Colombo, 1850.
The Christians of St. Thomas and their Liturgies ... ... *Howard.* Oxford, 1864.
The Syrian Christians of Malabar...*Philipos and Howard.* Oxford, 1869.
The Tulâpurushadânam, by a Travancorean ... ... Trevandrum, 1870.
&c., &c.

CONTENTS.

PAGE

CHAPTER I.

GEOGRAPHICAL SKETCH OF TRAVANCORE 1

CHAPTER II.

SUMMARY OF THE HISTORY OF TRAVANCORE 13

CHAPTER III.

THE PEOPLE—THEIR MANNERS AND CUSTOMS 25

CHAPTER IV.

MANNERS AND CUSTOMS (CONTINUED) 51

CHAPTER V.

THE NATIVE GOVERNMENT 66

CHAPTER VI.

NATURAL HISTORY 76

CHAPTER VII.

NATURAL HISTORY (CONTINUED) 93

CHAPTER VIII.

INDUSTRY AND COMMERCE 104

CHAPTER IX.

AGRICULTURE 115

CHAPTER X.

VERNACULAR LANGUAGES 128

CHAPTER XI.

LITERATURE AND POPULAR EDUCATION 141

CHAPTER XII.

HINDUISM IN TRAVANCORE 158

CHAPTER XIII.

HINDUISM (CONTINUED) 176

CHAPTER XIV.

DEVIL-WORSHIP 189

CHAPTER XV.

DEVIL-WORSHIP (CONTINUED) 213

CHAPTER XVI.

NATIVE MOHAMMEDANS 227

CHAPTER XVII.

NATIVE ROMAN CATHOLICS 230

CHAPTER XVIII.

THE SYRIAN CHRISTIANS OF MALABAR 236

CHAPTER XIX.

THE CHURCH MISSION IN TRAVANCORE 253

CHAPTER XX.

ESTABLISHMENT AND EARLY HISTORY OF THE LONDON MISSION IN TRAVANCORE 257

CHAPTER XXI.

EXTENSION AND PROGRESS OF THE MISSION 283

CHAPTER XXII.

RECENT HISTORY OF THE MISSION 295

CHAPTER XXIII.

MISSIONARY OPERATIONS, AND THEIR INDIRECT RESULTS . . 320

CHAPTER XXIV.

DIRECT RESULTS OF MISSIONARY LABOURS IN TRAVANCORE . . 350

LIST OF ILLUSTRATIONS.

Devil-dancer of Travancore	*Frontispiece*
View of Sea-coast from Muttam	*Vignette*
	PAGE
The Western Ghauts from Calcaud	5
Namburi Brahmins	30
The Reading-room at Kottār	53
Native Ear Ornament	59
The Rajah, First Prince, and Dewān of Travancore	*face* 69
Serpent Idol	88
Travancore Boatman	107
Native Coins and Chuckram Board	110
Palm-leaf Letter and Writing Implements	122
Palmyra Trees and Climbers	124
Native Chapel, Teacher's House, and Schools	140
Patmanābhan, the National Deity of Travancore	*face* 160
Courtyard of Trevandrum Temple	163
Karunkāli and Mallan	196
Pattirakāli	198
Veerapatran	199
Paramasattee	203
Magic Charms	211
Devil Temple at Agastispuram	*face* 219
Syrian Church	241
Mission Bungalow, Nāgercoil	266
Native Lace-worker, with Pillow	272
Christian Female, with Jacket and Upper Cloth	277
Pāreychāley Mission Station.	*face* 283
Seminary at Nāgercoil	285
Neyoor Dispensary	290
Medical Missionary and Students	313
Travelling Chair	325
Village Chapel and School-house	*face* 326
Pāreychāley Evangelists	*face* 328
Rev. C. Yesudian	332

ERRATUM.

Page 68, 14th line from top, *omit* "Knight."

MAP OF TRAVANCORE
COCHIN
COIMBATOOR
DINDICUL
TINNEVELLY
76.30
77.
77.30
10.0
9.30
9.0
8.30
Paravur
Verāpoli
Eddapali
Cochin
Mavallu
Cherllala
Ellu
Cottayam
Allepey or Alappara
Tiruvallā
Pantalam
Tirukunnapura
Kāyankullam
Karunāgappalli
Pallanapuram
Shengotta
Quilon or Kollam
Madavur
Varkkala
Attungal
Anjengo or Anjutengu
Trevandrum
Neyyāttunkara
Parcychāley
Pavār
Tiruvallur
Tengapallanam
Ooda gerry
Neyoor
Nagercoil
Kolachul
Kottār
Mullam
Agastispurom
Cape Comorin
50 miles

"THE LAND OF CHARITY."

CHAPTER I.

GEOGRAPHICAL SKETCH OF TRAVANCORE.

Position and Extent of the Country—Physical Features and Scenery—Climate and Seasons—Principal Towns and Villages.

"DHARMMA BHUMI," THE LAND OF CHARITY, or PIETY, is the poetic appellation bestowed by the Brahmans on the little kingdom of Travancore, in South India. In this term allusion is made to the generous scale of expenditure adopted by this native state toward the support of the Brahman priests, and the Hindu religion and ceremonial. Travancore is a country concerning which little is known in England, or even in the more distant parts of India, yet it is one of the most beautiful, strange, and interesting provinces to be found within the limits of that great empire. The country itself, with its varied and valuable productions, and the people, their languages, customs, and extraordinary laws, afford abundant material for study and research to all who take an interest in human nature and the works of God; while the remarkable spread of Christianity in the land invests it with great additional interest to the mind of the Christian philanthropist.

Cape Comorin, the southernmost extremity—the Land's End—of the peninsula of India lies just within the southern limits of Travancore. From the Cape the province extends southwards along the Western or Malabar coast of India. It thus forms the most southerly portion of the Western coast, being somewhat similar, in this respect, to the geographical position of Cornwall relatively to Great Britain, to which county, indeed, it bears some resemblance in general outline. Travancore is, then, a long, narrow strip of territory, measuring 174 miles in extreme length, and from 30 to 75 miles in breadth, lying between the Malabar Coast and the great chain of the Western Ghauts, a noble range of mountains, which, for hundreds of miles, runs almost parallel with the Western Coast of India, and which divides Travancore from the British provinces of Tinnevelly and Dindigul. It will be observed that Travancore thus occupies a very secluded position. The high mountain barrier on the East is almost impassable; the sea forms a protection on the West; it is therefore only from the North and the extreme South that the country is easily accessible. The area of Travancore is about one-thirteenth of that of Great Britain, or nearly as large as the principality of Wales, measuring 6,371 square miles, of which about one-third is occupied by mountains.

The physical aspect of this tract of country is strikingly diversified and beautiful. On one side the lofty mountains of the Ghauts rise to a height of from 3.000 to 5,000 feet, and present a magnificent background to the lowland scenery; on the other the Indian Ocean stretches its wide expanse of waters, its restless waves breaking perpetually in rollers of white surf on the sandy coast. The country is for the most part, except in the extreme south, undulating or hilly, and slopes down from the base of the mountains to the sea. Dense forests, or thick jungles of smaller trees and brushwood, cover the uncultivated land. The hill slopes are generally cleared and planted with the jack, the mango, cashew, and other fruit-trees, or are cultivated with a variety of grains and esculent roots. The valleys and low grounds, where brooks and rivers naturally run, are carefully levelled and terraced, so as to retain the water with which they are irrigated as long as may be necessary; and here is grown the nutritious rice, which forms so large a proportion of the food of the Hindus, yielding usually two, sometimes three crops in the course of the year.

Much of the scenery of Travancore is very picturesque, from its variety, romantic grandeur, or beauty. Many are the magnificent views of hill and dale, of wooded jungle and cultivated lands—verdant rice-fields gleaming in the brilliant tropical sun like lakes of rich emerald green, belts of noble forest, and isolated masses of rock rising abruptly from the surrounding country, with the lofty mountain peaks of the Ghauts shining calm and majestic in the distance. One of the finest and most charming views I ever beheld was from the summit of one of the mountains near Cape Comorin, on the slope of which our mission has a small bungalow, used as a sanitarium for the enfeebled, and as an occasional retreat from the labour and excessive heat of the low country. To the east lay spread out the wide plains of Tinnevelly, flat and arid, on the red sandy soil of which few trees flourish save the tall Palmyra palm; westward stretched the green and undulating country of Travancore, luxuriant with exuberant vegetation; northwards the noble range of the Ghauts expanded into a mazy group—a very ocean of mountain-tops; while to the south the whole coast-line on both sides from Cape Comorin showed clearly visible. At our feet lay dense forests, some still impenetrable, the abode of numerous wild beasts. Here and there portions of this primeval forest had been cut down to make room for plantations of coffee, and there rows of coffee bushes, with their glossy green leaves and beautiful white jasmine-like flowers, clothed the acclivities with perpetual verdure; while down from the heights, over rocky precipices, through green and shady valleys and deep ravines, gushed sparkling brooks, like streams of molten silver, the sources of those larger rivers which could be seen below flowing peacefully onward to the sea, now irrigating the fertile plains in their course, but in the rainy season to be transformed into swollen, rapid, and impassable torrents.

The vignette on the title-page gives a view of the coast-line from Muttam looking southwards toward Cape Comorin, showing the cocoa palm plantations along the coast, with the southern termination of the Western Ghauts in the background. The engraving opposite shows the Western Ghauts from the Eastern, or Tinnevelly side. Calcaud is in the same latitude as Trevandrum.

From its physical conformation Travancore is literally "a land of brooks of water, of fountains and depths, that spring out of valleys and hills." Fourteen principal rivers take their rise in the mountains, and before falling into the sea spread out, more or less, over the low grounds near the coast, forming inland lakes or estuaries of irregular forms, locally called "backwaters." These "backwaters" have been united by canals running parallel with the coast, and they are thus of immense value as a means of communication between the Northern and Southern districts. Travellers may in this way pass by water from Ponāny, near Calicut, to Kolachel, a distance of not much under 200 miles. The mode of conveyance consists either of canoes hollowed out of the trunks of large trees, pushed along by two men with bamboo poles, or of "cabin boats," built somewhat like English boats, with a neat and comfortable cabin at the stern, which are propelled by from eight to fourteen rowers, according to their size. Most of the traffic is carried on these canals and back-

VIEW OF THE WESTERN GHAUTS FROM CALCAUD, TINNEVELLY.

waters, and native passengers are conveyed at marvellously low rates. The principal road in Travancore also runs nearly parallel with the coast at a few miles distance.

The climate of Travancore is by no means the hottest in India, and presents, in several respects, a marked contrast to that of the Eastern coast. The temperature is moderated by the cool sea breezes which blow every forenoon, and by the abundance of rain which falls throughout more than half of the year. The thermometer does not often rise above 92 degrees Fahrenheit, and rarely sinks lower than 64 degrees. The annual range of the thermometer is about 20 degrees, and the average temperature of the whole year about 78 degrees Fahrenheit. In the mountains the temperature of course varies, diminishing in proportion to the height of the locality.

The south-west monsoon, or periodical wind from that quarter, commencing in May or June, and continuing for six months, brings with it the vapours of the ocean, and a consequent abundant fall of rain, which is, to some extent, intercepted by the lofty mountains from the Eastern coast. The rains of the north-east monsoon in October are less copious, but are still sufficient to maintain the delightful verdure and exuberant productiveness of the vegetable kingdom. The change of seasons usually sets in with tremendous thunderstorms and violent gusts of wind. At the capital the annual fall of rain averages sixty-eight inches, but in the mountains it is much greater, and strange variations have been observed in the amount of rainfall at different points not far distant from each other.

Practically the year may be divided into five periods:—(1) *The hot season*, from February to May; (2) *the rainy season of the south-west monsoon*, in June and July; (3) an interval in August and September between the rains; (4) *the rains of the north-east monsoon*, in October and November; (5) *the cold season*, December and January.

In December and January the nights and mornings are delightfully cool and pleasant, and very little rain falls. But in February the heat increases, and plants and flowers begin to dry up and wither, in preparation for the hot season, which is to the vegetation of the tropics a season of complete rest, as winter is in more northerly regions. A few trees, however, now appear in full bloom. The rice harvest is gathered in early this month.

In March and April a few light and refreshing showers fall, just sufficient to set and bring forward the fruits on the mango trees, which ripen early in May. The temperature is now at the highest point of the whole year, and much of the smaller vegetation is shrivelled and withered. The mountaineers embrace this opportunity for destroying the old grass and brushwood in the jungles and on the hills by fire, in order to clear the way for the new growth in the approaching rainy season. These fires are often visible from a great distance on a clear night.

The rains commence about the middle of May, and are ushered in by violent storms, with thunder and lightning. Rain falls almost incessantly for about three weeks. During this period little out-of-door work or exercise can be engaged in, and books, clothing, and furniture become mouldy and saturated with damp, and, if not carefully dried, rot away or fall to pieces. The rivers are swollen, and water is now stored up in tanks to furnish a supply for agricultural irrigation. All vegetation is invigorated and springs apace, but flowers are still scarce, and insects and birds are less plentiful than at other seasons. The rainfall in May, June, and July amounts to about thirty inches.

August and September are two of the finest months in the year, and are characterized by cool, refreshing weather, green vegetation, and abundance of brilliant flowers, with animal life in all its varied forms. This is the season appointed for the popular festivities connected with the Hindu new year. In the beginning of August the second rice harvest is cut and stored, and no time is lost by the farmers in again manuring and ploughing the fields, and in sowing the seed for another crop.

The rains of the north-east monsoon commence in the middle of October, and pour down heavily for a week or more. During this month and November rain is frequent; but little falls in December. The land winds, however, prevail during November, December, and January, and, if not guarded against, produce most unpleasant symptoms and disorders, such as rheumatism, cough, and local pains. These winds travel over the miasmatic swamps and valleys inland, and bring with them the seeds of disease. At the same time jungle fever, caused by the malarious exhalations of decaying vegetable matter in the forests, prevails near the base of the mountains, where it is almost certain death to remain overnight, or without taking the greatest precautions against this terrible and mysterious disease.

While the heat in Travancore is thus greatly moderated by frequent rains, and while the climate is therefore more agreeable, it is not, probably, upon the whole, more healthful than the hotter and drier climate of the Eastern coast. The moist heat is essentially enervating and depressing, lowering the action of the heart, and producing rheumatism, diarrhœa and dysentery where there is any constitutional tendency to those diseases.

The principal towns and villages in Travancore are mostly situated within a few miles of the coast. Farther inland the population is more sparse, and the proportion of uncultivated land much greater. Few of these towns are of great importance, but as there will be occasion hereafter to refer to some of them, a few remarks respecting the principal places may be useful.

A reference to the map prefixed to this chapter will bring to notice three prominent places, viz., Cape Comorin, Trevandrum, and Quilon. So far the missions of the London Missionary Society extend; all the country north of Quilon is occupied by the Church Missionary Society.

Trevandrum is the capital of Travancore, and is the residence of the Maharajah. Here are the head-quarters of the native government, and the chief courts and offices. A fuller description of this city is given in Chapter XXI.

From Trevandrum *southwards* will be seen on the map the following places, viz.,—*Neyyāttunkara*, on the main road—a considerable inland town on the banks of a river, with a temple and royal lodge. *Oodagerry*, near to Palpanābhapuram, a fort now dismantled and useless. Within its walls are the ruins of an old chapel in which was interred D'Lannoy, a European officer to whose genius Travancore owes much of its conquests. *Kolachal*, an ancient seaport, where the Danes once had a factory and a commercial resident, and from which a considerable trade with the coast and with Ceylon is now carried on. *Kottār*, a large and very ancient market town, mentioned by Ptolemy and Pliny, and still flourishing. Near to this is *Nāgercoil*, one of the principal stations of the London Missionary Society; and *Suchindram*, with its great temple, the largest in Travancore.

Cape Comorin is one of "the five renowned sacred bathing-places" to which pilgrims from all parts of India resort, though in smaller numbers now than in former times. *Quilon* is an ancient seaport town, mentioned by Marco Polo in A.D. 1295. This place is remarkable from the circumstance that the Malabar chronological era is reckoned from the traditional foundation of Quilon, the present year (1870) being the 1046th of that era.

About halfway between Trevandrum and Quilon, two places require special mention. *Anjengo*, on the sea-coast, a possession of the British Government, where a factory was established in 1684, but which was given up in 1813. It is now inhabited chiefly by a few Portuguese descendants in reduced circumstances. The remains of the old fort and several ancient monuments are worthy of examination. Here Orme the historian was born. The population is estimated at 2,000. *A'ttungal*, five miles east of Anjengo, contains a fort and palace, and constitutes, with seventeen surrounding villages, the hereditary domain of the *rānee* or eldest princess of Travancore, who formerly possessed the sovereignty of the country. In the earliest periods of the English factory at Anjengo, contracts were made with the *rānee* of A'ttungal.

North of Quilon numerous towns and villages lie scattered over the country. In most of the northern villages the houses are detached and straggling, each surrounded by its little garden and plantation of fruit-trees, cultivated for the pleasant shade and the food which they afford. On the backwater, a few miles north of Quilon, is *Kāyankollam*, a populous market town, formerly a Dutch commercial station. *Māvelikkara Fort* is about two miles in circumference; it contains a temple and the palace of a petty rajah, from whose family the present *rānees* of Travancore were adopted. *Pantalam* was once the capital of an independent principality, subjugated about a century ago. *Changanācheri* is a large market town, in which crowded fairs are held. The numerous rivers and canals maintain communication with all parts of the country.

Allepey is the chief seaport of Travancore. The produce of the forests is conveyed thither for disposal, and a large trade is carried on in timber, coir, pepper, cardamoms, &c. For the accommodation of shipping, which amounts to 74,000 tons yearly, a first-class lighthouse was erected in 1862. It is in the form of a pillar, about 100 feet in height.

The light revolves, and shows a bright flash once every minute, visible, in ordinary weather, to a distance of twenty miles. Allepey contains a very varied population, including a small proportion of Arabs, Negroes, and Malays. *Cottayam*, situated on the bank of a fine navigable stream, and in the midst of most beautiful scenery, is the principal seat of the Syrian Church, and is the head-quarters of the Church Missionary Society. *Eddapalli* is the capital of a small principality, governed by a rajah of the Nambúri Brahman caste. He is regarded as the family priest of the princes of Travancore.

The little island of *Verāpoly*, seven miles north-east of Cochin, is the head-quarters of the Roman Catholic religion in Travancore.

Parāvúr, now the largest mart of the northern districts, was once a military station. It was plundered and partly destroyed during the invasion of Tippu Sāib.

On the *eastern* side of the Ghauts lies a small but beautiful tract of territory belonging to Travancore, of which *Shencotta* is the capital. This is situated at a distance of sixty-five miles from Quilon, and is a tolerably large and compactly built town.

The total number of towns and villages in Travancore is about 3,000.

CHAPTER II.

SUMMARY OF THE HISTORY OF TRAVANCORE.

Early Traditional and Legendary History—Rise of the Kingdom in A.D. 1335, and its Advancement till 1780—Modern History—Invasion of Tippu Sāib, and Connection with the British Power.

TRAVANCORE, secluded by its geographical position, and distinguished from other parts of India by many peculiarities, has never been the scene of those great wars and schemes of ambition, nor of those displays of Oriental pomp, cruel revenge, and religious fanaticism, which occupy so large a portion of the history of India, and which have deluged its soil with blood. The history of Travancore, therefore, as distinguished from the rest of India, is not possessed of any very special interest or importance; still a brief summary of its history seems essential to the full comprehension of the present circumstances of the country. This subject naturally divides itself into—First, the mythological period. Second, the rise of the kingdom of Travancore, and its advancement to its present extent. Third, its modern history.

1. According to the legendary account contained in a celebrated Malayālim work called "Kerala Ulpatti"—the Creation of Kerala,—which professes to record the origin and history of the countries on the Western coast of India, but much of the earlier portions of which appear to be fabulous, the creation of the land on the Western coast between the mountains and the sea, anciently called Kerala, is ascribed to

Parasu Rāmen, the sixth incarnation of Vishnu. He appeared as a great warrior to destroy all the Chatriyas with their king, on account of their oppressive and wicked rule. After having gained twenty-one victories over these enemies, he retired to a mountain, and engaged in the observance of various penances and austerities to expiate the guilt of having shed blood. Here he obtained from the sea-god, Varuna, a grant of land as far in extent as the space over which he could throw his battle-axe. Exerting all his strength, he hurled the axe from Gokarnam (in N. Lat. 14° 32') to Cape Comorin, a distance of 500 miles; and the land of Kerala, which had been submerged under the ocean in a former age, again rose and was recovered from the sea. Of this country Travancore forms the southern portion.

Parasu Rāmen parcelled out the newly created land among the Brahmans whom he introduced. For their comfort and direction he made all necessary arrangements, and then departed. The Brahmans at first conducted the government on the principles of a republic, but afterwards a King or Perumāl was selected. Eighteen of these are said to have reigned for 216 years previously to the accession of the celebrated Cheramān Perumāl, the last of their number. His reign is supposed to have ended in A.D. 352. After his death the Malayālim empire was divided and portioned off among his descendants.

This legend probably refers to the conquest of the Western coast by a Brahman named Parasu Rāmen, after whose time the country was partitioned amongst his principal chiefs. From this ruler all the present rajahs and chiefs of Malabar profess to be descended, or to have received grants of land or titles. The native accounts go on to state that Cheramān Perumāl bestowed on his son, Veera Kerala, the southernmost part of his empire, lying between Quilon and Cape Comorin. This territory descended from Rajah Veera

Kerala by nephews, according to the custom of Malabar, for 300 years. From this time little is known of the history of the country. It was probably ruled over at various periods from the ninth to the twelfth century by Mysore, Madura, or Tanjore in turns, as each of these States succeeded in obtaining the ascendency.

2. The present kingdom of Travancore rose at the beginning of the fourteenth century, and advanced by degrees, by the conquest and absorption of the neighbouring states, to its present extent towards the close of the eighteenth century. The whole of the Malabar coast had been parcelled out into numerous rival states, all small and insignificant as to extent or influence, which were frequently engaged in petty warfare against each other. Nearest to Trevandrum, in the East and South, the country was divided amongst a race of subordinate chieftains called "The Chiefs of the Eight Districts." Immediately north of Quilon lay the principality of *Kāyankollam.* South and east of the great lake, *Changanācheri* and *Tekkunkúr* had their own rajahs; while *Vadakkunkúr* lay between Cochin and the mountains eastward. Still farther north were *A'langādu* and *Parāvúr.* Besides these there were a multitude of inferior states, so that it became a proverb that, "although two steps might be made on one territory, a third must pass the boundary."

The line of rulers descended from Rajah Veera Kerala, son of Cheramān Perumāl, had by this time become extinct. About A.D. 1304, two princesses, said to have been descended from Cheramān Perumāl by another wife, took up their residence in A'ttungal, and established that principality. From them were descended (or adopted, according to Hindu custom) the thirty-three sovereigns who preceded the present Rajah, and whose names are recorded in the native histories.

Veera Rāma Martānda Vurmah was the first of this line, and commenced his reign in 1335. He founded the Trevandrum fort and palace, which he made his principal residence. He was succeeded by twenty-two princes, of whom little besides the names and dates is recorded. Their rule occupied a period of 350 years. They were continually engaged in contending with the "Eight Chiefs," and had therefore little time to enter upon schemes of foreign conquest.

In 1684 Ravi Vurmah Rajah ascended the throne, after having escaped many dangers and enemies during his minority. Much of his long reign of thirty-four years was occupied in attempts to quell the turbulent spirit of his feudatories, some of whom, being unable to subdue, he treacherously assassinated in the temple at Trevandrum. The reigns of his two immediate successors, Unni Kerala Vurmah and Rāma Vurmah, were but brief, extending to six and five years respectively.

The next rajah, Vunjee Martānda Vurmah, was amongst the most successful in the subjection of his neighbours and severe in the government of his people. He received into his employment a Flemish military adventurer named D'Lannoy, and set himself to establish the power and extend the boundaries of his kingdom. The fortifications, garrisons, and arsenals at Trevandrum and other places were largely strengthened and increased, and the troops carefully disciplined. Additional customs duties were levied; a poll tax on the Shānars, a tax on the nets of the fishermen, and other rates, were imposed to defray the increased expense of the military establishment. During the lengthened reign of this prince, Kāyankollam, Tekkankúr, Vadakkankúr, Changanācheri, and other inferior states were subdued and annexed, notwithstanding the efforts of the Dutch at Cochin to restrain the advance or curtail the rising power of Travancore.

In the early part of this reign a contention arose between the Rajah and his sons on the subject of the succession to the kingdom. According to the Malabar law, *nephews* were the heirs and successors to all property and honours; but the sons of the Rajah sought to alter the law of succession in their own favour. They were aided in their ambitious schemes by several of the "eight chieftains," and by other adherents. Becoming aware of the conspiracy, the Rajah watched his opportunity, and ordered the execution of his two sons, one of whom he put to death with his own hand. Several of the minor chiefs were slain at the same time, their families sold into slavery, and their estates confiscated.

Yet this Prince was at the same time remarkable for his superstitious zeal in the service of the gods. He ever regarded the whole of his possessions as consecrated to Patmanābhan, the national deity, in whose honour he rebuilt and adorned the great temple and handsome pillared courts at Trevandrum. The splendid and costly sexennial festival, still observed by the native Rajahs, was first established in 1749 by Vunjee Martānda Vurmah. Other temples at Neyyāttunkara and elsewhere were built, and the whole expenditure of the religious establishment raised to the very liberal and even profuse scale which characterizes it at the present day. "He was," says Bartolomeo, "a man of great pride, courage, and talents, capable of undertaking great enterprises, and from his youth had been accustomed to warlike operations."

This Prince reigned for a period of twenty-nine years, and was succeeded in 1758 by Vunjee Bāla Rāma Vurmah. During his reign the authority of the petty chieftains was wholly extinguished, and he was enabled to direct his excursions northwards. By the aid of D'Launoy and an eminent native general called Martānda Pilley, the wide extent of country under the Rajahs of A'langādu and Parāvúr was subdued and annexed; and in conjunction with his ally, the Rajah of Cochin, he drove back the troops of the Zamorin of

Calicut. Thus Travancore was advanced to its present limits, and a line of fortifications, consisting of a wall and a ditch, was drawn across the whole northern military frontier. Thus, too, in the overruling providence of God, the anarchy and intestine feuds which had so long prevailed were brought to an end.

In religious enthusiasm, liberality in the erection of temples, and attention to rites and ceremonial, this Rajah imitated his uncle and predecessor. He is described as having been accomplished in Hindu literature and science, and bold and enterprising in character. He established the system of "Ootooperas," or free inns for Brahmans, in various parts of the country, and visited Rāmeeswaram and Alwāye to perform the ceremonies of bathing and sacrifice at those sacred places. Useful roads were made, and public buildings everywhere improved or rebuilt. Father Bartolomeo, a learned Romish missionary, who visited this Rajah in 1780, and knew him well, thus speaks of his appearance and habits:—"The king generally wears a turban of dark blue silk, a long white robe fastened at the breast with a string of diamonds, long wide drawers of red silk, and shoes, the points of which are bent backwards like those of the Chinese. A sabre is suspended from his shoulders, and in the blue girdle bound round his loins is stuck a poniard or Persian dagger, which can be used either for attack or defence. When he shows himself to the people in full state, he is attended by 5,000 or 6,000 men, together with a great number of palanquins and elephants. At the head of the procession is a band of musicians and two court poets, who celebrate in songs his great achievements. He is borne in a palanquin, and the principal gentlemen of his court must walk on each side of it. He is an affable, polite, and friendly man. It is the more to be lamented that he is so zealously attached to idolatry."

3. Travancore had now reached the acme of its political

power and extent, and at this period commenced its connection with the British power as an ally and tributary state. This occurred during the reign of Vunjee Bāla Rāma Vurmah Rajah, last mentioned. He had been a conqueror and spoiler of nations, and now his own turn came to be the object of the aggressions and spoliation of a mightier than himself.

Tippu Sāib, Sultan of Mysore, was the son and successor of Hyder Ali, who had risen from the ranks of the Mysore army by his military genius, and usurped the supreme power. Many of the kingdoms of Malabar had been conquered by Hyder or by Tippu, and fiendish cruelties perpetrated on the defenceless inhabitants. They seized the native princes, many of whom were starved in prison. Brahmans were forcibly circumcised and compelled to eat beef in order to destroy their caste; others committed suicide rather than submit to such indignities. Thousands were murdered; the lawless and licentious Mohammedan soldiery devastated the conquered territory and committed many acts of atrocity, polluting sacred wells and razing ancient temples to the ground.

The insatiable ambition and superstitious cruelty of Tippu Sāib induced him to attempt the invasion and subjugation of Travancore also. Cochin had previously been reduced to complete vassalage to Mysore, and part of that state lay within the northern rampart and defences of Travancore. The chief obstacle in the Sultan's way was the Government of Madras; for a defensive alliance had been formed in 1784 between the Rajah of Travancore and the English; to them, therefore, Tippu alleged various excuses for the invasion of the province. In December, 1789, he hastened with a powerful army to attack the Travancore lines. Reports of the barbarities of the Sultan had reached the Travancoreans, and they were nerved to put forth every effort in defence of their beautiful and sacred country, hitherto unpolluted by rude contact with foreigners. Their forces were, in the first instance, successful in driving back the Mysore army; but in April, 1790, Tippu, having received regular batteries of heavy cannon, breached the wall and overran the conquered territory as far as Verāpoly, committing his usual devastations and cruelties.

In the meantime Travancore had appealed to the British for aid. Lord Cornwallis, then Governor-General, regarding this attack on a stedfast ally as an act of hostility against the British Government, determined to interpose and to strike a blow at the very heart of Mysore by besieging the capital itself. Tippu was thus compelled to relinquish the prey which he had just grasped, and to hasten to the defence of his own dominions. The war resulted in the restoration of all that had been wrested from the Rajah of Travancore, in the death of Tippu, and the complete annihilation of his power.

The protection rendered by the English on this occasion was afforded on condition that the Rajah of Travancore should pay an annual subsidy to maintain a certain number of troops, to be stationed within his territory, and that he should receive a British Resident at his court. The following extract from the Treaty of 1805, renewing and confirming that of 1795, refers to one important stipulation:—"His Highness hereby promises to pay at all times the utmost attention to such advice as the English Government shall occasionally judge it necessary to offer to him, with a view to the economy of his finances, the better collection of his revenues, the administration of justice, the extension of commerce, the encouragement of trade, agriculture, and industry, or any other objects connected with the advancement of his Highness's interests, the happiness of his people, and the mutual welfare of both states."

This important provision for the good government of the

State has been, in the providence of God, the means of aiding the introduction of Christianity, and removing obstacles to its progress. Had it not been for the repeated exercise of the influence of godly and enlightened British Governors and Residents, and had the country been left wholly to native rule—or rather, misrule,—missionaries could have had little access to Travancore, caste injustice and social evils would still have been rampant, and slavery would still have enervated and corrupted the whole framework of native society. And yet, as far as the immediate parties were concerned, temporal interests only were regarded. The officials of the English Government merely sought the extension of British power, and a security for the due payment of the subsidy; the Travancoreans yielded to the conditions simply as a matter of unavoidable necessity; while the prime cause—Tippu's invasion—was entirely owing to his wicked and unscrupulous lust of power;—but the ultimate result of all, in the wondrous providence of God, has been the introduction into Travancore of civilization, justice, freedom, and Christianity. What an illustration is this of the inspired words, "Surely the wrath of man shall praise Thee; the remainder of wrath shalt Thou restrain"!

(Avittam) Bāla Rāma Vurmah succeeded to the throne in 1798, and occupied it for thirteen years. He was a weak and imprudent ruler, misled by selfish and ignorant favourites, and unable rightly to control his violent and corrupt ministers, yet withal rigorous and cruel in his treatment of the people.

The troops which had been levied for the defence of the kingdom against Tippu Sāib were, after the conclusion of the war, so numerous that, having no other employment, they overawed and harassed their more peaceable countrymen. "The military, exasperated by the reduction of some customary allowances, or instigated by leaders who concealed their views under this specious pretence, broke into open revolt against the Rajah in 1804. The ferment was allayed for a time by the concessions of the Rajah, but the views of the disaffected were soon afterwards directed against the British." They determined to make an effort to throw off the British alliance, and to repudiate the just obligations under which they were placed towards that power.

"The contest commenced by a treacherous attempt (Dec. 29th, 1808) to assassinate the British Resident, Colonel Macaulay, then residing at Cochin. The Resident had a narrow escape, which he owed to the fidelity of a domestic." Several attacks on Cochin were made by the Travancoreans; but reinforcements from Quilon and Malabar were speedily called in, and tranquillity was restored. "The state was called upon to defray the expense incurred by the British Government in this expedition; and a brigade, consisting of one European and three native regiments, with a detachment of artillery, was left in cantonment at Quilon as a subsidiary force, agreeably to the treaty concluded in 1795.

"After the restoration of peace the administration of affairs was still left in a most disorganized and unsettled state. So far did this proceed that the British Government at length felt itself called upon to remonstrate upon the non-fulfilment of the obligations under which Travancore was placed, and to intimate that further delay would render it necessary to assume the internal administration of the country, as the only means of insuring the satisfaction of those demands." *

The death of Rajah Bāla Rāma in 1811, and the accession of his sister, Gouri Letchmi Rānee, who was at that time without children, put a new and improved aspect on affairs. This Princess had the good sense to place the administration of the country into the hands of Colonel Munro, the British Resident, who acted for about three years in the capacity of

* Memoir of Travancore.

Dewān, or Prime Minister. The effect upon the administration and resources of the country, notwithstanding another attempt in 1812 to destroy the British authority, was most beneficial, and highly appreciated by the natives themselves.

In 1815 the Rānee died, leaving two infant sons and one daughter, and her sister, Gouri Pārvathi Rānee, was entrusted with the regency during the minority of the heir. She followed a similar policy to that of her predecessor, and sought the aid of able and upright advisers; so that the country continued, on the whole, peaceful and prosperous.

On attaining his majority in 1829, at the age of sixteen, (Choti) Vunjee Bāla Rāma Vurmah was installed as Rajah, and occupied the throne for eighteen years. In 1832, the country being considered safe from external attack, the greater portion of the subsidiary forces, including all the European soldiers, was withdrawn, and the entire responsibility of preserving the peace of the country was entrusted to the Rajah. "During the last few years of his administration the country was allowed to deteriorate, notwithstanding the vigorous remonstrances of the British Resident. Extravagance wasted the accumulations of former years of careful management; and a decreasing revenue, coincident with a lavish expenditure, led to the neglect of nearly all public works, however important or necessary. The roads and bridges were left to go to decay; and even the works for irrigation, so essential to the prosperity of the people and so closely connected with the immediate interests of the revenue, were not kept in repair." *

Towards the end of 1846 this Prince died; and in the following February his younger brother, Bāghiodya Martānda Vurmah, was installed as Rajah.

This ruler was personally of a kind and amiable disposition, and possessed many excellences of character; but

* Thornton's East Indian Gazetteer, Art. "Travancore."

he lacked decision and energy. He had enjoyed the benefit of a fair education, and was fond of the study of chemistry and medicine; but he was not less devoted to superstition than his predecessors. Sincere and devout in idolatrous worship beyond most of his people, he was lavish in his expenditure on religious ceremonials, and spent much of his time in devotional observances.

For some time after the succession of this Rajah, aided by an able though thoroughly unprincipled Dewān, he set himself to correct the improvident expenditure of his predecessor. But this course of improvement did not long continue. The reins of government were soon relaxed, and misrule began to produce its natural results. Public duty was neglected for festivals; the courts and police grew corrupt; the character of many of the high officials was bad; and monstrous evils in the system of forced labour, the collection of the revenue, and the administration of justice prevailed throughout the country. The state of affairs became increasingly worse, until the Madras Government was compelled again to interfere and urge reforms. Subsequent reforms were inaugurated in 1858 by the appointment of the present able and upright Dewān; and in the beginning of 1860 a British Resident, Mr. F. N. Maltby, arrived in Travancore. The talents and firmness, the political experience and Christian character of this gentleman were such as to warrant the expectation of considerable improvement in the state of the country. He has since been succeeded by others of like mind.

A few months after this the Rajah died, and was succeeded by his sister's son, (Ayilliam) Rāma Vurmah, the present Maharajah, a truly estimable and enlightened Prince, under whose rule, aided by his minister, Sir Madava Row, K.C.S.I., with the advice of the British Resident, the administration has been remodelled, and the condition of the country has visibly amended and promsies still further to improve.

CHAPTER III.

THE PEOPLE—THEIR MANNERS AND CUSTOMS.

Numbers and Density of Population—Caste; its Character, Origin, and Influence—Brahmans—Their Pride and Assumption—Bearing towards Europeans—Assault on Mr. Lee—Sûdras—Their Singular Customs—Ilavars and Shânars—Deed of Divorce—Slave Castes—Their Degradation and Sufferings—Hill Tribes.

A REGULAR census of the population of Travancore was taken in 1854, and showed a total of 1,262,647 inhabitants. There is reason to believe, however, that this number has since risen to at least a million and a half of inhabitants; but in any analysis of the elements of the population we must refer to the census, in which details are given. The average population, according to the more recent estimate, is 223 to each square mile of territory. The average density of the population of Great Britain is 274; of the Madras Presidency, 180; and of the whole of India, 130 to the square mile.

The population of Travancore is far from being uniformly distributed over the entire surface of the country. It chiefly occupies a strip of land, of a width of from sixteen to thirty miles from the sea. The maritime districts are the most wealthy and populous, while the mountains are uninhabited, except here and there by a few unsettled tribes of mountaineers, and, within the last few years, by the proprietors of coffee plantations and the labourers in their employment. The rocky, wild, and malarious districts near the base of the hills are almost wholly destitute of inhabitants.

Leaving out of view for the present the native Christians and the Mohammedans, to both of whom reference is made elsewhere, it is needful to give some account of the great body of the Hindu population, as separated into distinct *castes* or classes. The term "caste," be it remembered, is not always synonymous with employment, profession, or trade; nor does "high caste" imply the possession of wealth, nor "low caste" always indicate extreme poverty. Caste in India is but one of the innumerable manifestations of the pride, partiality, and selfishness everywhere natural to the unsanctified human character.

Some writers upon India have regarded caste as a mere social institution, corresponding in a measure with the division of labour amongst ourselves. They suggest fanciful theories respecting its supposed origin in the commencement of the framework of society; that it arose from the necessity of allotting to certain classes particular manufactures and employments, in order to increase and perpetuate from generation to generation the professional skill of artisans and labourers. Others, again, speak of this institution as being merely civil or political, not religious in its character, but rather corresponding to distinctions of rank and position amongst ourselves. But amongst the Hindus, caste is placed upon distinctly religious grounds, and is inseparably connected with the doctrines and traditions of Hinduism. Its origin is said to be divine. Its rules and sanctions are divine. It is supposed to exhibit the relative position in regard to holiness and purity, and the measure of salvation already attained by each individual. He who is now a "high caste" man must have performed meritorious acts in a former birth, on account of which he was again born into this higher position; and the degraded "low caste" man is now suffering the punishment of some former misdeeds. Thus the system of caste must stand or fall with Hinduism itself, and must be wholly and for ever rejected as heathenish and wicked by all genuine converts to Christianity. It were an easy task to prove from facts that the excuses and palliations of the system of caste brought forward by some European writers are utterly untenable, and are founded on error.

The origin of caste is doubtless connected with the early history of India, and the conquest of the aboriginal inhabitants by the Brahmanical race. In the present population of India there are two strata of people, distinguished from one another by physical characteristics, as well as by language, customs, and religion. The Brahmans and other higher classes migrated from a more northerly region, and are not distantly related to the European races; the lower classes are of remote Scythian or Tartar origin, and, in Southern India, are demon worshippers. The Brahmanical, or Aryan tribes in early ages subjugated the primitive inhabitants of India, and, to retain them in a condition of subservience and inferiority, invented the legends which are now related in the Hindu Purānas relative to the origin of caste. The Brahmans placed their claims to superiority on a religious basis; and the result has fully justified their shrewd and selfish policy.

Caste separates the people into many different classes throughout the whole of India. Each caste is supposed to be as distinct from others as are the various species of animals, such as the horse, the ox, or the ass. Those who belong to the highest caste enjoy extravagant privileges, and are almost worshipped as gods, while the lowest are regarded as degraded almost below the level of the beasts of the field. Individuals of different castes cannot intermarry. They are prohibited from eating together or in each other's presence, from drawing water from the same well, or even partaking of a cup of water from the hands of any of a lower caste. They cannot even worship in common; the man of low caste can never be admitted into a Brahman temple, nor even, in Travancore, touch its outermost walls; nor is he ever allowed to hear or to read the sacred books. Familiar hospitable intercourse between the different castes, or between high caste Hindus and Europeans, is impossible; the very touch of the degraded Pariah or Pulayan, even his shadow falling on the food of the Brahman, conveys pollution. I have known instances in which native gentlemen, or nobles, have ventured to sit at the table of Europeans, but dare not themselves partake of any of the food before them on account of the laws of caste. In Travancore, moreover, the most servile and humiliating language must be used by persons of inferior caste to those of high caste.

The fearful and aggravated evils of such a system must be obvious. It obstructs all progress even in civilization and arts; sea voyages are impracticable, manufactures in leather and other materials are prohibited, praiseworthy ambition and enterprise are repressed, patriotism is totally annihilated. The separate castes cannot unite even to repel an invader. Hospitality, kindness, the observance of the duties of common humanity, are extinguished by the rigid rules of Hindu caste. The whole system is, in every aspect, fraught with evil to high as well as low—is morally degrading to rich as well as poor; and, perhaps, nowhere is caste retained and defended with such tenacity, bigotry and jealousy as in Travancore.

The distinct castes and subdivisions found in various parts of this little state are reckoned to be no less than eighty-two in number. All these vary in rank, in the nicely graduated scale, from the highest of the Brahmans to the lowest of the slaves. Occasional diversities, arising from local circumstances, are observable in the relative position of some of these castes. But speaking generally, all, from the Brahman priests down to the guilds of carpenters and goldsmiths, are regarded as of *high* or good caste; and from the Shānar tree climbers and washermen down to the various classes of slaves, as of inferior or *low* caste.

To give some definite idea of these component parts of the population, *four* principal castes may be selected as typical or illustrative of the whole. These are Brahmans, Súdras, Shānars, and Pulayars.

According to the census of 1854, the BRAHMANS resident in Travancore number about 39,000. They are divided into two principal classes—Nambúris or Malayālim Brahmans, indigenous to the country, and foreign Brahmans, originally from the Canara, Mahratta, Tulu, and Tamil countries, but who are now settled in Travancore.

The Nambúri Brahmans, numbering 10,238, are regarded as peculiarly sacred, and as exalted far beyond the foreign Brahmans. They claim to be the aboriginal proprietors of the soil, to whom the ancestors of the present rajahs and chiefs were indebted for all that they possessed. Their head-quarters are at A'rāncheri in the Cochin state, where the chief Nambúri resides. The highest class of Nambúris, with rare exceptions, refuse to reside under the sway of the Súdra king of Travancore, and any of the females going south of Quilon are said to lose caste. Hence the Nambúris resident within the limits of Travancore are not recognised as being of the purest class.

These proud and arrogant Brahmans are not numerous in the south, but chiefly inhabit the central and northern provinces of Travancore. Their manner of life is usually very secluded, and many devote themselves especially to the performance of religious ceremonies in connection with the temples. In all the great religious observances of the Rajah, these priests are the principal celebrants, and are treated with every mark of reverence and respect. They rarely condescend to enter upon the arena of political life; and it was only in 1863 that the first instance occurred of a youth of this caste entering the High School at the capital, for the purpose of learning English. In consequence of their seclusion, caste prejudices, and strict attention to ceremonial purity, these Brahmans are inaccessible to the European missionary.

The Nambúris are often wealthy, and reside in large, comfortable houses. Their women are carefully concealed from the public gaze; and, when venturing out of the house, are enveloped in cloths, or are covered by an immense umbrella. The females are said to be distinguished by their beauty, and they enjoy the privilege of wearing golden bracelets.

The above illustration, copied from a native drawing, gives a fair representation of these people.

To keep down the numbers of this caste, the eldest son alone in a family is allowed to marry in regular form with a female of his own caste. The others form such temporary connections as they may find convenient, and are usually welcomed by the females of the Súdra caste, who regard it as a high honour to receive the visits of a Nambúri. Should the eldest son have no issue, the second marries, and so on till the object is attained.

Foreign Brahmans of various nationalities, attracted by the respect and attention paid to their class in the "Land of Charity," number 28,461. Some of them are engaged in trade, or in the employment of the native Government; others perform the minor duties of the temples. The Canara Brahmans are not accompanied by their families, but some of them associate with the Nair females during their stay in Travancore, giving to them a portion of their allowances, and remitting the remainder to their families. Others take up their residence altogether in Travancore, and never return to their respective countries.

Another numerous class closely connected with the Brahmans, and who might indeed be numbered with them, is that of Umbalavāsies, or "temple dwellers." Their caste position is intermediate between that of Brahmans and Súdras. They prepare garlands with which to decorate the idols, officiate as musicians in the temple services, and, like the Jewish Levites, perform various duties about the pagodas. They amount to 18,870 in number.

Very few Chatriyas and Vaishyas are found in Travancore, and it is not certain that these are the genuine descendants of the original castes so named.

The Brahmans in Travancore have secured for themselves a singularly high and unfair superiority over all other classes, —very different from their present position in British India. Though comparatively so few in number (little more than three per cent. of the whole population), they are the only class that are free from all social and religious disabilities, and enjoy perfect liberty of action. The whole framework of Hinduism has been adapted to the comfort and exaltation of the Brahman. His word is law; his smile confers happiness and salvation; his power with heaven is unlimited;

the very dust of his feet is purifying in its nature and efficacy. Each is an infallible Pope in his own sphere. The Brahman is the exclusive and Pharisaic Jew of India. He is professedly the pure and exalted priest, separate from all that is "common or unclean."

The traditional and *quasi*-legal rights and privileges conceded to Brahmans in Travancore, constitute a formidable barrier to the general progress and political improvement of the country. They are exempt in a native state from capital punishment for any offence whatever, and their crimes are very leniently dealt with, while those committed against them are severely punished. The laws as to *caste distance* also, as far as they are carried out, cannot but put a stop to the elevation of the lower orders, and necessarily limit the natural freedom of large classes of individuals. Fixed distances are appointed, within which persons of low caste dare not approach those of higher caste. A Nair, for example, may approach, but must not touch a Nambûri Brahman. A Shānar must remain thirty-six paces off, and a Pulayan slave must stay at a distance of ninety-six paces. Other intervals, according to a graduated scale, are appointed to be observed between the remaining castes; thus, for instance, a Shānar must remain twelve steps away from a Nair, a Pulayan sixty-six steps, and so on.

Even Europeans would be brought by Brahmans under the influence of these intolerable arrangements, did they only possess the power to compel the former to observe them. During the early intercourse of Europeans with Travancore, they were forbidden to use the main road, and required to pass by a path along the coast where Brahmans rarely travel; access to the capital was also refused as long as possible. I myself have been ordered to run out of the public road by the servants of a great Brahman priest who was passing along in his palankeen, but, of course, refused to do so. Other missionaries, however, have been assaulted and beaten for declining to yield submission to these arbitrary and despotic regulations.

The most recent occurrence of this kind took place about the middle of 1868, in the case of the Rev. W. Lee. One morning, attended as usual by his horsekeeper, a native Christian, Mr. Lee was riding to one of his congregations, through the Brahman street of Panjalingapuram, near Cape Comorin, a street which he had passed through repeatedly, as had other missionaries and Europeans for the last forty years, and which was the only direct road to the place he was about to visit. On this occasion the Brahmans assembled to prevent his passing through their street, and one suggested that he should go by an alleged back road instead of the direct route. Willing, if possible, to gratify the people, Mr. Lee consented to examine the by-road, so called, and found it was merely a path among the cesspools of the village, scarcely passable, of the existence of which he had never before heard, and by which under these circumstances he declined in future to proceed. When returning in the evening he was set upon and furiously attacked by a mob of Brahmans; stones and brass vessels were thrown at him, and he received some severe blows. He was struck at with a bullock pole, and his travelling bag was carried off by one of the assailants. After passing through the village he got off his horse and went back alone to the Brahmans, who had congregated at a little temple at the outside of the street, and asked in a conciliatory tone why they had committed the outrage, requesting them to return the bag. Again he was assaulted, and with difficulty escaped.

The question of right of way being one of essential importance, a complaint was lodged before the authorities, and duly investigated for nine successive days by the Dewān Peishcar. Everything went clearly against the Brahmans, and the case being fairly established was forwarded to the Dewān. Great excitement prevailed throughout the country during the trial. But the final decision of the Dewān was very unsatisfactory. A mere nominal fine of thirty rupees each was inflicted on five of the offenders, and although the street was proved in court to have been open to the public for a great number of years without any objection having been expressed by the Brahmans, and though Mr. Duthie had gone through it with his bearers but a few weeks previously, Mr. Lee was ordered to abstain from passing through it till he had first proved his right to do so in a civil court; a decision tantamount, in the present state of the country and its unequal legislation, to an absolute prohibition.

The stolen bag was discovered concealed at the bottom of a Brahman's well, but for the theft the men were simply punished with an insignificant fine of five rupees each, and the village watchman was allowed to retain his situation in the pay of the Government.

An appeal in the case was made to H. E., the Governor of Madras, in Council, and it was understood that his lordship's personal opinion was strongly in favour of the missionaries' right of way; but we have not heard the result of this appeal. It would certainly require some courage and determination on the part of the rulers of Travancore to repeal the unjust and partial caste laws which have hitherto prevailed to the serious detriment of so large a proportion of their subjects; but some such course is essential to the improvement of the country. While progress may be expected to be somewhat slow, any retrograde measures towards the old state of things will have to be vigilantly guarded against and avoided.

THE SÚDRAS constitute the next great division of the population. These were originally the lowest of the four true castes, and are still a degraded caste in North India. But in the South there are so many divisions below the

Súdras, and they are so numerous, active, and influential, that they are regarded as quite high caste people. In Travancore the Malayālim Súdras number 384,242; the Chetties, or Súdras from the Carnatic, 19,955; and the carpenters, weavers, herdsmen, smiths, and other castes, who may be regarded as belonging to the same great class, 78,210; making in all 482,407, or above one-third of the whole population.

The Súdras are the middle classes of Travancore. The greater portion of the land is in their hands, and until recently they were also the principal owners of slaves. They are the dominant and ruling class. They form the magistracy and holders of most of the Government offices—the military and police, the wealthy farmers, the merchants and skilled artisans of the country. The Royal Family are members of this caste. The ordinary appellation of the Súdras of Malabar is *Nair* (pronounced like the English word "nigher"), meaning lord, chief, or master; a marvellous change from their original position, according to Hindu tradition. By the primitive laws of caste they are forbidden to read the sacred books, or perform religious ceremonies, and are regarded as created for the service of the Brahmans. The ancient law of Manu runs thus:—"Men of the servile (Súdra) caste were created for the purpose of serving Brahmans. The Brahman who declares the law to a servile man, and he who instructs him in the mode of expiating sin, sinks with that very man into hell. If a Súdra reads the Vedas or the Purānas, then the magistrate shall heat some bitter oil and pour it into the Súdra's mouth; and if the Súdra listens to the Vedas, then boiling oil shall be poured into his ears." Accordingly, as a matter of fact, the Súdras never do read the Sanscrit Vedas, nor trench upon the duties and privileges of the Brahmans, though there are but few of them now in a position of direct subserviency to the priesthood.

Amongst the Nairs there are several subdivisions, with their distinguishing titles and characteristics, and their respective gradations of caste pre-eminence.

The four castes of goldsmiths, brassworkers, blacksmiths, and carpenters, form the lowest subdivision of the Súdras.

The Nair customs with respect to marriage are of a most singular and licentious character. In early youth the girl goes through the ceremony of marriage by having the "tāli," or marriage cord, tied round her neck, but this is not followed by cohabitation. It is a mere formality, and simply sets her at liberty to exercise and follow out her own inclinations in more mature years. When arrived at a marriageable age suitors present themselves, and the favoured individual offers to the young woman a cloth and other presents, and either resides with her or visits her at intervals in her brother's house. This is called "mundu koduttu pārppikka," "giving a cloth and residing together," and is the only practical substitute for marriage amongst these people. But this form cannot be regarded as constituting marriage in any true sense. It differs widely from the marriages of the Brahmans and Shānars, inasmuch as the engagement is not binding upon either party longer than they choose, and is readily dissolved. The woman is at liberty to dismiss the man, or the man to dismiss the woman, on very easy terms. A settlement of accounts as to presents, expenses of marriage, ornaments, &c., and a deed of separation, drawn up and signed in the presence of four witnesses of the same caste, completely dissolves this trivial connection. Many of these alliances are of course continued throughout life, but great evils result from the facilities afforded for change. Formerly, too, it was common for Nair females, while residing at their brother's house, to receive more than one visitor of the male sex, nor is this altogether unknown at the present day.

In consequence of these peculiar customs the law of

inheritance amongst the Súdras is equally strange. The children of a Súdra woman inherit the property and heritable honours, not of their father, but of their mother's brother. They are their *uncle's* nearest heirs, and he is their legal guardian. So it is, for example, in the succession to the throne. The late Rajah was not succeeded by his own sons. They received some private property during the lifetime of their father, but have no claim upon the throne or royal honours; and their descendants, in a few generations, will sink down to the level of ordinary Súdras, though they continue to be recognised by the title of "Tambi." The sister of the late Rajah left two sons, the elder of whom is now reigning. He will be succeeded by his younger brother, the heir apparent. Next in succession come the two sons of their late sister, who are entitled respectively the *second* and *third* princes of Travancore. Their mother had no daughters, so that it became necessary for the continuation of the succession by the female line to adopt some one into the family. Two daughters of the petty rajah of Māvelikkara were accordingly adopted, who are by Hindu law and custom regarded as the sisters of the second and third princes, and are called respectively the senior and junior Rānees of Travancore. The senior Rānee is without issue, but the junior Rānee has three sons,—the *fourth*, *fifth*, and *sixth* princes, who follow next in the succession. But unless daughters are born hereafter to the Rānee, there will be another break in this curious chain of sisters' sons, and it will be necessary again to adopt females into the family.

The monstrous custom of polyandry, or of one woman having several husbands, is sometimes practised in Travancore by carpenters, stonemasons, and individuals of other castes. Several brothers living together are unable to support a wife for each, and take one amongst them, who resides with them all. The children are reckoned to belong to each brother in succession, in the order of seniority. Such cases necessarily lead to jealousies and disputes, and other great evils; but they are much more rare now than in former times.

These peculiar usages of the Nairs naturally give to their females considerable social influence and liberty of choice and action. It is remarkable that most of the Súdra females are taught to read and write, though they can be expected to profit little by their training while no better books than heathen songs and foolish legends are within their reach.

This class of people cherish a most tenacious attachment to their native locality and country, and are rarely known to engage in travel, or to emigrate to other parts of India. They were once trained to the use of arms; they carried a sword and shield, and were noted as warriors, but little of the martial character is seen in them now-a-days. Able in the management of business affairs, they are crafty, unscrupulous, and deceitful. Polite and even respectful when an object is to be gained, they are often arrogant and oppressive toward their inferiors and to the weak. Hence they are greatly dreaded and disliked by the various classes beneath them, whom they treat in this severe and tyrannical manner, but who now, by British influence and by the progress of enlightenment and of Christianity, are gradually being freed from the power and domination of their hard and exacting taskmasters.

The Ilavars, Shānars, and others, form a third great subdivision of the population. These constitute the highest division of the low castes. The Ilavars number 168,866; the Shānars 82,861; and the potters, washermen, barbers, and mountaineers, who may be classed with them, 69,399; making in all 321,126.

The Ilavars and Shānars differ but little from one another in employments and character, and are, no doubt, identical in origin. The Shānars are found only in the southern districts of Travancore, between the Cape and Trevandrum; from which northwards the Ilavars occupy their place. These are the palm tree cultivators, the toddy drawers, sugar manufacturers and distillers of Travancore. Their social position somewhat corresponds to that of small farmers and agricultural labourers amongst ourselves.

The term Ilavar is derived from *Ilam*, a native name for Ceylon. The tradition is that they are immigrants from that island, who came over at the request of some of the early settlers on the western coast. They are also called Chogan-mār or serfs, and in other parts of the Malabar coast Teeyars and Billavars. Their labours are chiefly bestowed on the cultivation of the cocoa-nut palm and the manufacture of its various products. Many own or rent small plots of land, on which they cultivate a few trees and a small supply of kitchen vegetables, and some of them are in comfortable circumstances. They draw the fresh sap from the cocoa-nut palm, which is used as a drink, either fresh or fermented. It is also boiled into a coarse sugar, from which they distil the native spirits called "arrack."

The Súdra custom of a man and woman living together as husband and wife, with liberty to separate after certain settlements and formalities, has been adopted by most of the Ilavars, and by a few of the Shānars in their vicinity; and amongst these castes also the inheritance usually descends to nephews by the female line. A few divide their property, half to the nephews and half to the sons. The rule is that all property which has been inherited shall fall to nephews; but wealth which has been accumulated by the testator himself may be equally divided between nephews and sons. Some portion is usually left to the widow as a kind of legacy. She may, however, have received some property from her husband during his life, by deed of gift, or may have secretly accumulated her savings in anticipation of widowhood.

These strange customs have sometimes occasioned considerable difficulty to missionaries in dealing with them, in the case of converts to Christianity. Persons who have been living together after the observance of the trivial form of "giving a cloth" are of course required to marry in Christian form. The necessary inquiries are therefore made into their history, and into the circumstances of each case of concubinage; deeds of separation, drawn up according to heathen law, are read and examined, and all outstanding claims are legally settled. Many an hour have I spent along with my native teachers in such investigations. The ordinary form of divorce deed will be seen from the following translation of one in my possession:—

"This unalterable deed of separation is written and given by (woman) Valli Māthi, of Pandāratopu, in Neyyāttunkara District, to (man) Mallan Changili, of Valiavilei, in Kotukkal District, on this 10th day of Veigāsi month, M.E. 1034.

"Valli Māthi was married to Mallan Changili, and resided with him for some time. Afterwards she refused to live with him, and went to her relatives to reside. Shortly after she was taken as wife by one of her cousins, and cohabited with him. When the former husband, Mallan Changili, went and invited her to return she refused; and on his asking her to repay him the expenses incurred by him in marrying her, and to sign a deed of separation, so that he might take another wife, she consented to do so, on condition that he made an allowance for her support. Accordingly, the expenditure was inquired into and settled, and what was due to her was paid. She now signs this deed, saying, 'From this day I give liberty to Mallan Changili to marry or take as a wife any woman he chooses, according to caste rule, and she may inherit his property and debts, firewood and pots, and all that belongs to him.

"'But should either I or my children, contrary to this

agreement, make any claim hereafter on the property of Mallan Changili, the case, with this document, may be reported to the court, whose decision I shall obey, and again submit to the above terms.'

"Witnesses,— (Signed) VALLI MĀTHI.

"Mallan Karuman.

"Māttāndan Kāli."

The Shānars of South Travancore are of the same class as those of Tinnevelly, and in both provinces they have in large numbers embraced the profession of Christianity. Their employment is the cultivation of the Palmyra palm, which they climb daily in order to extract the sap from the flower-stem at the top. This is manufactured into a coarse dark sugar, which they sell or use for food and other purposes, as described at length in Chapter IX.

The general circumstances of the Shānar and Ilavar population in Travancore, especially of the former, have long been most humiliating and degrading. Their social condition is by no means so deplorable as that of the slave castes, and has materially improved under the benign influence of Christianity, concurrently with the general advancement of the country, but until recently it was very bad. To mark their degradation, their women were forbidden to wear any clothing whatever above the waist. They were not allowed to carry umbrellas, to wear shoes or golden ornaments, to carry pots of water on the hip, to build houses above one story in height, to milk cows, or even to use the ordinary language of the country. Their services were often demanded to labour or carry burdens for the Sûdras and the native Government, for which they were often unpaid, or received a mere nominal sum.

In consequence of long ages of oppression, the Shānars are, as a class, timid, deceitful, and ignorant. But they are usually faithful in the observance of the marriage bond, and are somewhat more chaste and truthful, more grateful and less prejudiced, than many other classes of the Hindus. Their superstitions, too, though gross and debasing, are less complex and fascinating to the native mind than those of the Brahmans, so that they appear to have been providentially prepared to lend a willing ear to the truths of the gospel.

The slave castes—the lowest of the low—comprehend the Pallars (3,736), the Pariahs (41,360), and the Pulayars (98,766); numbering in all 143,862.

Of these the Pariahs, a Tamil caste, are found, like the Shānars, only in the southern districts and in Shencotta, east of the Ghauts; but they appear to be in many respects inferior to those of the eastern coast. Indulging a depraved taste for carrion, they are in the habit of carrying off the carcasses of bullocks and cows left dead by the road-side and in the fields, which they regard as their peculiar perquisites. Their habits generally are most filthy and disgusting, and they have sometimes been suspected of kidnapping and entrapping into their number women of high caste.

The Pulayars, the lowest of the slave castes, reside in miserable huts on mounds in the centre of the rice swamps, or on the raised embankments in their vicinity. They are engaged in agriculture as the servants of the Súdra and other landowners. Wages are usually paid to them in kind, and at the lowest possible rates. To eke out their miserable allowances, therefore, they are accustomed to enter the grounds of their neighbours at night to steal roots, cocoanuts, and other produce; and they are but too ready to commit assault and other crimes, for the commission of which they may be sufficiently bribed by their masters.

These poor people are steeped in the densest ignorance and stupidity. Drunkenness, lying, and evil passions prevail amongst them, except where of late years the gospel has been the means of their reclamation from vice, and of their social elevation. They differ from the Pariahs, however, in abstaining from the flesh of all dead animals.

In former times slaves were let or transferred at the choice of the owner, were offered as presents to friends or as gifts to temples, and were bought, sold, or mortgaged in the same manner as the land on which they dwelt or as the cattle and other property of their owners. The price of a slave varied from six to nine rupees (twelve to eighteen shillings). In some parts of the country, however, as much as eighteen rupees were given. Being frequently engaged in digging and manuring, transplanting the young rice, repairing the banks, and performing other labours in the rice-fields, sometimes standing for hours in the water, they are subject to rheumatism, fevers, cholera, and other diseases, which carry off many long before the approach of old age. The survivors are often left, when past work, to beg or steal for their support, or to perish with hunger.

Cases of horrid and aggravated cruelty in the treatment of slaves by their masters, especially of those who attempted to escape to the mountains, were once numerous. Indeed, one of the usual clauses in the deed of transfer of slaves was "You may sell him or kill him." Both privileges have now, of course, ceased. One instance of savage cruelty by a Syrian towards a poor slave who had made his escape came under the cognizance of the Rev. H. Baker. This slave, after his conversion, went to visit his former master, carrying with him a few presents to avert his anger. He was immediately seized and fearfully beaten, then covered with hot ashes, and confined in the cellar of a granary. There he lay for three days, groaning and praying that God would forgive all his sins and his master's too. He asked for water, and they gave him some filthy compound from the cattle stall; at length he died of his wounds and starvation, and they buried his corpse to hide the deed. Some one told the facts of the case to the Puniāttu Rajah, who gave notice to the police, and it cost the owner some 500 rupees in bribes "to settle the trouble," as the natives call it.

Various measures for the amelioration of the condition of the slaves, and ultimately for their emancipation, have, through British and Christian mediation, been adopted by the native Government. In October, 1853, the Rajah's proclamation set free the *future* offspring of *Government* slaves, and somewhat modified the condition of other slaves; and in June, 1855, another proclamation was issued for the "amelioration of slavery," liberating all *Government* slaves, forbidding the courts of justice to enforce claims on any person as a slave, and providing for their holding property and obtaining redress for injuries the same as freemen.

Although thus legally emancipated the condition of the slave population remains very much as before; and perhaps it is well that there should be no sudden or violent convulsions of society. They have not the courage and enterprise, nor perhaps the industry, to avail themselves as a body of their legal rights. Nor, indeed, is it possible that they should rise to any considerable degree of improvement while the system of caste tyranny and oppression remains in full force.

Could we depict in true and vivid colours the miseries and woes of the Pulayars and other slave population of Travancore, the hearts of our readers would melt with pity and compassion for their temporal sufferings and spiritual danger. Mention can only be made of some of the bare facts as to how the inhuman system of caste affects the poor Pulayan in his person, his house and family, his business, his religious worship, and, in short, throughout the whole of his wretched life.

The very name expresses the idea of impurity; it is derived from the word "*pula*," funeral pollution.

With regard to his personal comfort and deportment, the only dress of the degraded Pulayan is a piece of coarse cloth fastened round the loins, and a small piece tied around the head as a head-dress. To women, as well as to men, it was forbidden, until 1865 (when, through the benevolent interposition of the British Government, the restriction was removed) to wear any clothing whatever *above the waist*. Their ornaments must be no more valuable than brass or beads, umbrellas must not be used to shelter the body from the scorching heat of the sun, nor shoes to protect the feet from the thorns and sharp stones of the jungle paths.

The Pulayan has no education, for who would be found willing to teach, or even to approach, the impure one? The language which he is compelled to use is in the highest degree abject and degrading. He dare not say "I," but "*adiyen*," "your slave;" he dare not call his rice "*choru*," but "*karikādi*,"—dirty gruel. He asks leave, not to take food, but "to drink water." His house is called "*mādam*," a hut, and his children he speaks of as "monkeys" or "calves;" and when speaking he must place the hand over the mouth, lest the breath should go forth and pollute the person whom he is addressing.*

The Pulayan's home is a little shed, which barely affords shelter from the rain and space to lie down at night, destitute alike of comfort and furniture. It must be built in a situation far from the houses of all respectable persons. Let him dare to attempt the erection of a better house, and it will immediately be torn down by the infuriated Sûdras. Very rarely has the Pulayan land of his own. It belongs to the Sûdra master, and the poor slave is liable to be expelled

* Compare Job xl. 4.

from the land which he occupies, and from his means of living, if he claims the freedom to which he is now entitled by law. I have known Súdras even take forcible possession of waste land which had been cleared and cultivated by Pulayars.

In the transaction of the ordinary business of life, the disabilities of the low caste man are such that it is hard to imagine how human beings could ever have been held in a condition of subservience to them. But we must remember the effect of thousands of years of oppression and tyranny. The Pulayan is not allowed to use the public road when a Brahman or Súdra walks on it. The poor slave must utter a warning cry, and hasten off the roadway into the mud on one hand or the briers on the other, lest the high caste man should be polluted by his near approach or by his shadow. The law is (and I was informed by a legal authority that it is still binding) that a Pulayan must never approach a Brahman nearer than ninety-six paces, and he must remain at about half this distance from a Súdra. I have often seen the Súdra master shouting from the prescribed distance to his slaves toiling in the fields. The Pulayan cannot enter a court of justice,—he must shout from the appointed distance, and take his chance of being heard and receiving attention. A policeman is sometimes stationed halfway between the Pulayan witness or prisoner and the high caste magistrate, to transmit the questions and answers, the distance being too great for convenient hearing.* As he cannot enter a town or village, no employment is open to him except that of working in rice-fields, and such kind of labour. He cannot

* Since these remarks were written, orders have been issued by the Government to allow the admission of the low castes to the public courts and a few of the English schools. No one, however, who understands the force of caste prejudice in Travancore can imagine that this concession will largely affect the condition of the low caste population for a long time to come. Nothing is yet being attempted for the education of the slave castes.

even act as a porter, for he defiles all that he touches. He cannot work as a domestic servant, for the house would be polluted by his entrance; much less can he (even were he by some means to succeed in obtaining education or capital) become a clerk, schoolmaster, or merchant.

Caste affects even his purchases and sales. The Pulayars manufacture umbrellas and other small articles, place them on the highway, and retire to the appointed distance, shouting to passers by with reference to the sales. If the Pulayan wishes to make a purchase, he places his money on a stone and retires to the appointed distance. Then the merchant or seller comes, takes up the money, and lays down whatever quantity of goods he chooses to give for the sum received,—a most profitable mode of doing business for the merchant, but alas for the poor purchaser! It calls to mind that old historic stone outside the walls of the ancient city of Winchester, which was used during the great plague. Upon it were placed letters, money, and articles of barter, to avoid the personal contact of the healthy with persons affected with the plague. But the pride and tyranny of caste produces a wider separation of heart and feeling between man and his brother man than the most deadly plague or disease. Only Jesus, by His love and grace, can reunite the hearts of men thus separated and draw all to Himself—"Unto Him shall the gathering of the people be."

Reference might be made further to the rites of religious worship, in which the "common and unclean" Pariahs and Pulayars are forbidden to unite with the holy Brahman; and of times of sickness and distress in which no aid will be rendered by those best able to assist. Were fifty Pulayars drowning in a river, the Brahmans and other caste men would stand aloof and witness their dying struggles with perfect indifference, and would never put forth a hand to touch and to save their wretched and despised fellow-creatures. I have known these poor people robbed, oppressed, beaten, put in the stocks, and tortured by their Súdra owners. I have seen a well-to-do Pulayan, who was suspected of desiring to avail himself of his legal freedom, falsely charged by his master, his house gutted of his little property, his family left destitute, and himself exposed to torture and suffering. The heart sickens at the thought of all that these poor people are compelled to endure. "So I returned, and considered all the oppressions that are done under the sun: and behold the tears of such as were oppressed, and they had no comforter; and on the side of their oppressors there was power; but they had no comforter" (Eccles. iv. 1).

The HILL TRIBES, numbering 14,348, we have classed with the low caste population, but perhaps they should be regarded as outside the whole system of caste, in which it seems rather difficult to assign to them their exact position. They are called Kānikārar (heritors), or Maleyarasar (hill kings), or hill Arrians. Most of them are migratory in their habits, cultivating, for a year or two, plots of ground cleared from the forest, and afterwards removing in search of other fertile lands. They also collect the honey and other spontaneous products of the forests. They have their fixed villages in picturesque sites on the slopes of the mountains, or in almost inaccessible ravines.

Some of their houses are good, substantial erections of wood and stone, but most are mere temporary huts of mud or bamboo ingeniously interwoven with leaves and grass. These people are employed in digging the elephant pits, and helping, with bark ropes, to conduct the animals into the taming cages. In the North many of them are comfortable, or even wealthy in circumstances, and are well formed in person. Large numbers in the Mundakāyam district have placed themselves under Christian instruction.

The hill tribes in South Travancore are exceedingly

wretched, uncivilized, and degraded. The men go almost naked, having only a few inches of cloth round the loins, and a small cloth on the head. They are short in stature, but strongly built. The women wear bracelets of iron or brass, numerous necklaces of coral or beads, and leaden rings in the ear. They are much overcharged in the purchase of those ornaments by the Mohammedan and other dealers, and are continually in distress through the almost universal prevalence of drunkenness. They lack even an ordinary amount of knowledge, being unable to read or write, or to count above a dozen; fibres of various climbing plants are knotted in a particular way, to express their wants. I have never met with one who could tell his own age.

Being remarkably addicted to the worship of the hill demons, they are supposed to have great influence with those evil spirits, and are therefore often dreaded by the people of the low country. When spoken to on religious subjects they seem hardly able to understand the distinction between good and evil. They say that, should they become Christians, the devils would kill them and spoil their cultivation by means of the wild beasts. They fear even to touch a printed book. One of them said to a native Christian teacher, "Do you come to destroy us by bringing the wrath of the demons upon us?" A poor woman pleaded on a similar occasion, "I have only two children, do not kill them by teaching them the Vedam, (Scripture)."

The Mohammedans, too, endeavour to prevent them from attending Christian schools by saying, "These people wish to make you all Christians; then the demons will desert you, so that you shall become the prey of wild beasts." This superstitious fear hinders them from all opportunity of improvement.

We have thus briefly sketched the *Hindu* population of Travancore. By the census of 1854 it amounts to about one million, but we should add at least a fourth more as the probable number at present. This one million is composed of some 60,000 Brahmans, or closely related castes, and 482,000 Súdras and others, so making the high castes rather more than half of the heathen population. The other half comprehends about 321,000 Shānars, &c., and 144,000 slaves.

The *Christian* and *Mussulman* population of Travancore, amounting to above a quarter of a million, will form the subjects of separate chapters.

CHAPTER IV.

MANNERS AND CUSTOMS (CONTINUED).

Native Houses—Costume and Ornaments of Men and Women—Food.

FEW native houses in Travancore can pretend to anything of magnificence or splendour in architecture or style. Even the residences of wealthy families are mean in external appearance, and insignificant as to size. The best houses consist rather of a series of small detached buildings, one or two stories in height, all contained within the walls of the outer enclosure. The dwellings of the poorest natives are more wretched and fragile than can well be conceived by those who have not had the opportunity of inspecting them. These consist of but four mud walls, with wooden rafters, and grass or palm-leaf thatch. Many huts are constructed wholly from the leaf and stems of the palmyra or cocoa-nut palms. A native hut of this kind would easily be contained within the limits of an ordinary English drawing-room, yet in such dwellings thousands of families in Travan core reside.

A painful but accurate picture of the deplorable condition of the dwellings of the poorest class is drawn by the Rev. C. Yesudian, in describing a visit to a slave village :—"While going about among them I with great difficulty got into and inspected an uninhabited hut, which was of the following description :—It was eight feet square, and was divided into three apartments. One of the rooms, intended for the accommodation of friends, was eight feet in length, and only three in breadth. The height of the top of the roof was not more than nine feet. Regretting that human beings should have been reduced to such miserable extremities, I turned round to get out, but I found it rather difficult to do so for some time, the door in the front, the only entrance to the house, being only three feet high, and two and a half broad, and the eaves of the roof still lower. I had first to stoop down very low, and then to drag myself carefully out. Several huts of this description are put together in lines opposite to each other, having in their midst a narrow street varying in breadth from six to eight feet. In the middle of this wretched pathway there is a gutter a foot broad, which is intended to serve as a drain for all sorts of filth. It would be almost impossible for persons unaccustomed to such habitations to remain and work any number of hours there. The reason why they make their doors so small is to keep themselves warm in cold weather, as they have very little clothing about them. To serve the same purpose the thatch of the roof is thickly covered over with straw. In fact, they were not allowed by their masters better clothing and dwellings, as improvements in these would have made them unfit for toiling day and night in the rice-fields, river banks, and threshing-floors, exposed to cold winds, rain, and dew."

The walls of the better class of houses are built of clay bricks dried in the sun or kiln burnt, or of a hard clayey material called "laterite," dug in abundance out of the hill-sides almost everywhere. It is cut into squares like bricks, and hardens by exposure to the air. "Chunam," or lime for plastering the walls, is procured by burning bivalve shells, found in abundance on the sea-shore and in the backwaters. This is very white and beautiful, and when properly applied and polished looks like fine white marble. These houses are often built two stories in height, with a verandah round the lower story to protect the walls from sun and rain, and to form an open hall for rest or recreation. The ceilings, rafters and beams are of teak, jack, or palmyra wood, and the roof is covered with small tiles of burnt clay.

The above engraving of the Reading-room at Kottār, recently erected through the indefatigable efforts of Rev. J. Duthie, will give a correct idea of the style of the better class of buildings.

Some houses are built wholly of wood, like immense boxes: in the woodwork of these handsome carvings are occasionally found. They are placed upon brick foundations, and with care last for centuries.

The principal dwelling-house is divided into several small rooms. One is used by the females of the family, another is more public, and another is the strong-room, carefully fitted with locks and bars, and upper ceiling, so as to form a secure repository for the cloths, jewels, weapons, coins, brass vessels, and other household valuables. Windows are either wanting, or are exceedingly small, and fitted with wooden bars or carved work. The interior is often dark, and ventilation is wholly disregarded.

Rarely, except in large towns, are native houses built in street rows, or quite up to the line of the roadway. Between the public road and the dwelling an open space or yard is left for various uses. Here rice is beaten in the wooden mortar, or spread out to dry in the sun. In one corner of the yard are sheds for cattle, and receptacles for rice, straw, cocoa-nuts, &c. Behind or at the side is a small cookhouse, unless indeed culinary operations are performed against the outer wall of the house, or even inside one of the apartments.

A well is often dug inside the courtyard for convenience of access. In front is the door or gateway, covered with a small roof-like frame, thatched, to protect the woodwork from the effects of rain and sun. Here, too, in most houses there is an open shed, in which visitors are received, and business of all kinds transacted. In these little sheds we have often engaged in worship with our Christian people.

In the more respectable native houses there are a great many separate buildings; some of them carefully secluded for the use of the various members of the family and their wives and children, with store-rooms, cooking-houses, and often a small domestic temple in one corner of the open courtyard.

Little furniture is required or used. A bench or two, a small native "*cot*," or bed-frame, on which a mat is spread, a brass lamp suspended by a chain, a wooden mortar for pounding rice, and a few cooking vessels (the whole costing but a few shillings), form the furniture of a small native hut.

European furniture, however, is coming into use in the houses of wealthy natives.

The ordinary *costume* of the people of Travancore is remarkably simple and primitive. While hard at work, many men, such as fishers, tree climbers, and others, wear but the scantiest shred of clothing demanded by common decency. A miserable covering of green leaves serves to hide the nakedness of some of the wildest of the mountaineers. Even the better classes ordinarily wear very light clothing. "This, you know, is our uniform," said a noble of high rank whom I visited once, and who received me dressed in a single piece of cotton cloth fastened round the loins. A Tamil man from the East is recognised in Travancore by the comparative abundance of cloths in which he is enveloped. On important occasions and in public, wealthy natives don a long coat or jacket of white or printed calico, with trousers somewhat in the European style. This is the usual dress of the Mohammedans and Christian teachers, and of the native police and Government messengers, or "peons." The latter wear also an embroidered belt with a brass or silver badge, having inscribed on it the department of state in which they are employed. The materials ordinarily used are common calico, or checked and striped coloured cloths, manufactured in the country. The better classes occasionally use fine silks, dyed or printed with brilliant colours.

A turban of white or coloured muslin, tightly and neatly folded in a great variety of fashions, is the usual head-dress of the Travancorean. This is very often simplified into a plain piece of white cloth, which may either be thrown over the shoulders or twisted round the head. The turban forms an admirable protection for the head from the burning heat of the sun. Another head-dress is a light cap of cloth fitting closely to the head, but somewhat conical at the top, and coming down low over the ears and back of the head.

Slaves and other poor people wear rude caps, composed of the thick, leather-like leaf-sheath of the areca palm tree.

Men of all castes are accustomed at regular intervals to shave the hair from the head as well as the face, for coolness and cleanliness. After a "clean shave" of this kind I have sometimes been at a loss to recognise my most intimate friends. A small portion of the hair is always left uncut by heathen natives. This is called the "*kudumi*," and is only cut off with certain ceremonies on the occasion of the death of a father.* Most missionaries regard this lock of hair as essentially a mark of heathenism, and require Christian converts to abandon the custom. The "kudumi" is usually worn at the *back* of the head, but the Nambúri Brahmans have it at the front of the head, over the forehead, where it is tied up in a loose knot. The tradition is, that in former times Parasu Rāmen introduced these Brahmans into Travancore from the other side of the mountains, lifting them up by the hair of the head, and hurling them over the mountains. Thus the "kudumi" was dragged from the back to the front of the head, where it has been worn by members of this caste ever since.

On the forehead of the Hindu a little dot, or horizontal or upright lines are drawn with sacred ashes, and renewed every morning. These are the sectarial marks denoting the particular deity worshipped. The upright lines are the marks of Vishnu, the horizontal lines of Siva, and so on. These signs are repeated on the shoulders and breasts, while a few who make pretences to special purity, rub the sacred ashes over the whole of the upper part of the body.

Small golden earrings are often worn by men. A few have the privilege of wearing large rings of gold in their ears. Rings are also worn by men upon the fingers. Around the necks of Brahmans and others specially devoted to religion

* Compare Deut. xiv. 1.

hangs a necklace, or rosary, made of the hard round nuts of certain trees strung together. These are used for reckoning the repetitions of the appointed prayers. The heathen use vain repetitions, "for they think that they shall be heard for their much speaking" (Matt. vi. 7). In passing a native house I have often heard the voice of prayer, if the mere repetition of "Nārāyanā—Nārāyanā—Nārāyanā!" or of the name of some other god several hundred times, can be regarded as prayer in any true sense of the word.

One is reminded by these heathen customs of the singular resemblance which they bear to some of the rites of the Roman Catholic Church. The Romanists, like the Hindus, rub the sacred ashes on the forehead, but only once a year—on Ash Wednesday. They use rosaries, exactly as the Hindus do. They have images in their worship, but repudiate the idea of worshipping the images themselves—so do the Hindus. Romish priests and monks shave the crown of the head, leaving a ring of hair on the *outside*. The Hindus have the long hair in the *centre*. Moreover, in the approval of celibacy and monachism, penances and pilgrimages—in the use of sacred lamps, and candles, and processions in worship—in regard to holy water, and sacred wells, and prayer in an unknown tongue (Latin in the case of the Romanists, Sanscrit amongst the Brahmans), and in the facts that the recognised Scriptures are forbidden to the laity, and all true progress prohibited, we see points of startling resemblance or identity between the superstitions of the East and those of the West. Human nature is the same in every land.

The mark of Brahmanical dignity is a cord composed of three treble threads of cotton, worn across the breast, running over the left shoulder and under the right arm. This cord, however, or "*púnúl*," is worn also by goldsmiths and several other castes, and by the males of the Royal Family. It is renewed from time to time as it wears out. The upper part of the body and the lower part of the legs are usually bare. Over one shoulder, or around the neck, a light scarf-like cloth is often thrown. The principal garment worn by men is the cloth fastened around the waist and covering the lower part of the body and the loins. This is a single piece of cotton cloth, not sewed or pinned, but merely fastened by having the extremity tucked in at one side.

Wooden or leather sandals and shoes, or rather slippers, of various patterns, form the protection for the feet. The shoes are peaked and turned backwards at the toes and "down at the heel," so as to be easily laid aside when entering a house, and resumed after the visit is over. Natives, up to the highest in rank, put off the shoes before receiving visitors or entering a house, just as Europeans uncover the head; while on the other hand they retain the turban, or head-dress, which is always worn according to the rules of Hindu etiquette on such occasions. Stockings are never used. Respectable natives carry an umbrella of palm leaf, or cloth, but these are forbidden, by ancient custom, to the lowest castes. They are permitted, however, to wear a kind of broad umbrella cap of palm leaves. Persons of official rank enjoy the privilege of having an umbrella of large size carried by an attendant, and in the case of the Royal Family and the Prime Minister this is formed of crimson silk.

Female dress in Travancore does not vary like the ever-changing fashions of European countries. For perhaps two or three thousand years it has remained unaltered. The Hindu woman has long, black, luxuriant hair, which she ties up in a knot at the back, or, in the case of some castes, at the right *side* of the head. When fully dressed, rich golden ornaments and a few handsome flowers are used to decorate the hair. Might it not be worthy the consideration of fashionable ladies at home whether it would not be a hitherto unthought-of novelty, amidst the innumerable fashions of "chignons" at present, to try the effect of wearing them, not at the back, or upper part of the head, but at the *side*, in imitation of this ancient, yet novel, Malabar fashion? Strange that none of the leaders of fashion in Europe have thought of this!

Ear ornaments, worn in a considerable variety of forms, are indispensable to the completeness of the costume of a Travancore lady. The views of the Brahman women as to the size of these ornaments are much more moderate than those of the Súdra and Shānar females. In the case of the latter the ear of the child is pierced in the usual place, and a heavy leaden ring, or weight, is then inserted, so as to draw down and extend the fleshy lobe and greatly to enlarge the opening. After some time another weight is added, then

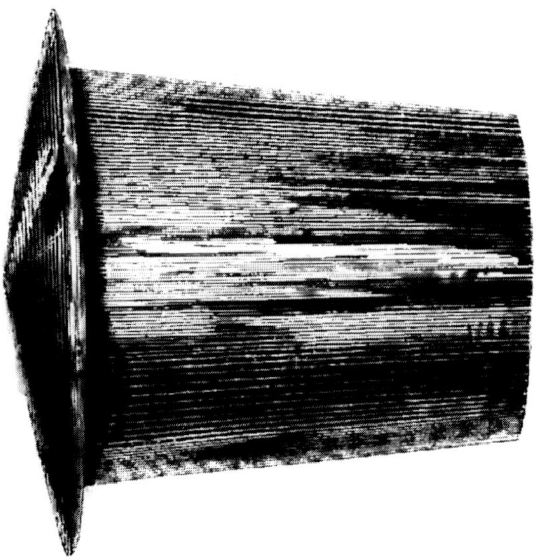

WOODEN EAR-CYLINDER.

another, and another, until, in the course of a year or two, the ear is drawn down almost to the shoulder; without this the appearance of the maiden is supposed to be very incomplete. The hole is enlarged and kept open by a piece of palm leaf rolled up so as to form a light spring, or by a heavy wooden cylinder, represented of the ordinary size in the illustration on the preceding page.

Occasionally the ring of flesh breaks under the operation, or is accidentally torn, and the ends have to be cut afresh and re-attached, bandaged with a small piece of the wing of a bat, anointed with oil, and carefully tended till they re-unite. In the opening of the ear thus unnaturally enlarged, a circular ornament of gold or other material, of monstrous size, is worn on marriage and other festive and full dress occasions.

Nose jewels, too, are required by the demands of female fashion in Travancore. These are sometimes mere studs, worn on one side of the nose, and fastened with a little pin inside. Or a large gold ring, two inches in diameter, is passed through the nasal cartilage, and hangs over a considerable portion of the mouth. This must be held up by one hand, or removed, while partaking of food. These golden ornaments are considered by the natives to form an admirable contrast with the dark complexion, and to add greatly to the beauty and bright expression of the countenance. Necklaces of gold, silver, brass, or beads are worn by all except widows, who are compelled to lay aside all ornaments and all coloured articles of dress. In the case of the poor slave women, the necklaces of beads, &c., hanging across the breast are so numerous as almost to amount to an additional article of clothing.

The "*tāli*"—marriage badge, or neck ornament—corresponds, to all intents and purposes, to the wedding ring amongst Europeans. It is composed of one or more small gold jewels and beads strung on a twisted thread. The "tāli" is tied on the bride's neck by the bridegroom at the time of the wedding, and is worn as an auspicious ornament. It is preserved with great care, and never removed except in case of widowhood, when it is torn off and not again resumed. In the Christian form of marriage the national custom of "tying the tāli" is allowed and generally followed, though a few prefer to use the European marriage ring.

As already stated, low caste females in Travancore were forbidden to wear any clothing whatever above the waist. This restriction has recently been removed by law, but a lengthened period must yet elapse before the poorer classes, excepting those who enjoy the protection and support of the Christian community, dare to avail themselves largely of this privilege, on account of the jealousy of the higher castes. Nor, indeed, do all the low castes, as individuals, care greatly for the use of the privilege, except on special occasions, as it involves some trifling additional expense and trouble. However, it is now left by the Native Government, as it ought to be, to the free choice and right feeling of the parties themselves. On his first arrival in the country a European must be greatly shocked by seeing so large a proportion of the people going about in a state thus nearly approaching to nudity, and it requires a long time to become familiar with such a state of things. The dark complexion of the natives, perhaps, makes this custom seem less unnatural than it would be amongst Europeans. Christian and Mohammedan women wear a neat jacket of white or coloured cotton.

The Súdra and other middle-class females place a light cotton cloth loosely across the breast and over one shoulder. This is called the "upper cloth." But in the presence of the Royal Family or persons of high rank, or when saluting such persons passing by, ancient usage actually required the removal of this cloth. Since 1865, however, by the good feeling and enlightened action of the Maharajah and his Minister, this degrading custom was discountenanced and completely abolished by a Proclamation of which the following is a translation :—

"Whereas Súdra women, when in the presence of persons in high office, and when serving in the Temple or Palace, lower their upper garment as a mark of respect, this appears to His Highness (the sacred mind) exceedingly immodest. We have informed the aforesaid persons that this offensive custom is henceforth unnecessary. It is our will that all the native people wear garments in accordance with propriety, and this we now make known, when women in temples, in the Palace, and other places, shall cover the upper parts with the cloth, in accordance with this circular, we hereby order that the officials do not oppose their doing so."

The Brahman women are, as might be expected, much superior to others in regard to the proprieties of dress. While imposing barbarous and often inhuman restrictions upon others, the Brahmans have taken good care that they themselves shall not suffer any diminution of comfort or honour. The upper part of the dress of a Brahman lady consists of a smart coloured jacket, fastening in front, and covering the bosom, and over this in addition the upper cloth is also worn. The principal garment of all classes of females is a piece of cloth several yards in length, usually of white calico—sometimes coloured or checked—occasionally of silken materials. This is tightly wound around the waist and turned in at one end in a variety of forms, with neat folds, making a kind of petticoat. The other extremity is used as an "upper cloth," or shawl, by being thrown over the shoulder so as to cover the shoulders and bosom. Considerable ingenuity and taste are displayed in the mode of enveloping the person in this cloth, and the whole forms a very graceful and appropriate female dress.

Sundry ornaments and jewellery, with the names and uses of which a European gentleman can hardly be expected to be familiar, are worn by Hindu females in various ranks and conditions of life. Besides ornaments for the hair, nose-rings, earrings, and necklaces, there are armlets and bracelets of various patterns and materials, numerous rings of shell or metal on the fingers, large hollow rings on the ankles (never of gold), and rings on the second toe of the foot. In fact, when a native girl or woman goes out to walk in full dress, the "tinkle, tinkle, tinkle," which attends her movements are a notice that all may see she is dressed "in the tip-top of the fashion." One is reminded of the list of Jewish female ornaments in the third chapter of Isaiah, the names and uses of which seem to have perplexed commentators quite as much as those of the Hindu ladies puzzle present writers on India.

On no subject are Hindus more vigilant and prejudiced than on that of *food;* this being one of the great tests of orthodoxy. Caste rules, as we have seen, forbid their partaking of food in company with persons of lower caste, or which has been prepared by such. The profession of a cook, as well as that of a teacher, is highly honourable in India. Hence the exercise of extreme caution as to the individuals with whom they eat, and as to the preparation of food. After coming into personal contact with a low caste man or a European, a caste Hindu must bathe and perform other ceremonies before he dare again eat or drink. Their difficulties in this matter, while on a journey and under other circumstances, are incessant and annoying; yet the law of caste is unyielding, even in the most extreme cases. A European physician was invited to visit and prescribe for a Hindu Prince, who was suffering under a severe attack of illness. The medical gentleman was duly warned not to touch or approach the noble patient; but in his anxiety about the case he forgot the prohibition, and in the course of conversation drew his chair nearer and nearer. At last, rising for a moment, and laying his hand upon the post of the bed, he requested the patient to show his tongue. A groan of sympathetic horror and distress was uttered by the native attendants, for now their master had become polluted, and it would be necessary, notwithstanding the suffering and danger of using cold water, to bathe ere he could again partake of nourishment of any kind.

Long voyages are impracticable, because, in accordance with the laws of caste, food cannot be cooked or eaten on shipboard, and it is, of course, impossible to land for the preparation of every meal. I have sometimes seen native dignitaries at the table of Europeans, by whom they were invited as an act of courtesy, or giving a dinner at their own houses to European guests. On these occasions they sit and converse with their European friends, but dare not partake of a single particle of food with them, or in their presence.

The Brahmans profess to reject animal food of every kind, including eggs, but they indemnify themselves, to some extent, for this self-denial by the use of quantities of milk, curd, and butter. Súdras partake freely of mutton and poultry, and even pork, but to all, except the most degraded Hindus, the flesh of the cow is the object of unmitigated abhorrence. This, no doubt, arose originally from the peculiar utility of these humble and patient creatures for agricultural purposes, and the consequent idea of sacredness which became attached to them. Hence it is that European "beef-eaters" cannot but be viewed, from a caste point of view, with the greatest abhorrence.

"*Curry and rice*" is one of the favourite and characteristic dishes of the natives of India, and a capital article of food it is when properly prepared. The rice is well boiled in water. Curry is a compound of spices—such as mustard, pepper, turmeric, ginger, coriander seed, tamarinds, onions, cocoanut juice, &c., in varying proportions, according to the flavour required. The ingredients being ground with a stone roller, on a flat smooth stone, are boiled and added to the meat, fish, or vegetable which is to be "curried." When eating, the natives sit cross-legged upon the ground. The rice is ladled out upon a large plantain leaf, and a small quantity of the savoury curry soup is added. Plates, spoons, and forks are not used. A small quantity of the rice is taken up in the right hand, mixed with the curry, made into a little ball, and deftly thrown into the mouth. For liquids, the firm hard leaves of the jack tree are puckered up at one side and fastened with a thorn, so as to form a rude kind of spoon. These leaves are thrown away after being once used. Wealthy natives have many different kinds of curries set before them at each meal.

Vegetables and fruits of all kinds, milk and curds, rice and flour cakes, are largely used by the natives as food; of late coffee also is coming into use. A considerable variety of sweetmeats are sold in the bazaars. A light meal of "conjee," that is, rice with the water in which it is boiled, is taken early in the morning; curry and rice are ready by noon; and at sunset, or later, supper is made of the same dishes with the usual accompaniments.

In India, men and women never eat together. After the males of the family have finished their repast, the women, who have meanwhile been attending upon them, retire apart to their own quiet meals.

CHAPTER V.

THE NATIVE GOVERNMENT.

Relation to the British Government—Legislation—The Maharajah—His Titles—Court and Levees—The Dewān—Revenue and Expenditure—Law Courts—Crime and Criminals.

TRAVANCORE, though nominally an independent state, under the rule of its own native sovereign, is in reality, as we have shown, tributary to the British Government, and under its control and protection. All important measures of legislation and finance, the appointment of the higher officials, and even the succession to the musnud, or throne, must be submitted to the British Resident for his opinion and sanction before being carried into operation. Sentences of capital punishment, too, must have the concurrence of the Resident before being executed. Without some such external restraint and stimulus, the country, with its rigid Hindu conservatism and barbarous caste laws, could never have improved as it has done for the last ten or twelve years, so as to be now, except in the matter of the low-caste population, who are treated as quite out of the pale of *human* society and laws, confessedly one of the best governed native states in India. In many instances it has been only after considerable moral pressure, both from public opinion and from the British representatives, that the native Government have yielded to accept the reforms urged upon them.

Notwithstanding all that has been accomplished, however, very much yet remains to be effected in the improvement of legislation, and the extension of freedom to all classes of the population. Large and liberal measures are still imperatively required for the benefit of the oppressed and down-trodden low castes. These are not, it should be remembered, in every instance, necessarily poor or destitute of capacity and moral character, in proportion to their position in the arbitrary scale of caste. The masses of the low-caste population have been as yet but slightly touched by the partial reforms of the Travancore Government. They ought, for instance, to have a fair share in the scheme of Government education, from which they are at present excluded solely on account of caste. Children of low caste are refused admittance into nearly all the Government English and vernacular schools; yet these contribute their fair quota to the public funds, which are wasted on Brahmanical rites, or expended almost exclusively on the education of the higher castes. Although permission to cover the upper part of the person has been given to the lower castes, they are still by law restricted to the use of *coarse* cloths, to the manifest detriment of the national commerce and manufactures. Any advance, too, in the use of richer ornaments, palankeens, and other luuxuries, on the part of wealthy members of these castes, is strictly prohibited. The public roads, also, ought to be opened freely to all classes, and admission to all the courts conceded to even the lowest and most despised of the population.* Moreover, the flourishing, peaceful, and loyal native Protestant Christian community claims recognition by the Government as a body with a status of its own, like the Mohammedans, Syrian Christians, and Jews. Native Protestant Christians should be specified in the census, and admitted to the police, the civil service, and any other employments and offices in the state for which they may

* See Note on p. 46.

prove themselves to possess the requisite qualifications. In short, the *half a million* low-caste people, constituting no less than *one-third* of the whole population, should be educated, enfranchised, invested with the rights of citizenship, and admitted to the enjoyment of the natural and indefeasible rights and liberties which belong to every member of the great human family.

The official titles of the MAHARAJAH of Travancore are sufficiently numerous and imposing. The title in full is as follows:—"His Highness Sree Patmanābha Dausa Vunchee Baula Rāma Vurmah Koolasekhara Kireetapati Munnay Sultān Mahārāj Rājah Rāmarājah Bahādur Shamsheer Jung, Knight Grand Commander of the Most Exalted Order of the Star of India, Maharajah of Travancore."

"Mahā" is the Sanscrit term for "great" or "mighty," as "rajah" means "king." The title "Maharajah" had long been used by native subjects, but it was only in 1866 that the British Government resolved that in recognition of the Rajah's excellent administration of the state he should in future be addressed in all communications as "Maharajah."

In the same year the order of the Star of India was conferred on his Highness as a mark of her Majesty's royal favour. The letter announcing the nomination as Knight Grand Commander was formally received at a grand "durbar," or levee, in Trevandrum, and the insignia were presented to his Highness by Lord Napier, Governor of Madras, in that city.

The personal name of the present Maharajah is "Rāma Vurmah," the names of two Hindu deities. "Shamsheer Jung" means "Chief in War." The remaining titles mostly refer to the names of Hindu gods, or are indicative of regal authority and dignity.

Durbars or levees are held by the Maharajah on state occasions,—such as the installation of the sovereign, mar-

THE FIRST PRINCE, MAHARAJAH, AND DEWAN OF TRAVANCORE.

(*Face page 69.*)

riages in the royal family, visits of the Governor of Madras, or the reception of state letters and documents. A brief description of the first durbar which the writer attended may interest our readers. This took place on the 2nd of May, 1860. The occasion was the reception of an autograph letter and handsome present from her Majesty the Queen to the late Rajah. Invitations had been issued by the Resident, on behalf of the Rajah, to most of the Europeans resident in the country, so that the unusually large number of thirty or forty were present at the durbar. The native houses in the town were decorated with bright-coloured flowers and plantain trees in fruit, and festoons of flowers and the green leaves of the palm tree cut and plaited into a variety of ornamental shapes, were strung across from house to house. At three o'clock we drove to the palace, and entered a magnificent pavilion which had been erected for the occasion. This was prettily adorned with garlands, hangings, mirrors and ornamental work, and supplied with showy European furniture. At the head of the room stood an ivory throne, with a shield and bow at the sides; above it was a glittering canopy supported by four silver pillars. In this hall the guests were already assembling, and a crowd of native officials stood around. The Dewān, a pleasant-looking man, short in stature, with a very intelligent countenance, fair complexion, and bright expressive eyes, dressed in white robes with gold spangles, and a white turban, engaged in polite conversation with the visitors.

Shortly afterwards, the Rajah, a rather stout and fine-looking man, entered the room, accompanied by the Princes, his nephews. He wore a robe of green satin, and a white turban, garnished with emeralds and a drooping plume of feathers, with two large pendent pearls. After bowing to the company, his Highness passed on to view his little army drawn up with military display in front of the palace, where also were the gigantic state elephants gorgeously caparisoned with howdahs and trappings of silver, ivory, and velvet, and an immense crowd of native spectators. On his appearance the troops presented arms, and the band struck up the national anthem.

At half-past three the British Resident arrived in procession, with his escort of British sepoys, and was saluted by the native troops. He was met and received at the door of the Durbar Hall by the First Prince, and a little farther on by the Rajah himself. Here he presented the Queen's letter to his Highness, who received and opened it, and taking the Resident's arm, proceeded up the hall to the throne. The Europeans, at the same time, took their seats in their order of precedence, on chairs ranged on either side of the room. There were present, besides the British Resident and Mrs. Maltby, Colonel Stevenson, who was charged with the safe delivery of the Royal letter, the commanding officers of the Nair Brigade and the residency escort, other military officers, judges, medical gentlemen, engineers, merchants, and missionaries, with their respective wives. The native officials stood behind as spectators.

The letter from the Queen acknowledged the present of an ivory throne, beautifully carved, which had been forwarded to the Great Exhibition of 1851, and was afterwards given by the Rajah to her Majesty. (It is now in one of the apartments of Windsor Castle.) The Queen sent, in return, a handsome ornamental belt, with rich gold embroidery and buckle, set with precious stones and containing a watch with the initials of the Queen and the Rajah, set with diamonds in blue enamel, on the opposite sides. The Resident then presented the case containing the belt to his Highness, who placed it for a moment on his head as a mark of great respect. The belt was put on the Rajah by the Resident, and his Highness in a short speech expressed his great gratification with the present, declaring that he regarded himself as the most fortunate prince in India, on account of it.

Three cheers for the Queen were then given, amid the deafening roar of a royal salute from the artillery and volleys of musketry. After a short time spent in formal conversation—the Rajah, addressing the Dewān, who repeated his remarks to the Resident, and carried back his answers in return—the durbar closed.

Before leaving, garlands of jessamine, fragrant leaves and tinsel ornaments were placed, according to Hindu custom, by the Rajah round the neck and on the wrists of the Resident and his lady. The Princes did the same for the remainder of the guests, each *salāming* and shaking hands with their Highnesses at the door of the palace.

The Dewān, or Prime Minister, is at the head of the whole administration of the State, and responsible only to the Maharajah, and indirectly to the British Government. The present Dewān, Sir Madava Row, Knight Commander of the Order of the Star of India, is a Mahratta Brahman of great talents and probity. Having enjoyed the benefit of a liberal education at the Madras University, he became English tutor to the present Maharajah and his brother. He afterwards received the appointment of Peishcar, and in 1858 became Dewān. It seems providential that his eminent talents, firmness, and political sagacity have for so long a time been devoted to the interests of Travancore. He has had a large share in the improvements which have taken place—in the removal of several long-established evils, the amendment of the laws and administration of justice, and in the establishment of valuable educational and benevolent institutions. His own example and personal influence in favour of popular education have also produced most beneficial results.

The country is divided, for purposes of government, into

four "divisions," or provinces, each in charge of a "Dewān Peishcar," or provincial governor, and these are subdivided into thirty-two "districts," or counties, with a "Tahsildar," or magistrate, at the head of each. There are also numerous minor subdivisions under the charge of inferior officers.

The annual revenue of the Travancore State amounts on an average to about forty-five lacs of rupees, or £450,000 sterling. For the last two years it has exceeded 50 lacs. Of this sum, above one-third, £165,000, or more, is raised by taxes on land, rice-fields, gardens, and productive trees—such as palms, jack trees, and coffee. Customs duties on imports and exports, by land and sea—especially the exports of cocoa-nut produce, tamarinds, and coffee, yield say £35,000. The import duty on tobacco brings about £80,000, and that on salt £85,000, besides which there are taxes on arrack and opium, pepper, cardamoms, timber, &c.

The usual annual expenditure includes about £56,000 (somewhat less during the past two years) for the maintenance of Hindu temples; £30,000, or more, for the Free Inns for Brahmans; and occasionally large sums in addition for extraordinary religious ceremonies, such as the sexennial Murajabam, which costs £16,000, the "Tulābhāram" ceremony £16,000, and others of a similar character. The Maharajah's personal expenditure is within £50,000 per annum. Public works, to the extent of between £50,000 and £60,000, are annually undertaken. The Nair troops, about 1,400 in number, with European officers, maintained for purposes of State and the preservation of internal peace, cost £15,000 a year. The annual subsidy paid to the British Government is fixed at about £81,000. The remainder of the income is expended on the civil, judicial, and police establishments, with some £30,000, or more, paid for various goods, as salt, tobacco, timber, &c., of which the Government retains the monopoly, or which it purchases and sells at considerable profit.

It will be seen that the taxes in Travancore amount to about three rupees, or six shillings, per head, a sum somewhat higher than the average taxation in British India.

The High Court, in which there are four judges, sits at Trevandrum, and receives appeals in both civil and criminal cases. One of the judges is always a Christian, as so large a proportion of the people are Christians of various sects. Subordinate to this court are the District Civil and Criminal Courts, each held at some central town in one of the principal divisions. Each court has two judges, of whom one is a Christian. There are in addition small cause courts, besides the various police courts at the head-quarters of each Tahsildar. Appeals may be made ultimately from all these tribunals to the royal justice and supremacy of his Highness the Maharajah.

Litigation is common amongst all classes. This arises from many causes, such as the minute subdivision of lands and the intricate tenures on which they are held, the peculiar laws of succession and inheritance, family partnerships and participation in common property, caste regulations, jealousies and oppressions, religious disputes, the injustice and partiality of inferior Government officials, assaults, forgeries and fraud, larcenies, and so forth. There are few natives who have not had, at some time or other, dealings with the law, and I have often marvelled at the pertinacity and dogged determination evinced by them in disputes which involved apparently very insignificant interests.

Crime is not at present particularly rife in Travancore. There is no organized crime, nor are there professional criminals. The commonest offences are those against the person and against property, and disputes regarding the possession of land, with cases of smuggling, forgery, perjury, &c.

In 1869, 542 persons, of whom a few were females, were charged with the graver offences. Yet this is not an unfavourable average in a population of a million and a half. There were 24 charges tried of culpable homicide, involving 62 persons, which (with the average of previous years) is a much larger proportion than in England. Of these, 3 were sentenced to capital punishment. The attempts at suicide were 16; and the actual deaths by suicide, so far as ascertained, were 52. The number of accidental deaths was 200.

The favourite mode of committing suicide is by hanging from a tree or drowning in a well. Natives frequently threaten this if thwarted or denied their requests, and the mere threat is often effectual for their purpose. It is sometimes actually carried out in revenge for some injury, real or imagined. The offended party kills himself on the premises of his adversary, under the erroneous impression that he will be held responsible for the occurrence. Indeed, in old times it generally did require the expenditure of large sums of money in bribing the police, who were ever ready to take advantage of the terror and misgivings of the party implicated, and of the uncertainty often necessarily arising as to whether the case was one of suicide or of murder.

There are generally 500 or 600 convicts in the several prisons, of whom above 400 are in the principal gaol at Trevandrum. Of the whole number, about 60 are under confinement for life. Most of the convicts are sentenced to hard labour, and go out daily under the charge of guards to work in gangs on the roads. Round the ankles of the male prisoners heavy iron rings are fastened, and these are united by cross bars which admit of their walking, but not with ease. Very rarely is solitary confinement resorted to. The prison at Trevandrum consists of a long, two-storied building, running round the sides of a square yard or open space with a noble banyan tree in the centre, under the shade of which stands a small temple for the use of the heathen prisoners. The ground-floor is supported by pillars, and is open towards the yard all round. The men sleep on mats on the floor, with a small wooden or stuffed pillow for the head. They are grouped according to their respective castes. In one corner may be seen a number of comfortable-looking Brahmans, some of whom are wealthy men, convicted of forgery and other crimes. These are allowed the privilege of going outside the prison to the Free Inn for meals, to avoid pollution by their fellow-prisoners of low caste. Next come Súdras and artisans. Another part of the long arcade is occupied by Mohammedans, who are often troublesome and unmanageable. Next, in a corner, you come to the Roman Catholics, with their little altar built into the wall, surmounted by a cross and a common coloured print of the Virgin Mary. These appear to be quiet people, and are often observed perusing devotional books. Next are the Protestant Christian prisoners, generally from fifteen to twenty in number, who have been more or less closely associated with the London Mission or the Church Mission, or have professed to receive Christianity in the prison itself. All the Christians have a holiday out of the prison on Christmas day and Easter Sunday. Our Sunday services are held in this part of the prison, so that any who wish may come over and hear; and this many are in the habit of doing. Further on are Pulayars and other very low castes. None of the regular European systems of discipline are carried out in these prisons.

For several years past the Government have very liberally granted us admission to the gaols at Trevandrum and Quilon for the purpose of instructing the Christian prisoners; these are rarely, it should be observed, baptized and recognised converts, but mere occasional attendants at our places of worship. Our efforts and instructions have incidentally, we believe, been the means also of much good to other classes of prisoners.

CHAPTER VI.

NATURAL HISTORY.

Elephants and Tigers — Deer — Monkeys — Jackals — Mungoose — Flying Fox—Sacred Kite — Weaver and Tailor Birds — Crows — Peacocks — Singing Birds—Crocodiles —Snakes — Serpent-worship—Fish—Sharks —Insects—White Ants—Conch Shell.

The natural history of Travancore is of the most comprehensive and instructive character. Air, earth, and water alike teem with animal and vegetable life. A few cursory remarks, therefore, on the most common animals, plants, and minerals will gratify many readers.

Throughout the dense and yet only partially explored forests of the valleys and table-lands of the Western Ghauts, wild beasts still abound. Many elephants are annually captured or destroyed; yet they still remain numerous, and are often dangerous to the life and property of the inhabitants of the mountain slopes. It may easily be imagined what would be the condition of a field of growing rice after having been trodden over by half a dozen of these gigantic creatures with their broad round feet. The hill people, therefore, are compelled to place watchmen at night in the tops of trees to frighten off these formidable visitors with cries and hideous noises. Indeed, in those parts where elephants and tigers most abound, the mountaineers are obliged to erect little huts in the tops of the trees for refuge and security. I have seen a house erected by the labourers at a coffee plantation which the wild elephants had actually walked right through one night, treading down the house as a stout boy might trample over the plants in a cabbage-garden. The poor men sleeping inside were glad to escape with their lives. To avoid similar rencounters, the hill people select a large tree with spreading branches. Light beams are lashed across from one branch to another, so as to form a rude platform, and upon this foundation a hut of bamboo or other light materials is built as a watch-house by day and sleeping-room by night. The ascent is by a long stout bamboo, with the side branches cut off to within a foot of the stem, thus forming a kind of rude ladder.

Solitary or "rogue" elephants are occasionally met wandering about alone in the forests. These are always dangerous. Not long since, four of the Nāgercoil Christians were descending the mountains from a coffee plantation in which they had been employed, when one of these "rogue" elephants rushed upon them. They ran, and did not venture to look back till they had gone a long distance. Then it was discovered that one of their party was missing. Hastening to the nearest chapel, they called some of the Christians to accompany them in search of the body of their comrade, and found it crushed and mangled by the savage brute. This animal killed altogether seven or eight persons.

Wild elephants are caught in large pits dug in the paths which they frequent, and concealed with a slight covering of twigs, earth, and grass. They are afterwards trained for six or twelve months, and accustomed by degrees to work and to enjoy a measure of liberty. The stud of elephants employed by the Travancore Government in dragging timber in the forests, labouring at public works, and otherwise, numbers about 120. Every year some are entrapped, and about 1,000 pounds of ivory collected. I have seen a single large tusk which weighed nearly 80 pounds.

Tigers and leopards, or cheetahs, are also common and often dangerous. Rewards are paid by the Government for their destruction. During 1869 the skins of 23 royal tigers and 112 cheetahs, killed by natives, were brought to the Dewān's office for the reward. Their depredations had been on the increase. Poor people are sometimes seized, carried off, and devoured by the tigers. An instance of the boldness and audacity of these beasts was related to me by the gentleman to whom it happened. He had a little house near his estate in the mountains, with a back room in which a milch cow was secured at night. One evening while sitting reading he heard a scuffling noise in the back room, and stepped into it to discover the cause. The cow was gone. A tiger had actually been bold enough to enter and carry it off. Next day he found the remains partly devoured, and watched the whole of the succeeding night in a tree to have a shot at the depredator; but the night was so dark that this proved impracticable.

The flesh of the tiger is supposed by the natives to possess medicinal properties, and its claws strung round the neck of a child are relied on to preserve it from the evil eye.

Black cheetahs are occasionally caught. Several of these are exhibited in the zoological collection at Trevandrum, where the female lately produced four cubs. These are probably a mere variety rather than a different species, as the spots can easily be seen through the dark hair when the light shines strongly on the skin.

Several species of deer are found in these mountains. The smallest is a beautiful creature about the size of a hare, and most graceful in its form and movements. Another species is the spotted deer, about the size of a calf; and a third, the *sambhur*, dark brown in colour, is as large as an ordinary ox. There are also antelopes, and the wild goat or ibex.

The wild oxen, found only in the more retired parts of the forests, are enormous animals, fully as large as the finest prize cattle in England. The bulls measure sometimes over six feet in height at the shoulder, and are possessed of immense muscular power.

Long-tailed monkeys gambol in the most amusing style in the lofty forest trees. The Hanuman, or sacred monkey, is about three feet in height, and quite black. They are generally vicious and intractable in a state of captivity. The Rāmāyana relates that Hanumat, a monkey chieftain, aided the hero and demigod, Rāma, in the search for his wife, Sita, who had been seized and carried off to Ceylon by Rāvana, King of the Giants. Visiting the city of Rāvana as a spy, Hanumat is detected and punished by having his tail oiled and set on fire, which appendage monkeys hold in great esteem. It was in extinguishing this fire, they say, that his face became blackened, and his posterity have been black ever since.

An isolated hill not far from Nāgercoil is said to have been brought from a distance of several hundred miles, and thrown down in its present situation by Hanuman. He was sent to the mountain to search for medicinal plants, but was unable to find them. Still, he knew that they were somewhere in the mountain, and to prevent disappointment he resolved to bring it entire, and get others to investigate the plants. He took it up and carried it through the air, but in putting it down he set it upside down, in which condition the people say it now is.

The following amusing story of one of these monkeys is told by Rev. J. Duthie :—

" One day a gentleman succeeded in catching one of these animals, which turned out to be of a very vicious disposition, and it was resolved to send him to a neighbour who had expressed a wish to have him. A strong basket was procured, into which, after no inconsiderable trouble and manœuvring, he was safely lodged. Jacko was furious; but the coolie who had been engaged to carry the load set off with it on his head, without any fear or misgivings, for the basket was strong and the lid carefully fastened down. He had not gone far, however, when, to our surprise, we heard screams proceeding from the direction in which Jacko had just been conveyed, and upon going out to see what the matter could be, we found the entire juvenile community of the station hailing towards the scene of the disaster, where stood the poor unfortunate coolie, screaming and gesticulating in a most piteous way. The people of India shave off all the hair of the head except a tuft on the crown, which on the present occasion proved to be very inconvenient, for Jacko, having torn open the bottom of the basket, seized hold of this tuft on the head of the coolie, to which he held on with relentless grasp. The more the poor man exerted himself to get rid of his basket, the more forcibly Jacko held on, till the friendly interference of the boys who had gathered to the spot succeeded, amid much merriment, in delivering the coolie from his perilous and ridiculous position."*

Another species is the small grey monkey, common throughout India. There is also a very pretty animal, called the wanderoo, or lion monkey. The body is covered with short black hair, and a long white beard or mane surrounding the face gives it a very odd appearance. The last two species are often tamed and kept as pets for children.

Other animals occasionally met with are hyenas, bears, sloths, wolves, and flying squirrels. The pangolin is a kind of armadillo, three or four feet long, which digs holes in the earth with its powerful claws with marvellous facility. Wild hogs are very mischievous to the cultivations near the foot of the hills.

* *Juvenile Missionary Magazine*, April, 1870.

The larger mammalia fortunately do not often descend into the low country. Here the greatest annoyances are jackals, with their diabolic howlings, which one can hardly distinguish at first from the cries of a woman in anguish or of children being murdered. These animals lurk in quiet retirement through the day, but come forth in the evening, and hunt about in packs all night in search of prey. The porcupine, or "spiny pig," as it is called, is very destructive to esculent roots, which it digs up and devours. Hares are not uncommon.

The mungoose, somewhat like a weasel, but larger, is very valuable as a foe to the cobra and other venomous serpents. Being wonderfully agile, it worries and torments the snake till it twists itself up in a coil; it then springs upon it, and seizing it by the neck soon despatches it. These nimble creatures are rarely bitten, but even then, strange to say, the venom appears to produce no effect. It was formerly supposed that there is a plant (*Ophiorrhiza mungos*) to which the mungoose resorted as an antidote to the poison; but recent experiments seem to demonstrate that the venom of serpents does not poison the blood of the mungoose as it does that of all other animals. If so it is a striking provision of Providence for reducing the numbers of these reptiles. The mungoose is easily tamed, and makes itself very useful about a dwelling-house in the destruction of snakes and vermin.

The flying fox is the largest of the numerous species of bats, measuring upwards of four feet in expanse of wing, the body being as large as that of a chicken. On the wide-spreading banyan trees, near temples, these creatures may be seen in multitudes hanging by one leg, with the head downwards and the wings wrapped round the body, looking very like black bottles hung in rows upon the branches. Here they sleep all day long. Towards evening they awake and fly abroad in search of fruits and other food. They are destructive to the ripening fruit in orchards and gardens. The flesh is said to be good eating.

Birds of brilliant plumage, graceful form, and sometimes pleasant song, abound in the forests, jungles, and cultivated lands of Travancore. The Brahminy kite, a very handsome bird with brown and white plumage, is regarded as the vehicle of Vishnu, to whom it is therefore sacred. On Saturday afternoons crowds may be seen assembled and looking up towards the sky; they fast and continue gazing upward till sunset. If the sacred kite appears, it is worshipped; if not, the unlucky gazers return home in great heaviness of heart.

Amongst other birds may be mentioned the tall adjutant, or marabou stork, some of the feathers of which are highly prized; the curious hornbills (sometimes incorrectly called toucans); herons and cranes in the marshes and backwaters, which are supposed to be very lucky to the beholder; owls, whose hoarse hoot is supposed to presage pestilence or misfortune; the woodpecker, constantly tap-tapping the trunks of trees in search of insects; the magnificent golden oriole, and the brilliant blue jay; splendid kingfishers, sitting patiently and silently on an overhanging branch, then darting down like an arrow into the water to seize the fish on which they prey; ringed parrakeets, in large flocks, harshly screaming as they fly; sunbirds, little larger than humming-birds, flitting gaily from flower to flower; with the rarer wild goose and duck, the quail, grouse and partridge, the cuckoo, dove, and hundreds of other species.

The mynah, which may be regarded as a kind of starling, is often taken young, caged, and trained to utter a few words. The jungle fowl, a small bird with brilliant plumage, but singularly shy in its habits, is perhaps the original of the common domestic fowl. The weaver bird, one of the family of finches, builds a long pendent bottle-shaped nest, which hangs from the end of a branch, and is entered from beneath, quite out of the reach of monkeys and serpents. The tailor-bird, a little warbler, actually stitches leaves together with cotton, which it gathers for the purpose, to form its nest in the cavity; I have sometimes found these in garden shrubs quite close to the window of my study. Crows abound everywhere: their impudence and thievery are astounding; I have known them carry off the wick and smaller portions of a brass lamp while it was being cleaned at the back of the bungalow.

One of the finest sights that can be enjoyed is that of a flock of peacocks flying about in the jungles. There is a curious fact connected with the name of this bird which throws some light upon Scripture history. King Solomon (1 Kings x. 22) sent his navy to Tarshish, which returned once in three years, bringing "gold and silver, ivory, and apes, and peacocks." Now the word used in the Hebrew Bible for peacock is "*tukki*," and as the Jews had, of course, no word for these fine birds till they were first imported into Judea by King Solomon, there is no doubt that "tukki" is simply the old Tamil word "*tokei*," the name of the peacock. This is therefore the first word of the Tamil language that ever was put in writing. The ape or monkey also is, in Hebrew, called "*koph*," the Indian word for which is "kapi." Ivory, we have seen, is abundant in South India, and gold is widely distributed in the rivers of the Western coast. Hence the "Tarshish" referred to was doubtless the Western coast of India, and Solomon's ships were the first "East Indiamen." From a very early period there has been maritime intercourse between the West coast and Arabia, and this was the first part of India reached in more recent times by European explorers, attracted by the valuable products of the East. A learned missionary, Dr. Caldwell, even conjectures that certain huge old specimens of the baobab tree (which is not indigenous to India, but belongs properly to Africa), found only at several ancient sites of foreign commerce, may, for aught we can tell, have been introduced into India, or planted, by the servants of King Solomon.*

It is often supposed in England that the birds of India do not sing, and are remarkable only for their fine plumage. But this is an error. The bulbul is a lively and agreeable warbler, as are other birds of the thrush family. A species of shrike sings most charmingly, and the Indian nightingale is exceeded only by the European species. The white-headed mynah, Indian robin, stonechat, and a species of flycatcher, are sweet songsters. The notes of the jungle mynah are very varied and pleasing. A species of lark which is frequently kept in a darkened cage, sings very sweetly, and learns to imitate exactly the notes of other birds and even animals. There are also several mimicking birds, and many others which utter strange or curious sounds or cries.

The largest and most formidable of the reptiles of Travancore are crocodiles, which may often be seen lying sunning themselves on the grassy banks of the rivers and backwaters, or swimming in the water with only the upper portion of the head visible, or lying in a hole in the bank of the river with the head protruded and the mouth wide agape, ready to snap upon any living thing which may come within reach. There are two species of crocodiles, the smaller and more common, generally six or seven feet in length, and not ordinarily dangerous to human life; the larger reaching the length of eighteen or twenty feet. The latter are more dangerous; still, one does not often hear of lives being lost by them in this part of India.

* "Comparative Grammar of the Dravidian Languages," p. 66.

A curious story is told of a crocodile which attempted to seize a cow that was grazing near its haunts fastened to a stake by a long rope. The monster had nearly reached the wooden post before it was perceived by its intended victim. On discovering its danger the terrified cow rushed round and round, and the rope caught the crocodile in such a manner as to wind around its body and the post, so that it was held firmly until seen and despatched by the owner of the cow.

In former times, when trial by ordeal was practised, one mode was to require the accused party to swim through a river infested by voracious crocodiles; if he succeeded in crossing in safety he was acquitted. Some of the people do not object to eat the flesh of these reptiles.

The guāna, a large lizard three or four feet in length, is not rare, and its flesh is considered excellent for food. Chameleons and many other lizards, tortoises, and turtles, are also found in their respective habitats.

But the most noxious of all the reptiles, and indeed one of the most incessant discomforts and ubiquitous perils of life in India, are the *snakes* and serpents of every kind, including the enormous boas, or rock snakes, which infest the mountains, measuring up to seventeen feet or more in length, the deadly venomous cobras, the beautiful bright-coloured and striped sea-serpents, and all the varieties of lesser snakes. Of course, all the species are not venomous, and perhaps those whose bite is speedily fatal form, in reality, but a small proportion of the whole. The boas, or pythons, destroy their prey by winding themselves around their bodies and crushing them. Others are perfectly innocuous, such as the pretty green tree snakes, with which children sometimes play, and which the natives suppose to be a good cure for headache when killed and tied around the head and over the forehead. But there is a sufficient number of cobras and vipers to cause great danger to the poor people who are compelled to walk abroad after dark, and in unfrequented places. When accidentally trodden upon they instinctively turn and bite, in self-defence as it were. Many deaths consequently occur. In 1862, in Bengal alone 2,394 persons met their deaths from snake bites. At this rate, it may be estimated that throughout the whole of India not less than 10,000 persons annually die from this cause, in addition to an equal number destroyed by wild beasts.

The Bengal Government spent at that time £2,000 annually in rewards, at the rate of sixpence for each snake killed. Yet, though multitudes of these reptiles are destroyed every year, they increase so rapidly in uncultivated lands, of which there is a large proportion everywhere, and are so lithe and slender, that they still find their way into villages and towns, and are frequently found in the vicinity of houses, so that it would be difficult, not to say impossible, wholly to eradicate them from the country.

Innumerable anecdotes might be related of these repulsive and insidious creatures. Indeed, it is a common remark that if conversation flags in society in India, one has only to introduce the subject of snakes, and every one present has some personal experience which he is eager to relate. I have on various occasions found cobras and other serpents in the garden, in the thatch of the bungalow when annually renewed, creeping about amongst the flower-pots, in the bath-room, in the soiled clothes basket, and once even under the bed. On one occasion I was climbing a tree to examine its flowers, and grasped a branch which felt unnaturally soft. It was a viper asleep on the branch. The last snake I killed was on the window of my bedroom. Rain had been falling all night, and the unfortunate snake no doubt expected to find hospitality and shelter, if anywhere, in the house of a missionary. Creeping in by the lattice of the window he quietly lay down to sleep on the frame. Finding the intruder there, on rising in the morning, I took a large knife, and at one blow struck off his head.

We take care to bury the snakes when killed, lest any of the natives with their bare feet should tread upon the fangs, which still retain their deadly venom. In short, one never feels quite at ease when walking through grass, sitting in the open air, or putting one's hand behind a shelf or box. Children are a continual source of anxiety to careful parents. One of the native children of our boarding-school while at home in the vacation, and walking about her brother's garden, leant her hand upon the wall of the enclosure. A cobra concealed in a hole bit her, and she died in about two hours. An illustration this of the expression in Amos v. 19, "As if a man leaned his hand on the wall, and a serpent bit him."

No certain specific is known for the cure of snake bites, though liberal rewards have been offered, and extended experiments made, with this view. Ammonia is probably the most useful medicine in these cases.

The serpent is very generally an object of worship to Hindus, especially on the Western coast. Many stone images of the cobra are found in temples and sacred localities. That represented in the illustration on the next page was renounced by some of the natives of Travancore on their conversion to Christianity, nearly forty years ago, and sent to England. A similar one is in the possession of the writer. The national deity, too, is supposed to recline on a great five-headed serpent. A large brazen gilt image of the serpent is worshipped at Nāgercoil, and carried out in procession, like other idols, once a year. Brahmans sometimes worship silver representations of Vishnu trampling a serpent under his feet. The cobra is called "nalla pāmbu,"—"the good snake;"—certainly on the principle that it is dreaded, and must be propitiated and pacified by gentle words and acts of worship. The account of the origin of this worship given in the "Kerala Ulpatti" is to the effect that in early ages serpents, increasing to an insufferable degree, killed many of the

SERPENT IDOL.

people. The surviving inhabitants refused to reside longer in so dangerous a country. Parasu-Rāmen, therefore, allotted certain localities in which these reptiles should be placed, and receive offerings and sacrifices. This being done, the serpents were appeased, and ceased to torment the people.

Serpents are now worshipped chiefly by Súdras, Brahmans officiating as their priests. When Súdras observe a snake, they catch it by a cord with a noose tied to the end of a long rod, place it carefully in an earthen pot, and bring it to the place of worship. Should they find others killing these sacred reptiles, they earnestly beg for their protection, or lavish abuse on the persons who have committed the sacrilegious act. Offerings of fruits, cakes, flour, milk, rice, &c., are made to the snake god.

No doubt the worship of serpents is similar in principle and is closely connected with the demon-worship of South India. Amongst the Hindus everything that is specially remarkable, either for good or evil, becomes the object of religious veneration.

No fish of the salmon order are to be found in India. But the pomfret, seir fish, mullet, mackerel, eels, and many others, both salt and fresh water species, are excellent food, and much relished by the natives. One celebrated fish is the "climbing perch," which has sometimes been found a little way up the trunk of a palm tree. The natives call it the "palm climber," and it seems endued with capacity of living long out of water.

Sharks are abundant and dangerous, as well as their congeners, the sword-fish and saw-fish. The latter occasionally attack fishermen. A case was brought to our medical missionary in which the fish had left several inches of its bony snout in the thigh of a poor man whom it had attacked. The ray, also, uses the powerful spine at the base of its long whip-like tail, and I have seen the hand of a fisherman torn open by this powerful weapon.

The insect world in Travancore is exceedingly diversified and prolific, and is at times a perfect pest. Butterflies and moths of brilliant colours and elegant forms, locusts, grasshoppers, mantises, &c., abound. Several species of wild bees produce large quantities of honey on branches of trees and in clefts of rocks. Beetles are of all sizes, colours, and odd shapes. Some are tinted with brilliant green, scarlet, or gold. The *longicorne* bore their way into the terminal bud of the palm, utterly destroying these valuable trees. The great stag beetle measures 4½ inches in length, and 1½ in breadth. The first specimen which I caught, I rolled up in a pocket handkerchief to carry home for examination, but on my arrival found the handkerchief completely cut up by the powerful mandibles of the insect. Mosquitoes are very troublesome, especially in localities embosomed in trees. Myriads of ants, red, black, and brown,—large and small,—stinging and stingless, fill the whole land, so as to make it exceedingly difficult to preserve articles of food from their attacks. The order, sagacity, and habits of the numerous species of these little animals, would fill a volume with interesting matter. Scorpions, up to six inches in length, millipedes, centipedes, and monstrous spiders (*mygale*) infest the jungles and waste lands.

But perhaps the most annoying of all the insect population are the white ants, or termites, small and insignificant in size, but all-powerful by their vast numbers, constitutional order, and almost incredible voracity. They are divided into at least three classes of individuals—workers, soldiers, and queens. The workers are about the size of a grain of wheat, the soldiers twice as large, with an immense disproportionate head and mandibles, and the queens (of whom, as amongst bees, but one is found in each nest or community) are swelled out to the length of three or four inches. Another class with wings issues at certain periods in myriads from the nest, but these are mostly devoured by birds and black ants. The queen occupies the central cell, which is built of extra strong tempered clay, and has no opening sufficiently large to admit of her egress. She is therefore continually imprisoned in the cell, engaged in laying eggs, of which 80,000 per day are said to be produced. A numerous train of attendant nurses wait upon her majesty, carrying off the eggs as fast as possible into the nurseries, where they are tended with great care. When annoyed the working termites retire into their galleries, and hosts of soldiers rush out, prepared valiantly to attack the assailant.

These tiny mischievous insects devour everything except stones and metal. They burrow through the ground, and up the interior of brick walls, working in relays, and removing the mortar, grain by grain, to reach the wookwork of the ceiling and roof.

A box of woollen clothing, which was laid aside for some months, was found completely riddled with holes, as if a red-hot iron had been thrust through the articles in all directions. I have laid my Bible down on the window-sill of a chapel after evening service, and found it partially eaten by the morning; numbers of books are thus destroyed. Carpets cannot be used, as even a thick coating of tar preserves a floor only for a year or so. Wooden roofs and beams must be frequently inspected and the ants beaten off, and all furniture carefully examined daily, and placed at a little distance from the walls of the house. Indeed, a house built and furnished as in England, left unwatched, would be eaten up by these weak, yet mighty insects in a couple of months, leaving perhaps the bones and outer skin of the more solid tables and beams. To such a state of distress and consternation were the good people of St. Helena reduced a few years ago by the ravages of termites, which had somehow been introduced, that the Governor of the island wrote urgent appeals to India for suggestions as to the destruction of the white ants. But little could be done. Most of the houses and churches in St. Helena have since been rebuilt with iron beams and girders, such as even the white ants cannot devour.

The only certain means of keeping down their numbers is by the destruction of the queen, which causes the dispersion of the whole community. But this is very difficult, as the galleries and passages extend to the length of many feet, and the central cell may be underneath some wall or building, and at such a depth as cannot easily be reached. I have found only two queens during a residence of several years in India.

Of course these insects have their own duties and value in the economy of nature, for the removal from the luxuriant forests of the tropics of dead and decaying matter, which might otherwise produce malaria and disease.

Crustacea and molluscs are found in due proportion in Travancore. Land crabs burrow in the rice-fields, and are used as food by the slave castes. Oysters of indifferent quality are produced in the backwaters. The marine shells are mostly small in size and of little interest. The conch, or chunk shell, however (*Turbinella pyrum*), like a monstrous white whelk the size of a man's fist, is remarkable. It is the sacred shell of India, used in Brahman worship and on funeral and festive occasions as a kind of trumpet, a hole being made at the smaller end of the shell and blown into. This, too, is the national emblem of Travancore, stamped on some of the coins, sculptured in enlarged proportions over the gateway of the palace, impressed on the Government seal, and used in a variety of ways as the emblem of the state. A representation of this emblematic form of the conch shell will be found on the cover of this volume.

CHAPTER VII.

NATURAL HISTORY (*continued*).

Indigenous Plants — Grains—Yams and Roots — Fruits—Palms — Spices — Medicinal Plants—Timber Trees—Flowers and Fragrance—Minerals.

THE flora of Travancore is a subject of very wide extent, which can, therefore, only be treated in the briefest and most superficial manner in such a work as the present. There are few Europeans who have resided for any length of time in the country whose interest has not been excited in its vegetable productions. Whether arising from the great variety, beauty, and economic value of the vegetable kingdom in Travancore, or the leisure and facilities which British officials occasionally enjoy, there has been quite a succession of amateur botanists there for some time past. A very useful and comprehensive botanical work, the "Flora Indica," has recently been published by Colonel Drury, late of Trevandrum. Although wholly unacquainted with scientific methods of investigation, the natives themselves take great delight in the study of medical botany. Annual flower shows have for several years past been held in the capital, and are likely to exercise a beneficial influence on gardening and agriculture.

The climate being moist and hot, and the country presenting great diversities of land and water, mountain and valley—situations dry and moist, exposed and shady, from the level of the sea to the height of fully 5,000 feet—a very considerable variety of species are, as might be expected, found indigenous in Travancore.

The principal orders exemplified are grasses (including the giant bamboos), sedges, arums, palms, plantains, gingerworts, orchids, lilies, yams, euphorbias, cucurbits, capparids, malvaceæ, water-lilies, amaranths, pepperworts, leguminosæ (including a large proportion of the regular-flowered cassias and acacias), apocynaceæ, solanaceæ or nightshades, asclepiads, convolvuluses, jasmines, labiates, verbenas, bignonias or trumpet-flowers, acanths, asters or composite flowers, myrtles, and cinchonads.

For oaks, fir trees, apples, gooseberries, and many other plants of temperate regions, one would search in vain. Potatoes, except in the mountains, will not bring their tubers to maturity, though the plants will grow for a time. Cabbages and English peas hardly yield as much as will repay the trouble of their cultivation. Wheat is not grown at all in Travancore.

An ample variety of valuable grains and pulse, roots, fruits, spices, and other edibles are cultivated. Amongst grains the principal are rice, ragee, and various kinds of millet. The species of native peas, beans, and other pulse are very numerous.

Yams—the tubers of Dioscorea, a slender climbing plant—I have seen grow to nearly four feet in length and six inches in diameter. On one species, commonly called the "Travancore potato," additional tubers grow attached to the climbing stem, so that it may be said with truth that the potatoes grow upon the tops of the trees in that country, rather than underground. Yams are very palatable, but hardly so fine in flavour as the potato. Several species of arums produce large and nutritious roots, weighing sometimes seven or eight pounds each.

The sweet potato is a kind of convolvulus (*Batatas edulis*), with a sweet mealy tuber at the root. The tubers of a ginger-like plant (*Curcuma*) ground into flour, steeped in water and dried, yield East Indian arrowroot. Tapioca is largely grown, and yields an abundant return. It is the farina manufactured from the large fleshy roots of a shrub which is propagated by cuttings, and arrives to perfection within a year. The fresh roots contain a virulent poison, used by the American Indians for poisoning their arrows; but happily this is dissipated when heat in any form is applied to the roots. A large proportion of the people, in districts where water is scarce, or in times of drought, live, to a large extent, on these esculent roots.

Many excellent fruits are grown,—not all, however, properly indigenous to the country. The fine graft mango, which resembles an immense kidney-shaped plum, the size of a man's fist, juicy, and of most luscious flavour, is perhaps equal to any fruit in the world. Pineapples have long been domesticated, and grow in whole fields almost wild. They sell at a rate equal to about three for a penny, but these are not equal in flavour to the superior varieties found in gardens.

Plantains are used in public and social festivities, as an emblem of plenty and fertility, and well deserve the distinction. They are a delicious and useful fruit, of all varieties of flavour and size, and are used both as a vegetable and as a fruit. They are in season all the year round, and are perfectly wholesome, even when freely eaten. The succulent stem grows rapidly, rising to the height of from twelve to twenty feet, and perishing when it has once borne fruit; suckers spring up around the old stem. The large smooth leaves are used instead of plates by the Hindus while eating. The fruit is produced in heavy clusters of several hundreds, the bunch weighing sometimes seventy to eighty pounds. One of these bunches will be observed in the frontispiece. The plantain is as valuable to the people of India as the bread-fruit is to the South Sea Islanders. There is a very handsome wild plantain (*Musa superba*), of which I brought seeds to England; the young plants from these are now flourishing in Kew Gardens.

The jack, an odd-looking fruit of immense size, covered with thick green skin with blunt prickles, is a species of bread-fruit (*Artocarpus*). Inside are many pulpy fruits, packed in a viscid fibre around the central axis; each of these inner fruits contains a nut about the size of a pigeon's egg. The jack fruit is oval in shape, measuring about a foot and a half in length, and nine inches in diameter; the weight is from thirty to fifty pounds. Being so heavy, the fruit cannot be supported by the smaller branches; but in young trees they grow out of the large branches, afterwards from the stem, and, in very old trees, even on the root. Europeans who venture to taste these fruits generally begin to relish them after a few trials; but most ladies declare that *the smell* is quite enough. They certainly emit a powerful odour; but the natives are fond of them, and they constitute an important and wholesome article of food.

Custard apples, guāvas, cashew nuts, cucumbers, melons, and gourds of every description, with limes, papaws, and other fruits, grow abundantly and in great variety. On the whole, for abundance, variety, and excellence, the Indian fruits may be said to excel even those of Europe. Oranges and lemons, the bread-fruit, cocoa bean (*Theobroma cacao*), mangosteen, and others appear to deserve more attention and more extended cultivation than they receive at present.

The tamarind is a large umbrageous tree, producing pods with an acid pulp, which is an indispensable ingredient in curry, and is also made into good preserves.

A coarse sago is made from the pith of the *Cycas circinalis*, and from that of the Caryota palm. The cocoa-nut and Palmyra palms are of so great economic importance that we must reserve a fuller description of them and their uses to the next chapter.

Several of the most precious spices of the East are grown in Travancore. The black pepper vine covers the stem of a large tree like ivy, and large quantities of the dried berries are exported. It is proverbially styled "the money of Malabar." Chilies (from which is made Cayenne pepper) are the fruits of a small annual shrub. Cardamoms are the seed of a ginger-like plant which springs up spontaneously in certain localities in the mountains. Ginger is produced in considerable quantities. Turmeric root, resembling a yellow ginger, is much used in making curry. Cinnamon, cloves, and nutmegs are little grown, but are worthy of more attention. Coffee is now largely cultivated on the mountain slopes by European capitalists.

The natives of India may be constantly observed chewing what is called "betel nut." The "nut" is the fruit of the areca palm, closely resembling in appearance the common nutmeg; and "betel" is the dark green, heart-shaped leaf of a kind of climbing pepper plant, which grows like hops on poles, but twice as high; these are chewed together with a small quantity of lime. The teeth and mouth are dyed red by the use of these spices, and European physicians believe that this habit often produces cancer in the mouth and other painful affections.

The medicinal plants of Travancore merit, and would, doubtless, repay judicious investigation and experiment. The native doctors are sometimes successful in the administration of indigenous remedies, but their practice is entirely empirical, and their opinions respecting the medicinal properties of plants generally require confirmation. A competent physician would in time be able to determine how far the statements in native works on Materia Medica are reliable, and would probably discover many plants readily and cheaply procurable and of great service in medicine.

It is already well known that there are powerful tonics

and febrifuges, such as the bark of the Margosa tree and of Cedrela, the chiretta herb, and others; the fruit of the bael tree, the cultivation of which the Government of British India have of late sought to encourage and extend, is a specific in cases of obstinate diarrhœa and dysentery; hydrocotyle has obtained considerable repute as a remedy for leprosy; the milk of the papaw is a useful vermifuge, and the root of *Plumbago rosea* a sharp and speedy blister. The thorn-apple, bryony, croton, dill, nux vomica, catechu, senna, and the Indian jalap, ipecacuanha, liquorice, sarsaparilla, squill, and galls have already been recognised and introduced into European practice.

The commercial and economic value of many of the native vegetable products is already considerable; and might, if thoroughly developed, be largely augmented. Several valuable timber trees are plentiful. At the head of these stands the strong, fine, durable Teak, which flourishes best in the mountains, large quantities of which are annually cut for sale and exportation. In the Trevandrum museum a slab of teak is preserved measuring eight feet in length by above four feet in breadth, and perfectly sound throughout. Jack wood is much used as a furniture wood, but is somewhat brittle. When polished, it is very beautiful, and darkens with age, so as to resemble mahogany. Black-wood is the timber of a Dalbergia, not unlike rosewood in appearance. It is in great request for furniture, but is becoming much more scarce and high-priced than formerly. Cedar wood is very light and strong. Ebony is rare, and not equal to the Ceylon article. Anjely wood (*Artocarpus hirsutus*) is strong, durable, and easily worked, and is particularly useful in house and ship building. Canoes are often hollowed out of the great trunks of the anjely. The wood of Thespesia is fine-grained and dark, and looks well in small articles of furniture. There are also the woods of Terminalia, Bassia,

Lagerströmia, and many others; some, however, being too heavy for ordinary work.

The Bamboo is one of the most useful and admirable plants in India. It combines to an uncommon degree lightness, elasticity, and strength, and is indispensable to the Hindu. The young green shoots are eaten or made into preserves. A single joint is commonly used as a bottle for honey, milk, and other articles, or as a case for rolls of paper; a section of a joint is the ordinary rice measure. A long bamboo, with the side branches cut off to within a few inches from the main stem, makes a light ladder. The stems of various diameters are also used as rafters, levers, beams, boat-poles, masts and oars, water-pipes, fishing-rods, arrows, &c. The broad grassy leaves are used for thatching; indeed, the whole hut of a mountaineer is often constructed of the bamboo, with elastic flooring and beds made of the same material, partially split lengthwise, opened and flattened out into a kind of planks. Slips of the wood are used in the manufacture of bows, window-blinds, &c., and are woven into mats and baskets. The thorny varieties, being planted around villages, form a high and almost impervious stockade or fortification.

Dye-stuffs, consisting of woods and other vegetable products, and vegetable oils in great variety, are also produced in Travancore. Abundance of fibrous materials might be manufactured from the plantain, agave, pine-apple, and many other common plants. Natives are never at a loss for substitutes for paper and twine. They will step into the garden or jungle, and at once select one or two broad leaves, in which they ingeniously fold their parcels, securing them with some creeper or fibrous stem. Milk has often been brought to me in a piece of plantain leaf pinned up at the corners, by means of thorns, into a neat but frail drinking vessel. The Indian grass matting for floors, now occasionally imported into England, is made of the flowering stem of a species of Cyperus, or sedge, which takes a red, black, or yellow dye, and is woven into pretty square or diagonal patterns.

Many beautiful flowering plants are indigenous to Travancore, and fill the jungles, forests, open country, and gardens with their beauty, their gay flowers and varied forms. The flowering trees especially are admired as singularly fine. Such are the showy Lagerströmia, which may most aptly be compared to a large oak tree covered with clusters of single roses; the Barringtonia, with its pendulous racemes of lovely pink tassels; the *Cassia alata*, with its tall upright spikes of bright yellow flowers; and the *Cathartocarpus fistula*, draped in graceful hanging yellow flowers, strikingly resembling our own laburnum. The Piney varnish tree, with white fragrant blossoms; the Michelia, with its rich orange-coloured flowers —famed in Hindu poetry; the Persian lilac; many species of Acacia; Bignonias, notably the Indian cork tree, with its long white fragrant flowers; the gaudy Poinciana, or peacock-flower—the two species of which have been introduced from the West Indies and Madagascar respectively; the large pea-flowered Agati; the flaming Erythrina, or coral tree, and many others, are equal in beauty to those found in any quarter of the globe.

Ornamental shrubs, too, are numerous; some of which are almost constantly in blossom. Especially may be named the various Bauhinias, Ixoras, and Jasmines; Henna (called in Holy Scripture "camphire"—Song of Sol. i. 14); Memecylon also, with its lovely azure-tinted feather-like flowers; the Oleander, Osbeckia, Mussænda, with its curious white calycine leaf, contrasting with the golden-coloured flowers, the Hibiscus, &c.

There are also the Canna, or Indian shot; Clitorea, or shell-flower; the gorgeous and elegant *Gloriosa superba*, the flowers of which bear some resemblance to those of the Martagon lily; many species of Ipomœa and Convolvulus, forming rich festoons from the trees and bushes, with their large and delicate flowers of every variety of colours; Plumbago, Costus, Hoya, and Roses, which are everywhere cultivated in gardens.

Water-lilies fill the quiet ponds with their floating leaves, and rare Orchids, with grotesque but beautiful flowers, gleam among the branches of trees, run over the rocks, or spring out of the earth. The Loranthus also, a plant nearly allied to the mistletoe, is a most beautiful object, with brilliant scarlet fuchsia-like flowers hanging from the branches of the trees to which it clings. Graceful ferns are abundant, growing often as epiphytes on the trunks of trees, or luxuriating in moist and shady nooks.

It is sometimes supposed that the flowers of India are gaudy but scentless. This may perhaps be affirmed with truth of many fine flowers, but those yielding a delightful perfume form a large proportion of the whole. There are, for instance, the roses, jasmines, lime, tuberose, orchids, amaryllis, bignonias, guettarda, melia, pandanus, oleander, henna; with sweet basil, lemon-grass, and others that have fragrant foliage. It must, however, be confessed that some of these flowers are too overpowering, and not sufficiently delicate in their perfume, for English taste. On the other hand, the poetical allusions sometimes made to the "spicy breezes" of India are founded upon error, for the leaves of cinnamon, clove, and other spice plants, emit no fragrance except when bruised.

Several plants are, on account of their beauty, or some legendary circumstance connected with them, held *sacred* in the estimation of the Hindus. The *Ficus religiosa* is a stately tree somewhat resembling our aspen, and, like the latter, its leaves also tremble in the breeze. It has not the descending roots of the banyan. The motion of the leaves is supposed to arise from the presence of the god Vishnu, to whom the tree is therefore sacred. Ocimum, or sweet basil, is the well-known Toolsee, dedicated to Vishnu and much worshipped in Bengal. The fragrant flowers of a handsome tree, *Michelia champaca*, highly venerated and planted near temples, are often referred to in native poetry. The leaves and fruit of the Bael tree, or wood-apple, are offered to Siva. Sandal wood is largely used in religious ceremonies. The cratœva, ixora, oleander, hibiscus, and others are also planted near temples, and offered in worship to the gods.

One of the most celebrated, as it certainly is one of the most beautiful plants in India, is the sacred Lotus, or rose-coloured water-lily. It is associated with much of its mythology, and furnishes many of the finest allusions and figures in Indian poetry. The sensitive plant (*Mimosa pudica*) is one of the commonest and most troublesome weeds in the country. It spreads with singular rapidity in gardens and fields, and one's footsteps may be traced for some time by the shrinking of this little plant. Another little plant, whose leaves possess a similar power, is *Oxalis sensitiva*.

The mineral products of Travancore are few, and do not require lengthened notice. A more careful and intelligent search may yet, however, disclose the existence of minerals of some value. The Western Ghauts being granitic, abundance of granite, gnéiss, syenite, and other formations of this series are readily procurable and extensively used as a durable building stone for the erection of temples and other structures, and in carved images and ornaments. In connection with the granite, mica (used in ornamenting fans and other articles) occurs in thin laminated flakes; and from the disintegration of the granite, fine porcelain clays are produced, some of which are found in a very pure state. The manufacture of porcelain might therefore be established with advantage.

A peculiar indurated iron clay called "laterite," or brick-stone, is found widely diffused everywhere near the coast, except towards Cape Comorin, where it ceases altogether. It lies at no great depth from the surface, ordinarily overlying the granite rocks. There are many varieties of laterite, some very compact and heavy, of a deep red colour, and containing a proportion of iron; others deteriorating into soft white and yellow ochrey earths. Often it has the appearance of numerous rounded pebbles united together by a clayey cement. Fossil shells have occasionally been found embedded in it. This hard clay is dug out in large bricks from the localities in which it occurs, and hardens still more after exposure to the air. As a building material it is easily worked and durable, and is usually stuccoed over with fine white lime, made of calcined shells.

Iron ore is plentiful but little worked. From the sulphuret of iron found at Varkkala large quantities of Prussian blue might readily be manufactured. Plumbago, or black-lead, is not uncommon, being found sometimes in lumps a few feet below the surface, at other times running in veins through the laterite. It seems, however, from the admixture of foreign matter, to be deficient in purity. Several sulphuric springs, with jets of gaseous air bubbling up through the water, have been discovered within twenty miles of Trevandrum.

CHAPTER VIII.

INDUSTRY AND COMMERCE.

Washermen and Barbers—Goldsmiths—Weavers—Carpenters—Ivory Carvings—Lace-making—Merchants—Weights and Measures—Monetary System—The Mint—Fisheries—Exports and Imports—Domestic Animals.

CONSIDERABLE activity in industrial and commercial pursuits, elementary arts and agriculture, prevails in Travancore, so that a large proportion of the people are usefully occupied in various forms of productive labour. All the ordinary occupations essential to civilized life are carried on, often in a style very primitive, and different from that of European workmen, but still practically efficient, according to native ideas.

A numerous body of washermen and barbers exercise their vocation for the personal cleanliness and adornment of the various classes of the community. Washing is principally performed by men, aided to some extent by their wives. The clothes are first boiled in a lye, then beaten on a stone at the brink of a river, and are soon, by the aid of a blazing sun, brought to a dazzling whiteness, without injuring the fabric so much as might be expected from this rude style of procedure. The clothes are carried home on the backs of donkeys. Barbers are in constant demand, as the men have their heads and beards closely shaven (always excepting the "kudumi") at regular and frequent intervals.

Goldsmiths also contribute to the personal adornment of

both sexes. As there are no banks in the country, thriving people lend out their money at heavy rates of interest, or hoard it up in the form of coin in a bottle or pot, concealed beneath the floor of the house. But as another means of security, they are accustomed to expend their savings on gold and silver ornaments of every variety of patterns and uses, which, being of small bulk, can be easily guarded or transferred or turned into money at any time. This practice, however, operates as a temptation to crime, as women and children going into unfrequented localities are occasionally robbed, and even murdered, for the sake of these costly decorations, which excite the criminal cupidity of their neighbours.

The goldsmiths are skilful workmen. One or a couple of these men will sit down in the verandah of a house, and with a few simple tools—a piece of broken pottery for holding fire, a reed for blowpipe, and a stone as anvil—will execute neat repairs, or turn out very creditable specimens of workmanship. Elegant filigree ornaments in silver, similar to the far-famed Trichinopoly work, are made in Quilon. Well-finished gongs, cups, waterpots, lamps, and other articles in brass, are made by braziers in several parts of the country.

Weavers in Travancore rarely attempt the manufacture of any but the coarsest and plainest descriptions of cotton cloth. Small quantities of silk cloth, checks, and huckaback are manufactured in Kottār. The colours are well dyed and permanent. The thread used is English, purchased from merchants and importers, but the machinery and tools are of the most wretched and imperfect description. Instead of a proper warping-mill, boys are employed to run with the spools of thread up and down a long path like a ropewalk, to form the warp. Instead of the ingenious but simple arrangement of machinery in the English loom, by which the shuttle is thrown rapidly and easily from side to side by a cord fastened to a "pluckstick," the shuttle is thrown, as was once the practice in England, from one hand and caught in the other alternately. The introduction of the English handloom would at once treble the manufacture of cloth from the Indian looms, and would be a great boon to the weavers themselves.

By far the largest proportion of skilled artisans are those employed in connection with the building trades. Wood for the roof-work, doors, windows, pillars, and carved decorations, enters largely into the peculiar style of house architecture in Malabar. Rice-bins, ploughs, carts, and other articles, are made, and must be kept in repair. Native vessels, also, are built in several of the seaports, and cabin-boats and canoes are common on all the backwaters and rivers.

The carpenters are clever and handy with the tools at present in use,—which, by the way, might be vastly improved. They sit at work, holding the materials on which they are operating with the left hand and the toes of the foot. Their tools are almost exclusively rude chisels, of various sizes and breadths. With these they cut or chop through, instead of sawing across, a piece of timber; of course with great waste of material. Planks are smoothed or planed with the broad chisels; narrower tools are used for piercing holes, into which pins of palm wood, instead of iron nails, are driven to fasten the pieces together. When carefully superintended, and allowed to take their own time, the more experienced of these workmen make strong and handsome articles of furniture. Their wood carvings are often strikingly correct, elaborate, or curious.

In the erection of temples and wayside rest-houses, and for images and decorative carvings, stone is largely used. It is of course expensive to work, but is imperishable. Noble and imposing works of art in the peculiar Hindu style exist in some of the ancient temples, but the stonecutters of the present day seem hardly equal to the execution of artistic productions of equal merit.

TRAVANCORE BOATMAN.

Blacksmiths and potters are the remaining classes of skilled artificers. The latter produce the common red "chatties" and other vessels of clay for drinking, eating, cooking, storing oil, and other purposes. As these are exceedingly fragile, and are besides frequently thrown away, and the household stock renewed on account of imaginary defilement, immense quantities are used throughout the country. They are moulded by hand on a wheel, and burnt in a small furnace.

The ivory carvings of Travancore have of late years come into notice at exhibitions and elsewhere. The work is well executed, and the designs are often artistically composed of animals, foliage, and geometrical patterns; but these articles are very expensive, only one or two families of high caste being acquainted with the art. Arrangements have recently been made to preserve and extend this branch of industry.

Lace-making, introduced by Mrs. Mault in her boarding school at Nāgercoil, and by Mrs. Lewis at Sānthapuram, has succeeded to perfection. Admirable specimens of fine pillow lace, in cotton and gold and silver thread, manufactured at the Mission school, were shown at Madras, and in the great London and Paris Exhibitions, in all of which they gained prize medals. Being sold for the benefit of the female schools, the profits have greatly assisted this department of our work. The employment has also spread to Tinnevelly. A suggestion has recently been made that it might be more profitable, instead of merely copying and repeating, as has hitherto been done, the old standard English patterns and styles, to get up real Indian designs in accordance with the purest national taste and styles of art, so as to establish the Nāgercoil lace as a purely indigenous production. The suggestion seems important, and worthy of being carried into effect.

The trade of Travancore is chiefly in the hands of the chetties or merchants. But in every part of the country there are innumerable shops and bazaars where small articles of native provisions, clothing, and household convenience are retailed; besides which men and women of the lower classes purchase sugar, rice, fish, fowls, &c., in the periodic markets and fairs, and hawk them about for sale at a small profit wherever they can find a purchaser.

The weights and measures in common use are in a most unsatisfactory condition of uncertainty, confusion, and variation, though of late efforts have been made by the native Government to determine and supply verified copies of several of the established measures. Those used in one part of the country are quite unknown in other parts. Different weights of the same denomination are used for metals, for pepper, and for salt. The introduction of uniformity in this matter throughout the bounds of so small a state appears to be quite practicable, and is certainly much to be desired.

The coinage also is rather unsettled and fluctuating in its relative value as compared with British currency, and some skill and practice are required readily to perform calculations of this kind. Poor people, too, have often difficulty in procuring change at equitable rates.

The smallest coin in use is the copper "*kāsu*" (*c* in engraving, p. 110), called by Europeans "*cash*," and equal in value to about one-nineteenth of a penny—less than a quarter of a farthing. On the obverse of this coin is a figure said to represent the god Krishna; on the reverse a curious geometrical figure composed of two triangles, to which some notion of sacredness or good luck appears to attach. Coins of this minute value are indispensable for so poor a people: even a single cash will purchase a determinable quantity of fruit, tobacco, vegetables, or other cheap commodity. Many a noisy quarrel between two poor women takes its rise about a cash or two in their petty dealings.

The only other coin largely circulated is the "*chuckram*" (*a* and *b* in the engraving), a tiny silver coin, about the size of half a small pea, and weighing under six grains. The impression on one side appears to be merely a fancy design. On the other side are ten dots and two curved lines, interpreted by the natives as representing the legs and toes of the national deity Patmanābhan. A chuckram is worth sixteen copper cash, and 28½ chuckrams are reckoned to be equal to one rupee (two shillings), so that a single chuckram is worth about six-sevenths of a penny.

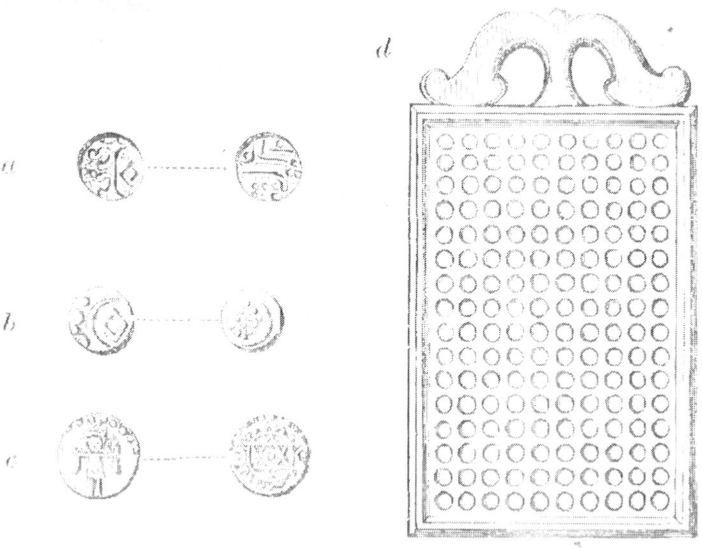

NATIVE COINS AND CHUCKRAM BOARD.

These are the only two coins in popular daily use in Travancore. British Indian rupees pass current, and the native Government are just now introducing into circulation a quantity of the copper coinage of British India. Within the last two years another native coin, in silver, called "*panam*," or "*fanam*," equal in value to four chuckrams, and about the size of our threepenny piece, has been struck. Gold coins of the size of the cash, and worth about sevenpence, were formerly in circulation, and a variety of other coins have occasionally been tried for a time.

Chuckrams being so small and globose are exceedingly

troublesome to count or handle. They slip out of the fingers and run over the floor, and are only discovered again with difficulty. £100 sterling amounts to 28,500 chuckrams, weighing twenty-four pounds avoirdupois; and hours would be wasted in reckoning this number of small coins. They are therefore measured, or counted, by means of a "chuckram board,"—a small square wooden plate (*d*), with holes, the exact size and depth of a chuckram, drilled in regular rows on its surface, as shown, of reduced size, in the illustration; a board contains fifty, a hundred, two hundred, or more of these holes, according to convenience. A small handful of coins is thrown on the board, and it is then shaken gently from side to side, so as to cause a single chuckram to fall into each cavity, and the surplus, if any, is swept off with the hand. A glance at the board, when filled, shows that it contains the exact number of coins for which it is intended. The rapid manipulation of this simple but ingenious implement requires some practice, but the Government clerks and native merchants are surprisingly expert and exact in its performance.

The Mint Department was established about eighty years ago. Its operations are now conducted within the fort at Trevandrum. Chuckrams are coined from dollars and other silver coins bought up for the purpose. These are melted in clay crucibles, which are each used but once, then ground to powder, and the atoms of precious metal which adhere to the clay carefully remelted and collected. The molten silver is suddenly poured into cold water, where it falls into grains and dust. These are then weighed out in delicate scales to the exact weight of a chuckram, and the separate quantities thrown into small cavities in a large earthen plate, which contains several thousand holes of the proper size, closely arranged on its surface. The plate, with its whole contents, being put into the furnace, is exposed to a high temperature for three hours and a half, so that the grains of metal are fused and formed into separate globules, of which there may be 3,000 in a single earthen plate. When cooled these are taken out and punched by hand into chuckrams, one of the dies being firmly embedded in a stone underneath the coin, the other held in the workman's hand.

Copper is purchased in sheets and melted in a similar way, but double the time is required for its fusion. The copper globules are partially flattened by a single blow of a hammer previous to the operation of stamping. Two men will make 20,000 chuckrams in a single day. A good press, with feeding machine, for the manufacture of fanam pieces, has recently been procured from England, and strikes off 8,000 coins in a day. The acid of tamarind fruit is used for cleansing the coins.

The fisheries of Travancore are productive, and afford employment and support to multitudes of people all along the coast. The fish are caught with nets and hooks, and are carried inland on the heads of the women to be sold. Large quantities are also dried in the sun, or salted for home use or exportation; the value of the fish annually exported amounting to about 75,000 rupees. The curing of the fish is, however, insufficiently done, so that its use as food at certain seasons tends to increase the ravages of cholera and dysentery. Greater attention to the process of curing would soon enlarge the profits and importance of the trade. Fish oil is manufactured, the best quality of which is now coming into medicinal use, as a cheap and effectual substitute for cod liver oil.

The exports by land and sea amount in value to about 60 lacs of rupees, or £600,000 sterling; in 1869 the amount was 72¾ lacs. The imports reach about 25 lacs, or £250,000, and are also on the increase. The exports consist chiefly of the various products of the cocoa-nut, areca, and palmyra palm trees; such as the dried kernel, fibre, and oil of the cocoa-nut, the nuts also, the leaves (for thatching purposes), and the cordage or "*coir*" spun from the fibre, besides coir matting, palm sugar, &c. Great quantities of cocoa-nut oil are now shipped to Bombay for the manufacture of gas in that city, and to England for use in the manufacture of stearine candles. Pepper, formerly a monopoly of the native Government, but now an article of free trade, although very heavily taxed; is exported to the value of £25,000 yearly. It is an important staple of the country, and holds a high place in the French market. The quantities, however, vary much according to the seasons, the pepper vine being said to bear with greater profusion in alternate years.

Arrowroot, hides, molasses, tamarinds, ginger, rice, &c., are also included in the list of exports. Cardamoms, ivory, and salt are Government monopolies. The trade in coffee is of recent growth, the quantity produced having been very insignificant until about seven years ago. It is now, however, rapidly and steadily advancing as the estates in the mountains come into bearing, and promises to become of great future value to the State. Over 15,000 acres are now planted. Coffee to the value of £25,200 sterling was exported during 1869, and a large increase may shortly be expected.

Most of the imports are from British India; and these, by a commercial treaty, are exempt from duty to the Travancorean Government. They consist principally of raw cotton, cotton thread and piece goods, metals, chilies, opium, and cattle, with salt and tobacco. The consumption of opium appears to be on the increase.

Domestic cattle are abundant in Travancore. Black cattle, according to the last enumeration, number about 400,000; buffaloes, 100,000; sheep and goats, 28,000. The native breed of oxen, however, is wretchedly small; nor would it be easy at present to provide sufficient pasturage for larger animals, if introduced. They are kept and reared for their milk, so largely used by Brahmans and others, and for farm work and agricultural labour; but never, of course, for slaughter.

Buffaloes, powerful but sluggish creatures, almost amphibious in their habits, are of great service in ploughing the mud of the rice-fields. Their milk is made into the native butter or "*ghee*," which forms a kind of substitute for flesh-meat to those whose religious prejudices forbid their eating such. Sheep do not thrive in Travancore; while goats, on the contrary, do. The flesh of both is used by the middle classes of natives. They are sold at about eight shillings each. Common poultry are reared in great numbers for their eggs and flesh, which the people say is "good for medicine," and on this point all will agree with them; for the very best "medicine" one could recommend to a poor ill-fed native would be a fowl nicely boiled or roasted. They are sold at the rate of sixpence to a shilling each, but are diminutive and badly fed.

For horses the climate is unfavourable; these animals are therefore very rare. Even Europeans usually keep the handsome and docile Pegu ponies, as large horses often become weak in the loins in consequence of the humid climate and unwholesome winds of the Western coast. Donkeys are kept chiefly by lime-burners and washermen. Nor do superior specimens of the dog readily increase in India; but the native "pariah dog," a wretched, ugly, annoying brute, abounds in every village.

CHAPTER IX.

AGRICULTURE.

State of Husbandry—Price of Labour—The Palm Tree—Its Mode of Culture —Products and Manifold Uses.

Agriculture, as a science, is utterly unknown in Travancore, and the implements in use are wretchedly inefficient; yet the natives are pretty well acquainted, from experience and observation, with the best practical mode of cultivating their various crops.

Most of the common vegetable productions are grown in small holdings by the cottagers and small farmers. Almost every native, however poor, has some little property in land. The principal crop, cultivated on an extensive scale throughout the country, is rice, of which valuable and nutritious grain there are many varieties—white, red, black, bearded and smooth, early and late, suitable for wet or dry lands, hill or plains. Sixty-four distinct varieties were exhibited in one case at an exhibition of fruits, flowers, and vegetables in Trevandrum.

Three crops of rice in the year are procured from the best land. This grain, as is well known, is grown in fields flooded with water; in fact, rice is grown in mud and water from the sprouting of the seed till the crops begin to ripen, when the water is run off. The fields are therefore made perfectly level, and are surrounded with narrow banks of clay. The seed is sown thickly broadcast; when the young plants have reached the height of several inches, they are gently pulled up and transplanted in small bunches.

The rice-grounds are subjected to repeated ploughings, and are well manured with ashes, dung, green leaves, and twigs chopped small—in short, with whatever can be procured for this purpose. The Pulayar slaves do the rough work in the mire for their masters, such as repairing the outer banks, ploughing, manuring, and threshing; the females of this caste assist in the transplanting, reaping, and carrying the grain. Rice cultivation is very profitable, except in seasons of excessive drought.

The rice or "paddy" fields, as they are called, form an exceedingly beautiful feature of the Indian landscape, quite as much so as fine corn-fields in England, usually presenting, in addition, a marked contrast with the surrounding declivities and high lands. They look like lakes of bright, soft green, afterwards assuming the golden tinge indicative of a rich and satisfying harvest. The fields lie on various levels, so as to allow of a slight current of water running from one to another; in sloping ground they have the appearance of terraces of different widths and outlines according to the conformation of the ground. Rice straw makes good fodder and bedding for cattle.

The price of labour, both skilled and unskilled, and indeed of every commodity, has largely increased within the last twelve years. Whether this is owing to enlarged intercourse with other parts of India; to the abolition of slavery and the spread of education and civilization; to the emigration of many of the Shānars to Ceylon and the Mauritius; to the introduction of coffee-planting, the building of bridges and other important public works which bring labour more into demand, and consequently increase its value; or to other less obvious causes, producing a slow but general equalization of the value of money throughout the world, it is not easy to say. But the wages of day labourers, which in 1858 were, in rural districts, 2 chuckrams a day, have by degrees risen to a minimum of 5 chuckrams = 4½d., while even more is paid to labourers on the coffee plantations. The prices of rice, meat, cloth, and other necessary articles have also doubled at the least within the same period.

The value of money is, on the whole, about six times as much as in England, except to European residents, who are compelled to purchase the articles of food and clothing to which they are habitually accustomed from native merchants at double the English rates, or to procure them from Cochin, Madras, or even from London; in other respects, too, their necessary expenditure has enormously increased.

Considering the position which the Palm tree occupies, we cannot pass on without giving some fuller account of it, especially as many of the native Christians of South Travancore, like those of Tinnevelly, are largely supported by its various economic products.

The Palms are amongst the most interesting productions of the vegetable kingdom, whether "we consider the majestic aspect of their towering stems, crowned by a still more gigantic foliage, the character of grandeur which they impress upon the landscape of the countries they inhabit, their immense value to mankind as affording food and raiment, and various objects of economical importance, or, finally, the prodigious development of those organs by which their race is to be propagated."* They have been rightly styled "the princes of the vegetable world." Several species of plants belonging to this noble order are found in Travancore. The lofty Bastard Sago, with its graceful leaves and immense pendulous strings of nut-like fruits; the Talipot, or Fan palm, with its gigantic leaves, each of which is large enough to cover

* Lindley's "Vegetable Kingdom," p. 134.

ten or twelve men; the dwarf Phœnix palm, and the long trailing Rattan, have each their appropriate uses;—but all dwindle into insignificance beside the three principal palms which constitute a large proportion of the vegetable wealth of the country—the Areca, the Cocoa-nut, and the Palmyra palms.

The Areca is the most graceful and elegant of all the Indian palms. It yields the "betel nut," which the natives are in the habit of chewing as a stimulant spice. Within the limits of Travancore alone nearly ten millions of these trees grow, the value of the annual produce of which is estimated at over £50,000 sterling.

The Cocoa-nut is very extensively cultivated, the number of trees in Travancore amounting to nearly ten millions. There seems no end to the economical uses of the various parts of the plant. These trees thrive only in the neighbourhood of the coast, and best under the influence of the cool sea breeze, and when their roots are almost laved by salt or brackish water. In such localities the whole country seems a forest of stately cocoa palms, with their beautiful crowns of leaves, like gigantic ostrich plumes, gently waving in the breeze, and clusters of great nuts hanging from every tree. This palm having been so frequently described, and being consequently so well known to all readers, it will not be needful to dwell upon its uses.

The Palmyra palm (*Borassus flabelliformis*) ranks next to the Cocoa-nut in importance and value. There are about 2,500,000 Palmyras grown in Travancore, almost all of which are in the districts south of Trevandrum. Whether from superabundance of rain and moisture, or from the absence of Shānars to cultivate the tree, it rarely occurs in the Northern districts, where it is sometimes regarded as sacred in consequence of the sojourn of local demons. The Palmyra is also found in Ceylon and various parts of Asia and Africa.

This palm furnishes the principal means of support to several millions of the human family. It flourishes best, not like the Cocoa-nut in well-watered grounds and fertile soil, but, by a remarkable providential arrangement, in inferior and especially sandy and arid ground, where scarcely anything else will grow, and where its long roots, penetrating to an immense depth, draw perennial supplies from hidden sources of nourishment. "The righteous shall flourish like the palm tree" (Psa. xcii. 12).

The Palmyra is a tall, branchless palm, with a stiff radiating head of fan-shaped leaves;—

"A column, and its crown a star."

It rises to the height of from 60 to 90 feet, and begins to produce when 25, or, in favourable soil and circumstances, 15 or 16 years old. Very rarely does a Cocoa-nut palm grow quite upright, the stem being usually curved or inclined more or less; but the Palmyra, on the contrary, like the Date and most other palms, is almost always perfectly upright in growth—"upright as the palm tree" (Jer. x. 5). The trees are always diœcious, that is, bearing male and female flowers on separate plants; one tree producing only barren or staminiferous flowers, another bearing the pistil and fruits. The male flowers are minute, and are produced between scales closely set on a branched flower-stalk. Each stalk is estimated to bear 90,000, and as there are usually seven of these on each tree, the male flowers on a single tree are probably 630,000 in number; but not one of these produces a fruit.

The fruiting, or female palms, bear on each flowering stalk from 10 to 20 fruits. About 10 of these bunches are produced in a year; so that over 200 fruits are sometimes obtained from a single tree. The fruit is dark and globular, is four or five inches in diameter, and generally contains three good-sized nuts or seeds.

Every part of this palm is turned to account by the natives. The wood, for example, is one of the best and strongest known for rafters and roof-work, and is employed for this purpose in most of our chapels and mission-houses. It is very hard and durable, with wire-like fibres, and freely splits up lengthwise. The hard wood is the outer portion of the stem, the centre being filled with soft, spongy, useless pith; just the reverse of exogenous timber trees, in which the toughest wood is in the centre. The stem of the Palmyra, generally about a foot in diameter, is split up into three or four pieces; these are smoothed with the adze or chisel, the pith being cleared off, and are then ready for use as rafters.

As the tree is so many years in arriving at maturity, the people say it will live and bear for 1,000 years; but this is scarcely credible. A common Tamil proverb is "Nattāl āyiram; vettāl āyiram," "If you plant it, (it will grow) a thousand years; if you cut it, (it will last) a thousand years." I have never been able to find sufficient data for calculating the probable period of the life of this palm, as no record can be found of its age, and the trees are usually cut when old for timber instead of being allowed to die of age. Probably it lasts for at least 150 or 200 years. Reliable information on this point would be most interesting and acceptable. The timber is not thoroughly ripened till the tree is 80 or 100 years old. When cut it will no doubt, with reasonable care, last for 1,000 years. It is really better after being in use for a century, if preserved from rain and white ants, than when newly cut. The whole stem of a tree is occasionally polished and used as a pillar in building. The wood is also made into walking-sticks, bows, bed-frames, and other articles.

The pulp of the Palmyra fruit is eaten by the poor, but is rather unsavoury. The nuts are singularly hard and strong; it is a common proverb that even an elephant cannot break one. They are therefore planted somewhere near the house, and after four months commence to grow. They are then dug up and split with a heavy knife; the kernel, now soft and tender, is eaten, and the edible sprout, or young growing stem, somewhat like a small parsnip inverted, is boiled, roasted, or dried and ground into meal.

The large fan-shaped leaves are of service to the people in innumerable ways. The petiole, or leaf-stem, is 3 or 4 feet in length, and the fan-like expansion over 3 feet in diameter, containing from 60 to 80 double slips or rays. From 12 to 15 leaves are annually pruned off each tree; these are used for fuel, thatch, &c. The outer skin or fibre of the leaf-stem is exceedingly tenacious, and is used in narrow strips for caning bed-frames, and as cordage. The rays of the leaf, cut into narrow slips like straw, are plaited into mats and baskets; they are also made into folding fans, umbrellas, tobacco pouches, and ornamental work, and the slips form the ordinary writing material. These are three feet in length, and about an inch and a half broad, of a very smooth, leathery and satin-like texture. The best for writing purposes are those which are cut while young and soft, and afterwards dried in the sun. The writing is scratched into the surface by an iron pen, or stylus,—a "writing nail" it is called; when desired, the characters can be blackened by rubbing over them a mixture of lamp-black and oil. This is as if we in England wrote our letters on large leaves, or the bark of trees (as was once done*) with an iron nail, and then darkened the writing by rubbing ashes over it.

The engraving on the next page represents these writing implements, with a palm-leaf letter of the ordinary style, such as are constantly received in India:—*a* is the small knife, used to trim the slips of palm leaf; *b*, the iron stylus, often inlaid with silver or even gold; *c*, the piercer, with which small holes, about a quarter of an inch in diameter, are made in either end

* Compare *folium*, leaf, folio; and *liber*, bark, book.

of each leaf, for the purpose of tying or binding them together; *d*, the writing-case for holding these instruments, usually worn stuck in the folds of the waist-cloth.

The letter itself (*e*) is neatly folded up, with the ends turned inward, and fastened outside with a strap of the same material. For books, the slips are cut into lengths, say 10 or 12 inches long, a small round hole is pierced at both ends, through which a cord runs to string them together, with two narrow slips of wood at either side, similarly pierced and fastened, to form a kind of binding.

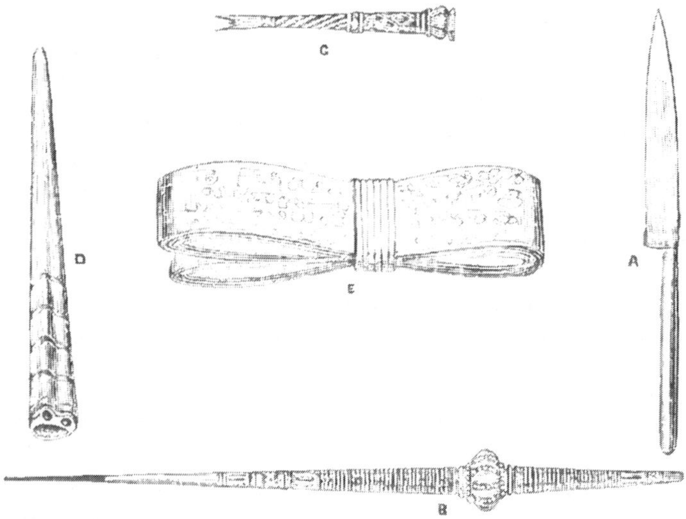

The natives are very rapid writers on the "*olei*," or palm leaf, and write standing or walking as well as sitting. An odd scratching noise is made by a number of men writing simultaneously. I have seen a European missionary almost put out in his early attempts at Tamil preaching by the sound of the iron pens of the native teachers taking notes of his sermon. Deeds and documents are all written upon this material, and if kept in the smoke of the fire, or otherwise out of reach of the white ants, they will last for two or three hundred years, which is the age attributed to some documents of this kind still extant.

Small specimens of the palm leaf are also smoothed and flattened, the ends of the rays being cut off, then ornamented with mica, tinsel and peacock's feathers, and made into beautiful fans.* The leaves are also folded up so as to make light buckets for carrying water, or small temporary drinking vessels. The central leaf-bud makes a tender and delicious pickle; but of course this is only to be had when a tree is cut down for timber, as the removal of the crown destroys the life of the palm. But perhaps the most profitable product of the palm is the sap, or "palm wine," which is drunk fresh or fermented, boiled into sugar or distilled into spirits. The last manufacture is chiefly in the hands of Ilavars, and is never practised by Christian Shānars, whose ordinary occupation is the climbing of the Palmyra to tap the tree, to collect the sap, and manufacture the palm sugar. The "climbing season," during which the sap flows, extends over a period of about seven months in the year, from August to February, and this is a busy time with the Shānar. He begins before daylight in the morning, works hard till nearly noon, and again late in the afternoon till night, manipulating from 30 to 50 palms, which he must ascend twice—sometimes even thrice, in the course of a day.

The Shānar's tools consist of a large curved knife for cutting off old leaves and the extremity of the unexpanded flowering stalk, from which the sap exudes; a pair of wooden pincers for slightly crushing the sap-bearing branch, so as to aid the ready flow of the juice; a small basket with lime, and a brush, with which a small quantity of lime is rubbed inside each pot, to prevent the too speedy fermentation of

* See palm-leaf fan and umbrellas in engraving on p. 30.

the palm juice. These instruments are placed within a light basket or tool bag, formed from the spathe or flowering sheath of the same tree, and fastened on one side to the climber's waist-cloth. Another leaf basket, or bucket, plaited double, to hold the sap, is fastened at the other side. In his hand the climber carries a staff, or crutch, with horizontal top.

Arrived at the foot of the tree, he lays his crutch against the stem, then placing one foot on the top of the crutch, rises two or three feet. Placing his feet in a loop of fibre to keep them close together, and clasping his arms round the trunk of the tree, he draws himself up a little way. Extending his arms again, he reaches higher up and draws up his feet again, so that rising alternately with hands and feet, a practised climber in a few moments reaches the top of the tree. The agility of these men is really marvellous. The Shānar takes down the little round earthenware pot, holding about a quart, which had been suspended to the flower-stalk, empties its contents into his basket, cuts the extremity of the stalk afresh, and again ties up the little pitcher till evening. In this way from five to fifteen pints of "sweet water" are drawn daily from each palm (compare Psa. civ. 16). This is an agreeable, harmless drink, tasting just like sugar and water. Other palms besides the Palmyra yield a similar juice. When set aside for a day the "sweet water" ferments, and is then called "*tădi*," or "toddy." It is a pleasant acid drink, corresponding in a measure to our beer, but with a larger proportion of intoxicating quality; it makes an excellent yeast for bread. Toddy spoils in two or three days, but is then laid aside for some months, till it passes into vinegar by acetous fermentation.

It is matter for great regret that this work is everywhere carried on on Sundays as well as week days during the climbing season, which very much reduces the attendance on public worship at this time of the year, and is a hindrance in many respects to the improvement of our people. To test the practicability of dropping this Sunday work, I made careful and extended experiments with a number of trees, but found that the omission of a single day's tapping seriously checks the flow of the sap, and reduces the quantity to less than one-half. Still, some of our Christian people attempt, by various arrangements, to reduce the Sunday work to a minimum, while others distribute to the poor the whole produce of this day's labour.

Boiling the sap into sugar is the next process, and is performed by the laborious Shānātti, or female Shānar. She first gathers firewood in the jungles, and bears it home on her head; then, when the juice has been collected, the climber's wife commences to boil it down over a slow fire in large earthen pots, till it becomes a thick syrup. This is then poured into moulds, each formed of half a cocoa-nut shell, in which it hardens into lumps of very dark coarse sugar. This "*jaggery*," or palm sugar, is largely used as food. Bearers and workmen when unable to spare time for cooking curry and rice, eat a lump of "jaggery" as a refreshment. They use it also with salt fish as a regular meal, and in times of famine, when rice is scarce, we have occasionally given a light meal of jaggery to the children of our boarding schools. Jaggery is also an essential ingredient, in fixed proportions, in good mortar, to which it imparts adhesive strength and tenacity. It is sometimes imported into England as an excellent manure.

The dark palm sugar is sometimes refined and clarified with animal charcoal, eggs, or lime; and this might well become a staple trade of Travancore. Small quantities of sugar-candy are also prepared, of which a handful is often presented by native gentlemen, as a friendly gift and token of respect, when visiting Europeans.

Arrack, or native spirits, a transparent, colourless liquid like gin or whisky, is distilled from jaggery. The sugar is first broken up and put in water for four days to ferment; it is then boiled in an earthen pot, the vapour being caught in a bamboo tube which falls into another vessel, in which the liquor is cooled and condensed. This operation is repeated a second time when necessary. Arrack is a most injurious beverage, and there is reason to fear that it is largely used by some classes of the people; a single pennyworth will intoxicate a native.

The economical uses of the noble Palmyra are almost endless. The natives say that there are 801 uses of the palm, and I have no doubt that this number might be reckoned. A hundred trees will support two families; and the produce is not, like that of some other plants, readily affected by change or inequality of seasons. "A native," says Dr. Winslow, "if he will content himself with rather ordinary doors (windows he wants none) and the common mud wall, may build an entire house—wanting no nails or ironwork—with posts, plates, roof, and covering of the Palmyra tree. From this tree he may store his grain, make his bed, furnish his provisions, kindle his fire, draw or bring his water; and also, by the help only of an earthen pot set on three stones, cook his food, sweeten it if he chooses, procure his wine (such as it is), and live day after day dependent only on this tree."* Thus bountifully does the wise and paternal providence of God supply the wants of man, and provide for his sustenance and enjoyment in every climate, according to its special requirements and circumstances.

* Ferguson's Popular Description of the Palmyra Palm.

CHAPTER X.

VERNACULAR LANGUAGES.

Vernacular Languages—Tamil—Its Peculiarities and Idioms—Malayālim—Comparison with Tamil—Ludicrous Blunders in Speaking—Proper Names of Places and Persons.

Two languages, Tamil and Malayālim, are spoken in Travancore. The former, vernacular in the south-east of the Indian peninsula, extends round the corner, as it were, of Cape Comorin into Travancore, and for a distance of about forty miles along the Western coast. The Neyyāttunkara river may be regarded as the boundary of the two languages; so that, when labouring in the district of Pāreychāley, the writer studied and preached in Tamil; but, after removing over the borders of the Tamil country to Trevandrum, a distance of only twenty miles, it was necessary to learn Malayālim, which is spoken throughout the remainder of the principality, and is the language in which the missionary services at Trevandrum and Quilon are conducted. The Tamil-speaking portion of "the Land of Charity" may be estimated at one-fourth of the whole population. In the capital itself almost every native is acquainted with both languages. Malayālim extends altogether to the vicinity of Mangalore, a distance of about 300 miles along the Western coast, and is vernacular to three millions of the people of India.

Tamil is, strangely enough, called by old writers the "Malabar" language. The word "*Tamil*" or "*Tamir*" signifies "sweetness" or "melodiousness," intimating the high estimation in which this language is held. The languages of Southern India are not derived from Sanskrit, but from that which was spoken by the early inhabitants of the peninsula before its conquest by the Brahmanical, or Sanskrit-speaking race; and Dr. Caldwell, in his learned and able work on the Comparative Grammar of these *Dravidian* languages, shows that they are distantly related to the Scythian or Tartar tongues, as also in some measure to Hungarian and Finnish. The South Indian languages have, however, engrafted upon the original stock many Sanskrit words, the proportion being greatest in Malayālim, next in Telugu, and least in Tamil.

The Tamil language, spoken by at least twelve millions of people, is very pleasing and euphonious in character, though it is more circumlocutory and diffuse than English; a page of the latter, when translated, generally occupies 1¾ pages of the same size in Tamil.

The Tamil alphabet has 30 letters (12 vowels and 18 consonants), and 216 combined or compound characters. The characters are read from left to right, as in English and other European tongues. Dr. Winslow's Tamil Dictionary contains 67,452 words. In native books the words are printed without separation, certain letters being altered, omitted, or doubled, according to the connection; thus, "*vanthu irukkiren*," "I have come," becomes "*vanthirukkiren*;" "*solla ponan*," "he went to tell," becomes "*sollapponan*;" "*kadalthirei*," "wave of the sea," becomes "*kadaltirei*," and so on. Tamil grammarians divide the words into four classes or parts of speech, viz., Noun, Verb, Adjective, and Particle.

This language has many peculiarities of grammar and idiom. There is no word corresponding to our relative pronoun "who" or "which," the deficiency being abundantly supplied by participles used only with the noun, somewhat like the Greek participle in *ōn*, *omenos*, &c. Thus "the labourer who digs" is "the digg*ing* labourer." The collocation of words is also very different from that of English, being often the very reverse of ours. Sentences usually end with the verb,—just as the participle or infinitive is put at the end of a sentence in German.

"And" is expressed by the addition of "um" to the various nouns, like the "que" subjoined to the last of two nouns in Latin, as "kuthireiy*um* manithan*um*"—"The horse and the man." There is no definite article in the language; but "*oru*"—"one," is used for the indefinite article "a." To denote quotation, the conjunction "that" is not used, but "ondru," "saying;" thus, "he said *that* he would come" would be expressed—"I will come, saying, he said."

Some idea of the structure and style of the Tamil language may be gathered from the following popular story, transliterated into Roman characters:—

"Entha uyireiyum kollātha oru sanniyāsi oru
What-(ever) life (even) not-killing, an ascetic

eri karei mele ponān. Pogumpothu oru sembada
pond bank upon went. Went-when a fisher-

van antha eriyile meen piditthān. Sanniyāsi
man that pond-in fish was-catching. (The) Ascetic,

sembadavanei (p) pārtthu Eiyo! nee eppothu karei
fisherman seeing, "Alas! thou when bank

eruvāy? endrān. Eiyā en pari nirambi
wilt ascend (get to heaven)?" said he. "Sir, my basket fill-if

nāl karei eruven, endrān.
bank ascend will I," said he.

The humour of the story consists in the pun on the double meaning of the words "ascend the bank," which are often used to denote the attainment of future happiness—"get to heaven." The ascetic is shocked at the criminality of the fisherman in destroying the life of the fish, but is at once silenced by his ready and witty reply.

The word "*vendum*," corresponding generally to "*must*," is also used in urgent but respectful solicitation; but the newly arrived European is rather astonished, if not, indeed, provoked when he is told by a poor native that he *must* do so and so, while an urgent entreaty is all that is intended by the humble suitor. In fact, this word "must," with the addition of the emphatic "*e*," is the form used in Malayālim in prayer to the Supreme Being.

There is a set of onomatopoetic words much used in Tamil, expressing by their very sound the idea intended. Thus they say, "He cried saying *ko*,"—that is, he cried like "ko" or "koo." He walks "*takku takku*,"—that is, stepping heavily as stout persons. He walks "*tattakka pittakka*,"—that is, tottering as an old person. He shut the door like "*padār*," and so forth.

One of the great difficulties of Tamil consists in the correct and appropriate use of the honorific forms of address. The pronouns and verbs which you use, as well as some of the names of objects, at once reveal your estimate of the relative rank of the person whom you address. If he is evidently your inferior or junior, you say, "nee pogirāy,"—"thou goest," and the use of the honorific in such circumstances would be simply inappropriate or ludicrous. If he is your equal in rank, or you wish politely to treat him as such, the form is "neer pogireer,"—thou (sir) goest. If superior, "neengal pogireergal,"—"ye go," or "tangal pogireergal,"—"themselves go,"—which is the customary form of address from natives to European gentlemen. If higher still, as, for example, in addressing the Maharajah, the most respectful form would be, "Is the Maharajah *themselves* going?" unless one were to use the customary native form of address to his Highness—"golden god" or "sacred mind."

Should the person addressed be an entire stranger, and his rank not be apparent from his dress, pronunciation, or attendants, the pronoun "it" may be used without offence; "enge pogirathu?" "where does *it* go?" afterwards rising to "neer" or "neengal" if necessary. There are yet other forms, such as "pogirathundu"—"there is a going," which are occasionally used without any pronoun, or intimation of either respect or disrespect; but this style is rather troublesome and roundabout.

It is by no means polite or respectful to call a person by his proper name in Tamil. Individual missionaries, for instance, are spoken of as the "Neyoor eiyar," or "missionary"—the "Cannamoola pădre," or "minister" (from the name of our mission premises at Trevandrum), and so forth (compare First Samuel, 9th chapter, 11th and 18th verses). Letters are addressed "to the very reverend teacher gentleman themselves." Other European gentlemen are recognised as "the *great* gentleman" (the Resident); "the *second*" or "*little* gentleman" (his assistant); the "Tyecăd Doctor," the "Engineer gentleman," and so on. I have experienced difficulty at times in inducing uneducated natives to mention the personal name of the catechist of their congregation, when I have been uncertain as to the person indicated. One of the rules of native etiquette which females are taught is that they must never be so disrespectful toward their husbands as to mention their names, and this often causes little difficulties. When, for example, a woman whose husband's name is Matthew is asked to read "the Gospel according to St. Matthew," she hesitates to pronounce the evangelist's name, and is only induced to do so after some expostulation and advice.

There are in Tamil, as in Malagasy and the Polynesian languages, two distinct forms of the personal pronoun "we"—"*nām*," *in*cluding, and "*nāngal*," *ex*cluding the party addressed; as, for example, "We (nām) are men," or "we (nāngal) will not go with you." These distinctions, though somewhat difficult to the learner, are yet useful in practice, and of essential importance. In preaching to a congregation one must say, "Our (*nam*mudeiya) Saviour;" while in prayer addressed to the Divine Being, one must be careful to say, "We ("*nāngal*," not "nam") are sinners;" otherwise the persons respectively addressed are wrongly excluded or included in the "we."

The Malayālim letters (pronounced Ma-lay-ā-lim) are 53 in number, of which 16 are vowels; the double letters are 592. Many are aspirate letters, as *gha*, *kha*, *bha*, &c., which do not exist in Tamil. The great number and intricacy of these characters, as compared with Tamil, is rather puzzling to a beginner. In Bailey's Malayālim Dictionary there are 43,000 words, but being the first work of the kind it is less accurate and complete than the present Tamil dictionary. In essential structure this language closely resembles Tamil, and the roots are nearly identical in both. The chief distinction lies in the grammar and inflections, and in the large proportion of Sanskrit words used in Malayālim. The difference is about as great as between the Spanish and Italian languages, in both of which the roots are identical, while the details of the grammar are quite diverse.

The question as to which is the preferable language, Tamil or Malayālim, is often discussed, and I have noticed that most of those who are acquainted with both languages give the preference to the one which they had learnt first, and to which they had naturally become attached. This seems to show that both have their merits. It is indisputable, however, that Tamil is the more highly cultivated, exact, and euphonious of the two; while Malayālim is the more terse, and adopts Sanskrit words in their most correct form, without the corruptions and alterations to which they are necessarily exposed by the rules of Tamil. To the Malayālim speaker, Tamil appears needlessly to lengthen out its words; to the Tamil scholar, Malayālim sounds harsh, nasal, and full of aspirates, and appears deficient in exactness, especially in the terminations of the verbs. There are fewer honorifics in Malayālim, so that one at first feels awkward in addressing the Divine Being in prayer, in this language, as "Nee," which in Tamil would be exceedingly irreverent and unbecoming.

These languages were doubtless once identical, the most ancient forms of Tamil and Malayālim almost coinciding. This is ingeniously demonstrated by Dr. Caldwell, who shows that the word for *east* in both languages means literally *down*wards, and for *west up*wards—thus proving that both nations were originally located on the *eastern* side of the Ghauts; in which case eastwards is really "downwards" to the coast, and westwards "upwards" toward the mountains.

It is interesting to note that in our own language we have adopted several words of Tamil origin. A certain stimulating mixture is called *toddy* (in Tamil "tādi"); cigars are called *cheroots*, from the Tamil "churuttu," a roll; *cot*, now occasionally used in England, as in India, for "a small bed," is from the Tamil "kattil," a very different word from our own "cot,"—a house or cottage; *rice* is the Tamil "arisi,"—written by the Greeks "oruza,"—in English "rice."

On the other hand, many English, Portuguese, Arabic, and other terms, learned by intercourse with these nations, are now in common use amongst the people of South India.

It will readily be seen that much study and attention are required to attain proficiency in Tamil or Malayālim. Not that the Indian languages are by any means equally intricate and perplexing as Arabic and Chinese; the difficulty is really not extreme, and can in every case be surmounted by care and constant practice. In the pronunciation, Europeans err chiefly in interchanging one *d* or *t* sound for another; in omitting aspirates; in mistaking the long and short vowels; and in confounding the hard and soft and hissing *r*. With industry, living amongst the natives, and freely associating with them, and with daily reading and conversing, a European should be able fairly to commence regular extempore speaking within a year after his arrival in the country, and two years may suffice for a fluent and moderately accurate command of the language.

At first, egregious blunders are unavoidable, but the natives are very polite and lenient in their criticisms, and are delighted with any earnest attempts to overcome the difficulties of the language. The exact intonations and idioms are, it must be confessed, rather difficult of acquisition. For example, different words are used for "the sun," and "the *heat* or *rays* of the sun," while in English we apply the same term to both. A European, therefore, using the wrong word may be insisting on having his towels put into the *body of the sun* itself, instead of into its *rays* merely.

In English we are accustomed to speak of both "mirror" and "tumbler" alike as "glass," so that the tyro in Tamil may inadvertently call for "a *mirror* of water;" or, by a slight mispronunciation, he may speak of "pilleigal," *children*, as "puligal," *tigers*. Mistakes will occasionally be committed even after some practice in speaking. I remember on one occasion observing a gentle twinkling smile steal over the faces of my hearers, and on afterthought recollected that I had made a mistake of half a letter in a text which I had quoted, "Riches make to themselves wings like an eagle," —a "karugei," I should have said; but "karuthei," a *donkey*, was the word which, by a slip of the tongue, I uttered; and as the good people had never seen wings on a donkey in that part of the world, it was no wonder that their fancy was tickled by the ludicrous idea.

The long and strange names of places in India often seem very puzzling, but most of the Indian geographical names given in English maps and other publications are much altered and corrupted, or abbreviated from the real form of the word. This arises from carelessness and insufficient acquaintance with the language on the part of the early British residents in India. Thus Travancore is called by the natives themselves Tiruvithānkodu; Trevandrum is Tiruvanantapuram; Quilon is properly Kollam; (Cape) Comorin is Kumari; and so on with most of the names of well-known localities in India. Our English form of many words has become established through long use, and cannot now be well altered or corrected.

It is interesting to observe that the Hindus have given names to localities very much resembling those in use in our own country. There are many villages and towns with names similar (when translated) to some of our own. In Travancore, as well as in Great Britain, I have known or visited Newmarket (Puthukadei), Hillsborough (Maleivilei), Newport (Puttentorei), Smithfield (Kollanvilei), and many others of like nature; thus showing that the Hindus are like ourselves in mental structure, as also in the essential characteristics of their languages.

Although it is impossible, from the various changes which words undergo in course of time, to discover the meaning of every local name at present in use in India, yet most of these long and formidable-looking names have a definite signification. They are generally compound words, and may readily be resolved into their elements.

Many of our English geographical terms end in *ham*, *stow*, *ton*, &c., each of which has its appropriate meaning. So also will be found in South Indian local names such terminations as *kodu*, ridge or stronghold; *palli*, temple; *vilei*, field; *puram*, town; *oor* or *úr*, village; *patnam*, town;

kurei, river bank; *konam*, corner; and *pettah*, a village attached to a fort.

The position or other circumstances of a locality are often indicated in these local terms. Such are Valiatory (Great Port), Kulivilei (Hollow Field), Udayagiri (Eastern Hill), Pārcikonam (Rock Corner), A'ttūr (River Village), Manakādu (Sand Desert). These resemble in character such English words as Springfield, Blackwater, Bath, and others. Cochin, properly *Kochi*, is from "kochu," "little"—the town being built upon a very small piece of land between the sea and the backwater.

Some of the Tamil local names are, like the English Newcastle and Chester, suggested by forts, palaces, and great and important edifices by which the localities were distinguished. Thus Aranmanei means The Fortifications; Kottāram, The Palace; and Cottayam, The Fort.

The names of traditional or fabulous heroes and gods, or allusions to legendary tales related of the localities, furnish many geographical terms. Trevandrum is "The City of the Sacred Snake," where a great serpent is said to have sheltered the god Vishnu, who there became incarnate; Patmanābhapuram is "The City of Patmanābhan," the national god of Travancore; Devikodu, "The Goddess's Town;" Nāgercoil, "Snake Temple," where the serpent god is worshipped; Māvelikkara, "Great Bali's bank;" Alagiapāndipuram, "The Beautiful City of Pāndi," &c. Compare with these our Peterborough, St. Albans, Holywell, &c.

Animals and plants common in India give names to numerous localities. Anjengo, properly *Anjutenga*, means "The Five Cocoa-nut Trees;" Tāmareikulam, "The Water-lily Pond;" Kānyirankulam, "Strychnine Tree Pond;" Vāreitottam, "Plantain Garden;" "Nellikākuri, "Gooseberry Hole;" Mungilvilei, "Bamboo Field." One might almost by these names discover what plants most abound in each place.

Sokankāni is "Monkey's Land;" Meilādi, "Peacock's Dance;" Pāmbādi, "Snake's Dance;" Kolitottam, "Fowl Garden;" A'neikādu, "Elephant Forest;" and Kilūr, "Parrot Village." In like manner we in England have Primrose Hill, Ivy Bridge, Oakley, Oxford, Otterton, Foxham, &c.

In India localities are often named after the class of persons who formerly or at present reside in them. Accordingly, Vannānvilei means "Washerman's Field;" Pāreicheri or Parcherry, "Parian's Street;" Pitcheikudiyiruppu, "Beggar's Dwelling-place;" and Tattānvilei, "Goldsmith's Field."

The Hindus frequently indulge in fanciful and poetical names for their villages, which are sometimes strikingly inconsistent with the matter-of-fact or miserable appearance of the places themselves. Butter and milk are frequently referred to, probably as emblems of fertility and prosperity. Such are Pālūr, "Milk Village;" Pālār, "Milk River;" Neyoor, "Butter Village;" Neyyāttunkarei, "The Bank of the Butter River;"—the very figure used in Holy Writ, "a land *flowing with milk* and honey," Exod. iii. 17. One village which I have often visited is called Chandramangalam, "Moon's Rejoicing"—evidently a mere poetical compound.

Many of these names are very long and formidable-looking, but of course to those who have studied the language they are quite as easy as our longest English words. Others, longer still, are by no means difficult to pronounce. Here are one or two of the longest:—Koleishegaramangalam, Chinnamartāndaputtentorei, Anantanādānkudiyiruppu.

As the British Indian Government have decided that all Indian names shall henceforward be simply transliterated into Roman characters, and as this is the only remedy for the confusion and diversity in this respect so generally complained of by English readers, this system has been adopted in the present work, except in the names of places frequently referred to in geographical works and missionary reports, of which the less accurate orthography has become established and familiar.

In like manner proper *names of persons* have their several significations, and those often very pretty and poetical. Many of the people receive names in honour of popular Hindu gods and goddesses, as Nārāyana, Rāmā, Mādava, Perumāl, Pārvathi, Latchmi; or of demons, as Mādan, Sāttan, Isakki. Others are elegant and poetical compounds, and these, as well as Scripture names, are favourites amongst Christian converts. Such are Masillāmani, "Pearl without a flaw;" Vethamānikkam, "Gem of Scripture;" Gurupātham, "Feet of the Teacher;" Karuttudian, "Possessor of thought, or judgment;" Gnānakkan, "Eye of wisdom;" Gnānamuttu, "Pearl of wisdom;" Sebattiān, "Praying one;" Devadāsen, "Servant of God;" Sattiyāyi, "True one;" &c.

Other names are suggested by the personal appearance of the individuals who bear them, as Karuttān, "Black one;" Velleiyān, "White one;" Ilayan, "Tender one;" Kochukutti, "Little one."

Many names are given on the principle of bestowing an humble cognomen, as a kind of protection from envy, or the evil eye, which might injuriously affect those who assume to themselves lofty and sounding titles: such are Ummini, "a small particle;" Valli, "a creeping plant;" Podipen, "a minute woman—a *bit* of a girl;" Pichei, "alms, or charity," —unless indeed this last alludes poetically and beautifully to children being the charitable gifts of God's bounty, for which the parents may have offered their humble petitions.

VILLAGE CHAPEL, SCHOOL-HOUSE, AND NATIVE TEACHERS' HOUSE IN TRAVANCORE.

CHAPTER XI.

LITERATURE AND POPULAR EDUCATION.

Classical Literature—Proverbs illustrative of Scripture—Astrology—Native Poems—A Royal Author—Moral Sentiments—Poetical Figures—Metres—Specimens of Christian Lyrics and Native Tunes—Village Schools—System of Instruction—Government Schools and College—Female Education—Mission Schools.

THE Tamil vernacular literature is of considerable extent and variety. No less than 1,755 distinct publications (including tracts, &c.) have been put into *print* by Hindus, Mohammedans, Roman Catholics, and Protestants, in addition to many works still found only in manuscript. Of these the largest proportion are Protestant religious works, next those on Hinduism, with poems, plays, philosophy, fables, proverbs, and works treating of medicine, grammar, and educational subjects. The first book printed in the Tamil language was by a Portuguese Jesuit, in 1577. The Tamil translation of the Holy Scriptures was the first rendering of the Scriptures in an Indian language, being published by the Danish missionaries in 1715—above a hundred and fifty years ago.

The Malayālim indigenous literature is very scanty in amount, and is inferior in literary character; this language having been chiefly cultivated by Brahmans rather than by native Malayālis. A few good works, including a translation of the great Hindu epic, "Rāmāyanam," exist in manuscript. There are one or two printing presses conducted by natives, but there is no such sale for vernacular books as amongst the Tamil people.

The works most popular in Travancore are portions of the great epic poems, the Rāmāyana and the Mahābhārata, the Story of King Nala, and other fabulous histories of Hindu heroes and gods, together with religious works expatiating on the benefits to be derived from the strict observance of the prescribed ceremonies and prayers. Other popular and much-read books treat of omens, incantations, astrology, and so forth.

Many Hindu *proverbs*, as well as common customs, furnish admirable illustrations of the language or statements of Holy Scripture. The following may be selected out of many of a similar character :—

1. "A knife within and piety outwardly." (Compare Psa. lv. 21 ; Matt. xxiii. 28.)

2. "The king administers instant punishment, but God delays His judgment." (Eccles. viii. 11.)

3. "Will words of commiseration cool the head?" (Jas. ii. 16.)

4. "The future fruit may be known before it is ripe." (Prov. xx. 11.)

5. "Like standing upon two boats." (Jas. i. 6.)

6. "Though the bitter gourd be washed in the Ganges, it will not become good." (Jer. ii. 22.)

7. "They who give have all things ; those who withhold have nothing." (Prov. xi. 24 ; Matt. xiii. 12.)

8. "The fowl is not aware of danger till it is seized by the hand." (Prov. xxix. 1.)

9. "The moon shines even in the house of the wicked." (Matt. v. 45.)

10. "When a thing is given out of love, it is like nectar." (Prov. xv. 17.)

11. "Are there any bars that can confine love? The tender tears of the loved one cause a very tempest in the soul." (Cant. viii. 6, 7.)

12. "Purity of mind alone is virtue." (Matt v. 8.)

13. "The unloving live to themselves, the loving live wholly for others." (Rom. xiv. 7.)

14. "Soft words are better than harsh : the sea is attracted by the cool moon and not by the hot sun." (Prov. xv. 1.)

15. "Where there is a stain on the heart, even good deeds will be all received as evil; but those of spotless minds will still look upon it as good." (Tit. i. 15.)

16. "If those who confess the existence of God enter on an evil action, God will rebuke them. Not so those who say, 'There is no God.' Is it not to their own dear children that men patiently repeat instruction?" (Heb. xii. 8.)

The school books in general use ordinarily contain lessons in *Astrology*. One of these in Malayālim is entitled "Vākkiam"—Astrology. It is divided into four parts, of which the first and the third consist of tables to facilitate computations of the relative positions of the moon and planets—the data and formulæ being represented by Sanskrit mnemonic words and letters. The second part contains tables of the days of the week; the twenty-seven stars or constellations through which, according to Hindu astronomy, the moon passes; the twelve signs of the zodiac; the age of the moon, and other information. The fourth part is exclusively astrological, giving rules for finding out lucky times for the performance of every necessary action,—such as bathing, shaving, marriage, domestic events, house-building, lending money, journeying, and so forth.

The following specimen of information of this kind from the Malayālim almanack for M.E. 1039 may not be devoid of interest:—

"*Propitious times for marriage, &c.—1st Chingum*, 1039 (16th August, 1863). After sunset, between 18½ and 20 hours, and 22 and 23¾ hours, the moon being in the first quarter of the star Uttiram, and the sign Gemini rising,—

a good time for children's teething. Between 19½ and 25¼ hours, Gemini and Cancer rising,—fortunate for giving names.

"11*th.*—From 8 to 9¾ hours, and 11½ to 13 hours, the moon being in the third quarter of Uttrādam, and Libra rising,—good for giving children rice for the first time (weaning).

"9*th Vrichigam*, 1039.—After sunrise, 14⅝ to 15¾ hours, the moon being in the fourth quarter of Aswathi,—lucky both for commencing the erection of a house, and for first entrance into a new residence.

"11*th.*—After sunset, 8¾ to 19 hours, the moon being in the second quarter of Rohini, Cancer and Leo rising,—good for marriage, excepting ten minutes at midnight."

A curious specimen of a thoroughly native production is a Malayālim poem in my possession, composed by a Súdra native of Trevandrum, Mādavan Pillei, in honour of the late Rajah Martānda Vurmah, and written in the most inflated style of fulsome panegyric. Opening, as usual, with invocations to Vishnu and other deities, the poem proceeds to describe, in the most exaggerated terms, the public reception of the present from her Majesty the Queen to the late Rajah,—to which we have already referred in Chapter V.

The Rajah's fame for wisdom and virtue had, it appears, attracted the attention and excited the admiration of the gods themselves, several of whom came down to have the pleasure of witnessing these excellences, bestowing upon the Rajah at the same time the nectar of the gods, so that thenceforth his words seemed to the hearers as heavenly ambrosia flowing from his lips.

Victoria is represented as Queen of the Húnas, or Europeans. (In former ages, according to tradition, the monkey gods in the army of Rāma married the female Rākshasas or giants of Ceylon, and to their descendants Rāma allotted the remote West as their place of abode. These are the European nations, and they still evidently retain the characteristics of both the original races from whom they are descended, inasmuch as, like the monkeys, they select elevated sites for their abodes, and delight to sit upon chairs and benches instead of the ground, and, like the giantesses, they habitually devour flesh for food.) To this Húna Queen the Rajah had sent a beautiful ivory throne, richly carved and inlaid, and in token of her Majesty's regard for him she kindly sent in return a handsome embroidered belt and watch. Details of the Durbar are then given, but, it must be confessed, without much regard to historic accuracy; the Rajah is represented upon this occasion as shining amongst his attendants like the moon amongst the stars.

The second part of the poem describes a visit paid by the Rajah to the sacred temples at Suchindram and Cape Comorin. He is described as no less than an incarnation of Deity itself, and his learning, courage, and piety are highly extolled. This kind of thing is no doubt the origin of much of the hero-worship and idolatry which have prevailed amongst ancient nations. The royal procession being witnessed by strangers, a dialogue is introduced, in which the spectators, ignorant of the person of the Rajah, inquire who this glorious and extraordinary personage is. One hints that it must be the god Indra on a visit to the presiding deity of the temple; another, that it is the god of riches, but that he is not so fair as this glorious person. Others suggest that it may be the great hero Rāma or Kāmadeva, the god of love, but for the report that the latter is without material body or form. At last they meet with one who sets them all right upon the subject.

This extravagant production exhibits few signs of true poetic ability, and possesses little merit as to literary composition or style.

More special interest naturally attaches to a poem composed and published by H. H. the late Rajah Vunjee Bāla Rāma Vurmah, elder uncle of the present Maharajah, who died in 1846. It is considered by native scholars to be a good specimen of modern Sanskrit poetry, the compound poetical terms being formed according to standard rules, the sentences skilfully constructed, and the whole adapted to be sung to the most popular and melodious Hindu tunes. This work contains hymns in praise of Patmanābhan, the tutelar deity of "the charitable kingdom;" but of course is thoroughly superstitious, and after a fashion devout in sentiment and tone. The first hymn commences thus:—

"O thou, Lord of Earth, Husband of Sree (the goddess of prosperity), thou, O God, who hast lotus-like eyes—save me! O holy Patmanābhan, whose chariot is drawn by birds—save me! O thou who art worshipped by the king of the Suras (celestials), thou who art full of goodness, Subduer of enemies, Giver of blessings to thy servants, thou who hast arms admirably powerful, thou who art adored by the holy ones—save me! O thou Upholder of mountains, thou Enemy of Mura (a demon), thou Seat of Mercy, Remover of the suffering arising from births and deaths. . . .

"Remove my manifold sins, O Souri! (a name of Vishnu,) who walkest in the most holy gardens of bliss and happiness. Remove my manifold sins, O thou Destroyer of Kashipu, who was a terror to the three worlds, thou who shinest like gold. Remove my manifold sins, thou Purifier from sin, thou Joy of the shepherdesses, thou who art adorned with beautiful features, thou who art devoid of passions, whose lotus-like foot measures the universe. Remove my manifold sins, O my Lord, who takest away sorrows; thou, O Souri, who hast the sun and the moon for thine eyes."

The last hymn is an address to the soul, as follows:—

"O my Mind! be thou always fixed upon God. Ah!

tell me, art thou not incessantly fixed on self? O my Mind, know that this thy body is fragile; be not over-anxious. Do not covet earth. Delight in the history of Mādhava (Vishnu), which is full of joy, holy and divine. O my Mind, cherish not rude ignorance; let not dreadful sins have place in thy thoughts; avoid evil communications. O my Mind, be kind to every one. Consider all things as thou considerest thyself. Put away thy sorrows, and with all thy strength incessantly serve the azure-tinted Patmanābhan. O my Mind, be thou always fixed upon God!"

It should be borne in mind that this poem is the production of one well acquainted with many of the truths inculcated by the Christian religion.

Excellent sentiments are contained in the Tamil ethical poems, studied as classics, several of which are of considerable antiquity. But it must be remembered that the Hindus have had considerable opportunities of learning something of revealed truth from their intercourse, in ancient as well as modern times, with Jewish and Christian colonists and merchants. Beautiful and appropriate *poetical figures* abound in these works. Gratitude, for instance, is set forth in the following verse:—

"The cocoa-nut bears heavy bunches, and gives men its nectar-like water its lifelong time, in grateful remembrance of the water given to it in its younger days: likewise, virtuous men never forget former favours."

The evil of association with the wicked is thus described:—

"Even the blameless are despised on account of their associations. The sweet sandal-wood tree and the fine timber trees are burnt up with the rest of the jungle."

The benefit of association with the good is illustrated as follows:—"When the rice-field is watered, the grass on the borders is also profited. If there be one good person, for his sake the rain falls."

Many works on medicine, grammar, jurisprudence, and other subjects, in Tamil and Malayālim, are composed in a poetic form, to aid the memory of students. The poetical dialect of Tamil is, however, very different from the language in common use at the present time; it is the ancient form of the Tamil language, and contains very few, if any, Sanskrit words. Malayālim poetry, on the contrary, employs a large proportion of Sanskrit, in consequence of the influence of the Brahmans in Malabar, by whom the language has been cultivated.

In both languages a great variety of metres are in use, to which are attached ancient and appropriate tunes, sung in temple worship and on other occasions. Alliteration is introduced, often to the absurd extent of sacrificing sense to sound. The rhyme, like that of the Welsh poetry, comes not at the end but at the beginning of the lines, as in the following verse:—

> "Roll, O rill, for ever;
> Rest not, lest thy wavelets,
> Sheen as shining crystal,
> Shrink and sink to darkness."

It will not be difficult to perceive a similar rhyme and alliteration in the following verse of a Christian lyric in Tamil, viz.,—

> "Múvarāy arúbiṣāy mun úri úri kālam vār
> Pāva tār vilā valā parābarā tayābarā."

Amongst the Tamil people several eminent Christian poets have, in the providence of God, been raised up, and their delightful hymns and spiritual songs are exceedingly popular amongst our Christian people, who sometimes sit up all night, at weddings and other festivals, singing and hearing these lyrics. Their partial use in public worship has for some years past been encouraged by many missionaries, and the

English prejudices against them which formerly prevailed are rapidly disappearing.

We are accustomed to sing these hymns at our open-air services, and many heathens are attracted and instructed by the Christian truths presented in so captivating a form. This is literally "singing for Jesus," like that sweet singer and Christian poet, Philip Phillips, of New York. Many instances have come to our knowledge of heathens taking with them printed copies of single lyrics, published as hand-bills — notably one on "The Day of Judgment," — and learning and singing these in their own houses and villages.

The favourite Tamil poet and most voluminous writer was the late Vethanāyagam Shāstri, of Tanjore; next stand John Palmer, of Trevandrum, formerly a catechist at Nāgercoil, and many other writers of popular hymns. A few original Malayālim poems have been published, and the writer had a number of the best Tamil lyrics translated into that language by a Syrian Christian friend, and published for the use of native Christians in Malabar.

One or two specimens of the lyrics and tunes most popular amongst our people will perhaps be interesting. The first line of each verse is generally repeated, and the chorus is always repeated at the conclusion of each verse. Some of the tunes are slow and grave, others very quick; or else a part of the tune may be slow, and then a line or two be sung in very quick time; but they are mostly a kind of rapid chant. Native musicians do not sing in parts, but in unison merely, the best of them keeping time with wonderful accuracy. The following are among the simplest and shortest of these tunes, but their peculiar character is to a large extent lost by their reduction to the English notation, and by their disconnection from the original words.

No. 1.*

CHORUS. M. 96, *twice to a measure.*

The above words form the chorus of a hymn, written to this tune, by Vethanāyagam Shāstri, containing earnest desires and humble petitions for the Divine presence. The literal meaning is as follows :—.

> "Grant at this time the abundant manifestation of Thyself,
> Eternal! Divine! All-righteous One!"

The verses all through are sung to the same tune as the chorus.

No. 2.

CHORUS. M. 136.

* Nos. 1 and 2 have been written for this work in English musical notation by Mr. W. E. Clift.

The lyric sung to this lively tune is a hymn of praise to Christ, also composed by the Tanjore poet. The following is a literal translation of the above verses :—

CHORUS.

"O worthy of praise! O heavenly gospel name!
O excellent joy! great splendour! Our health, beauty, happiness!"

VERSE.

"O soul filled with exceeding loveliness! heavenly Lamp of grace!
Renowned One, whom celestials praise for thy sweet grace!
O worthy, &c."

No. 3.

The above tune (written in English musical notation by

Rev. J. P. Ashton, M.A.) is sung to another of the Shāstri's compositions, part of which translated is as follows :—

CHORUS.

"Why art thou bewildered, O my soul? why art thou bewildered?
As the wild deer is bewildered (or confused), why art thou bewildered, O my soul?"

VERSE.

"The God who made space, air, heavens and earth,
If thou knowest who He is, why, as if not knowing him?
Why art thou, &c."

The following is a more complete specimen of a characteristic composition by Vethanāyagam Shāstri, on the subject of

Christ worthy of the Confidence of Sinners.

CHORUS.

"Jesus (Thou art my) strength—O grant Thy grace!"

VERSES.

"Surrounded by the holy excellent ones, Thou rulest in the great Mount Zion,
Sweet Sea of grace, Helper of men!
Blessed Being, glorious, magnificent, formless Spirit,
Effulgence, Beginning, Righteousness—who camest by Thine own power in form of a sacred man.
Jesus, Thou art, &c.

"Fulness of good, Stream of wisdom!
Sea of might—Head of the heavenly hosts!
Adoration to Thy greatness (which is) beyond the praise of Thy servants!
O Word, Love, Jesus, King—Object of men's daily worship and praise and honour!
Jesus, Thou art, &c.

"Thou didst create heaven and earth, and destroyest the work of the great serpent;
Thou dost impart spiritual blessings and grace to men,
Loving, friendly, gracious One! Plant who destroyest the sin of the world!
Desiring, enduring, seeking, accompanying, Thou art the King who givest grace, the kind Friend!
Jesus, Thou art, &c."

We conclude with a translation of a favourite hymn on the work of the Holy Spirit by Rev. S. Winfred, a native minister labouring in connection with the London Mission in Madras. It is sung to the first tune.

CHORUS.

"The evil heart to change, O Holy Spirit, come,—Great loving One!"

VERSES.

"Cleaving to the bondage and illusion of sin, pining, dying the death,—
A greatly deceived sinner was I.
The evil heart, &c.

Measureless sin I did, resisting knowledge,
With great desire infringing,—
The evil heart, &c.

Worldly prosperity I reckoned perpetual, in it took pleasure;
My heart was absorbed and exhausted.
The evil heart, &c.

Heaven to view I had no mind; mere chaff I sought, O Lord—
A sinner am I, O Lord.
The evil heart, &c.

My deceitful heart desired but evil. O thou refuge,
Who wilt end my delusion.
The evil heart, &c.

Darkness to remove, inward light to grant, Thou didst come;
To soften the mind Thou dost wait.
The evil heart, &c.

Now thought, new desire to renew and preserve
To Thy praise,—
The evil heart, &c.

As Thou didst give grace to Lydia, show mercy to me! So open my heart
That conformity to Thee may begin.
The evil heart, &c."

How encouraging and delightful to think that men who might, but for the gospel, have been sunk in the dense darkness of Hindu idolatry and superstition, have been led by the grace of God thus to write the praises of our adorable Saviour, and to seek the influences of that divine Spirit who is the author of all good and grace in the hearts of men!

Vernacular schools conducted by private teachers are found in almost every village in Travancore. Throughout the whole of India, indeed, the profession of a teacher is held in high repute. In 1865 I had occasion to make careful and detailed inquiries as to the number of heathen schoolmasters in the districts of Trevandrum and Quilon, in order to carry out in my own neighbourhood the effort which was then being made by the Bible Society to supply a New Testament, in his own mother tongue, to each heathen schoolmaster in India. Above 160 copies were distributed in these districts, and there may have been a few other teachers whom we did not discover. These men were chiefly of the Súdra and Ilavar castes, with a few carpenters, vellālars, goldsmiths and others. Very few Brahmans were found engaged in educational pursuits.

In most of these schools there are from 20 to 30 or more boys. I was pleased to find also in almost every school from 2 to 4 or 5 Súdra and Ilavar girls. The total number of pupils under instruction in schools, other than those maintained by the native Government (including all mission schools), is roughly estimated at 40,000.

The system of instruction in the common village schools is very defective, and consists chiefly in imposing rote lessons, without sufficient explanations of the meaning or *rationale* of what is taught. In addition to "the three R's," the principal studies in the better schools are astronomical calculations and vernacular poetry.

The first lesson of the juvenile pupil is writing on sand. He is made to strew a handful of sand over a part of the floor, smooth it, then write the letters with his forefinger, and at the same time sing out the name of each letter;

thus learning to read and write at the same time. After a time the scholar is advanced to writing on "oleis" or palm leaves; few of them use paper.

The native system of arithmetic is ingenious, and, as far as it goes, rapid in its processes; but generally I have not found those educated in the common schools good arithmeticians,—they are easily puzzled by a long sum in addition or multiplication.

The schools supported by the native Government are of a superior class. At the head of these stands the Central Institution, or High School, at Trevandrum, commenced by Mr. Roberts many years ago, and in which, at his request, the then Rajah liberally gave permission to have the Bible read and explained by the Christian teachers. This practice, I am happy to say, is still continued. In the junior department of this institution nearly 700 boys of all castes, except the lowest, receive a good English education; and in the senior or collegiate department, under the care of the principal, Mr. John Ross, A.M., there are ninety-six youths, of whom thirty-nine are undergraduates of the Madras University. This institution takes a high position in the Government examinations amongst the schools and colleges of South India.

For the accommodation of the senior pupils, the foundation stone of a new college at Trevandrum was laid, with appropriate ceremonies, by H. H. the Maharajah, on 30th Sept., 1869. English education early took root in the country, and the standard has by degrees been raised higher and higher during recent years. There is now a large and increasing number of native youths and men well educated in English, some of them being graduates in arts and law of the Madras University.

Sixteen District English Schools and twenty-nine Vernacular Schools are supported by the Government in various districts of Travancore; in these above 4,000 boys receive a good education. There are also twenty vernacular village schools, with 1,300 pupils, receiving grants in aid.

Female education, too, is spreading. There has never been any decided objection on the part of Súdras or Ilavars to the elementary instruction of females, probably in consequence of the influential position of women in their singular system of inheritance by the female line. One or two thousand girls of these castes attend the ordinary village schools. It is from the Brahmans, principally, that objections to female education come. Of course the lowest classes also are without the means of obtaining instruction, except in Mission Schools; their children being refused admission to all respectable native schools, and, with rare and recent exceptions, to all Government schools.

From the commencement of missionary operations in Travancore, great attention has been paid to female education by missionaries both of the London Missionary and the Church Missionary Societies, the former being liberally aided by the Society for Female Education in the East. Within the last few years much good has also been accomplished by the agents of the Indian Female Normal School and Instruction Society, who have induced numbers of the very highest families in Trevandrum to send their children to their school, or to receive instruction at their own homes, like the "zenāna" teaching of Northern India. This good work has enjoyed the patronage and benefited by the personal example of H. H. the Maharajah, the first Prince, and the Dewān; and there are now, in addition, two schools for Brahman and other high-caste girls, under their more immediate patronage, conducted respectively in the fort and in one of the suburbs of the capital.

Mission schools are numerous and influential. According to information furnished by the missionaries themselves, for insertion in the Calendar for 1867, the schools of the London Missionary Society then contained about 8,000 pupils, of whom 1,600 were girls; those of the Church Missionary Society, 2,200, of whom over 400 were girls; the Roman Catholic Mission Schools over 2,700, of whom 270 were girls; and the Syrian Christian Schools 2,000 children, of whom 900 were girls. The aggregate, therefore, amounts to 13,000 boys and 3,200 girls; to all of whom more or less of religious as well as secular instruction is imparted. The Church Missionary Society have an excellent English College and Vernacular Institution at Cottayam, and the London Missionary Society an English and Vernacular Seminary at Nāgercoil, both of which have largely aided the cause of popular education in Travancore.

Education is thus spreading in a remarkable degree in this interesting country, and must inevitably bring with it, by the blessing of God, the downfall of superstition, error, and oppression, and be the means of introducing an era of national enlightenment, progress, and freedom.

CHAPTER XII.

HINDUISM IN TRAVANCORE.

State Support of Idolatry—Worship of Vishnu as Patmanabhan—History and Description of Great Temple at Trevandrum—Principal Ceremonies and Festivals—Sexennial Murajabam—Royal Regeneration Ceremony.

THE thought of the general prevalence of idolatry throughout the vast empire of India is a solemn and depressing one to the Christian mind. In the little kingdom of Travancore alone there are at least a million of heathen idolaters, living without God and without hope in the world,—knowing not the Giver of every good and perfect gift, but turning from the great Fountain of all life and happiness to endeavour to hew out for themselves "broken cisterns that can hold no water." How terrible to think of such a multitude, generation after generation, bowing down to worship false gods, "the work of their own hands, that which their own fingers have made;" to see—

> "Immortal men
> Wide wandering from the way, eclipsed in night—
> Dark, moonless, moral night—living like beasts,
> Like beasts descending to the grave, untaught
> Of life to come, unsanctified, unsaved!"

Oh that they may be brought speedily to return unto the Lord, and find in Him peace and eternal salvation!

Hinduism is the established religion of the state, and is sustained and supported by all its power, wealth, and social influence. The theory is that all other classes are created for the service of the Brahmans, and that the highest possible virtue consists in obedience and homage being rendered to them. Their influence and authority are supposed to extend over all the acts and relationships of life, and everything enjoyed or possessed by others comes, they affirm, from the favour of the Brahmans, and belongs properly to them. Manu says (i., 100, 101, 105), "Whatever exists in the universe is all in effect, *though not in form*, the wealth of the Brahman; since the Brahman is entitled to it all by his primogeniture and eminence of birth. The Brahman eats but his own food, wears but his own apparel, and bestows but his own in alms. Through the benevolence of the Brahmans, indeed, other mortals enjoy life. He alone deserves to possess this whole earth." In accordance with these and other principles of the law of Manu, so far as it is possible to carry them out in human society, the attempt has been made to shape out the whole civil polity of the state.

Occupying, as it does, a secluded corner of the peninsula of India, and having thus escaped the modifying influences of conquest and political change, Travancore retains the observance of most of the laws and institutions of Hinduism in their primitive form and obligation. It has yielded but very slowly, and with intense and unconcealed reluctance, to the few inevitable national reforms which have been effected, to the introduction and extension of Christianity, and to the consequent gradual decrease of Brahmanical domination and influence. This state is still therefore one of the great strongholds of Hinduism and caste in the South of India, and is distinguished as "The Land of Piety and Charity" for its liberal support of the Brahmanical religion and priesthood. No less than one-fifth of the whole annual revenue of the state is expended on the support of the Brahman temples and priests, and the influential classes are united in the support and defence of this formidable system of imposture and superstition.

Vishnu, the second deity of the Hindu triad, is worshipped as the national deity of Travancore. He is usually represented by the Hindus as a black or blue man with four arms. In one hand he holds a war-club; in another a "chakra" or circular missile weapon, like a quoit, sharp at the edges, with which he is said to cut off the heads of his enemies. A third hand holds a lotus water-lily, the emblem of emanation,—unfolding—creation. A conch-shell is in the fourth hand; and this has consequently been adopted as the national emblem of Travancore, as the rose, thistle and shamrock are for Great Britain and Ireland, the peacock for Burmah, and the dragon for China.

Vishnu is said to have appeared under nine several incarnations, viz., as a fish, tortoise, boar, &c. He is expected yet once again to appear as a great reformer, mounted on a white horse, and bearing a sword and shield. He has 1,000 names, such as Rāma, Krishna, Nārāyanan, Hari, Perumāl; and one of the lessons of boys at school is to commit these to memory. In various parts of India Vishnu is worshipped under local forms and attributes. In the character of the patron god of Travancore he is called Patmanābhan, and is represented as reclining upon a great snake, called "Ananta" (endless), which is coiled up to form a couch for the deity, while its many heads stretch upwards over his head as a canopy. Our copy of a native sketch, drawn in India, in a very primitive style of art, shows the god reclining on the king of serpents, surrounded by attendants and by glorified worshippers and gods celebrating his praise. Patmanābhan means "the lily-navelled one," and the sacred lily is accordingly depicted as proceeding from the navel of the god. From that flower Brahma, the creator, springs. The original allusion of the symbol probably is to the deity in quiescence,

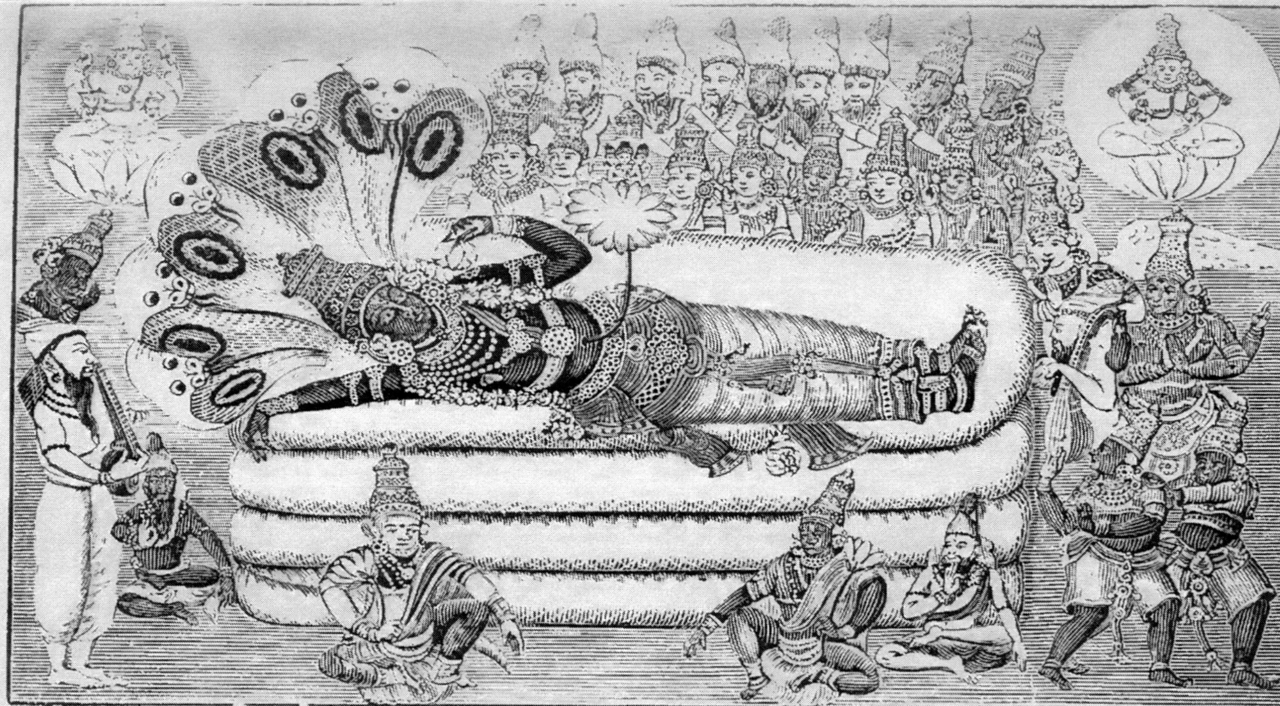

PATMANABHAN—THE NATIONAL DEITY OF TRAVANCORE.

(Face page 160.)

before the production or evolution of the universe, as represented under the emblem of the growth of the water-lily.

The head-quarters of the worship of this god are at the great temple in the capital, Trevandrum. The correct native name of this place is "Tiruvanantapuram"—"the town of the sacred snake." This refers to the legend respecting the origin of the national worship in this locality, which is as follows:—

The place where Trevandrum now stands was formerly a jungle, called Ananta Kādu. In the centre of this desert dwelt a Pulayan and his wife, who obtained a livelihood by cultivating a large rice-field, near to their hut. One day, as the Pulayan's wife was weeding her grounds, she heard the cry of a babe close to her, and on search, found it so beautiful that she supposed it was a divine infant, and was at first afraid to touch it. However, after washing herself, she fed the babe with milk, and left it again under the shade of a large tree. As soon as she had retired a five-headed cobra came, removed the infant to a hole in the tree, and sheltered it from the sun with its hood. It was an incarnation of the god Vishnu. While there, the Pulayan and his wife used to make offerings to the babe of milk and conjee in a cocoa-nut shell. Tidings of these things reaching the ears of the sovereign of Travancore, orders were issued for the erection of a temple at the place. The natives add that the cocoa-nut shell used by the Pulayan is still preserved in the royal pagoda at Trevandrum.

Few temples in Travancore equal those of the eastern coast in extent or grandeur. That dedicated to Patmanābhan at Trevandrum may be regarded as a favourable specimen of other edifices of this kind. It is the centre and the holiest part of the capital. Corresponding care is therefore taken to guard and preserve its immaculate purity from all contamination by contact with low castes or Europeans. It covers a space of about a square furlong in the centre of the fort,—in which the palace, the official residence of the prime minister, the great offices of government, and the houses of many Brahmans are situated. Several roads lead to the temple, but natives of low caste and Europeans are prevented, by native prejudice, from approaching too nearly even to the outer walls. A lofty wall surrounds the sacred enclosure. The principal entrance, on the east side, opposite the great gate of the fort, is illuminated at night. A handsome flight of stone steps leads up to the lofty entrance door, which is surmounted by a great stone tower, pyramidal in form, and 80 or 100 feet in height. This is the "pagoda," or steeple, and stands, not over the most sacred portion of the temple, but above the entrance gateway. The tower is covered with elaborate sculptures and ornamental work, and has window-like openings in the centre of each of its seven stories. Within is an extensive, well-swept courtyard, surrounded by open porticoes supported on carved stone pillars, which are covered with grotesque or natural representations of gods, warriors, and animals. In various parts are shrines dedicated to various deities—as Krishna, Ganesha, Patmanābhan; for although a Hindu temple is dedicated to and recognised by the name of one particular deity, numerous smaller fanes for the worship of other gods are often included within the same enclosure. So true is it that "their land is *full* of idols."

In the highest of the inner buildings, the golden image of Patmanābhan, in whose honour the beautiful and costly edifice has been erected, is treasured and worshipped with daily offerings and services. In one part of the courtyard stand two brazen pillars, thirty or forty feet in height, with niches for the display of lights on festive occasions, also a gold-plated flagstaff, on which is raised the flag that announces the inauguration of the principal ceremonies. A covered way runs round the courtyard, for protection from the weather during the solemn processions of the idol. In one of the open halls, called the *kulaseghara mandabam*, or "portico," the more important ceremonies are celebrated.

It is said that there is a deep well inside the temple, into which immense riches are thrown year by year; and in another place, in a hollow covered by a stone, a great golden lamp, which was lit over 120 years ago and still continues burning.

COURTYARD OF TREVANDRUM TEMPLE.

Outside the temple, on the north-east, is the great "tank," or pool of holy water, in which the Brahmans bathe daily. Such a reservoir, or a stream in the near vicinity, is essential to every Hindu temple, as frequent ablutions are necessary to both priests and worshippers.

The greater part of the buildings in connection with the temple of Patmanābhan are of no considerable antiquity. It is probable that the locality has been regarded for ages as more or less sacred, and used as a place of worship. Native historians date the first erection of a temple in the year 225, Malabar era—that is A.D. 1050 :—

"In 225, M.E., a priest from the Tulu country, named Divāgaran, set out to visit sacred places, and happened on his way to come to Ananta Kādu. His patron deity, Krishna (or Vishnu), there appeared to him as Patmanābhan. He determined thereupon to offer worship and dedicate a temple to this god. There were already two temples here in honour of Krishna and Shāstāva. To the priests of these temples, therefore, Divāgaran applied. With their aid he built another temple, made images from the heart-wood of the forest trees, and consecrated and worshipped them with the usual ceremonies. He also laid out a flower-garden, and erected dwellings for Brahmans. The place soon became celebrated under the name of Ananta puram. It is reported by ancient tradition, that even before this time temples had twice been erected on the same spot, but had gone to ruin, and the site became overgrown with forests."*

The more costly portions of the temple are said to have been erected by Vunjee Martānda Vurmah Rajah in 1729, and the great tower completed in 1779, after many years of labour in its construction.

In this "temple royal" the great religious ceremonies of state are observed. Splendid processions feasts, shows, and royal gifts, tend to attach the people to the worship and superstitions with which these are associated. The average annual expenses incurred on account of the daily "poojah," or worship, and the periodic festivals and ceremonies in this pagoda alone are, reduced to pounds sterling, as follows:—

Daily poojah (or worship)	£7,573
Feast of Lights (twice a year) ...	2,750
Bathing Festival (twice a year) ...	4,780
Total,	£15,103

—a sum equal, in relative value, to about £90,000 in England.

* Malayālim History of Travancore.

In this temple the coronation oath is taken. Immediately on his accession to the throne, the Rajah proceeds to the temple with his offerings to the presiding deity. He receives from the high priest a sword and a belt, a cloth and some rice, as emblems of protection and power, sustenance and support, received from the favour of Patmanābhan; and he solemnly promises to reign as the vicegerent of the national god. His Highness is then invested with the first of his official titles—"Sree Patmanābha Dausa," "the servant or slave of the holy god Patmanābhan."

The "A'rāttu," or bathing festival, occurs twice every year, in April and in October. It lasts for ten days each time, concluding with the ceremony of bathing the idols in the sea. The first day of the feast is called the "Kodiyettu," or raising of the flag of crimson silk on the golden flagstaff in the court of the temple.

During the first nine days of this festival special offerings are made, the idol is anointed, and incessant rites and devotions are performed in the temple by the Nambúri priests. The Rajah remains, as far as possible, in a state of seclusion and partial fasting. At night the people are entertained with dramatic shows, feats of jugglery and skill, and other exhibitions within and near the sacred enclosure.

The tenth day is the principal one of the festival, on which the god Patmanābhan is carried in solemn procession to be bathed in the sea, at a distance of about two miles from the fort and temple. All necessary preparations having previously been made, the royal *cortége* sets out at four o'clock in the afternoon, and is saluted by the firing of twenty-one guns. The procession is composed of the Maharajah, with his personal attendants and body-guard; the whole of the infantry and cavalry sepoys of the Nair brigade, their swords drawn, banners flying, and band playing; the state elephants magnificently caparisoned, and bearing howdahs of gold, silver, and ivory; the Brahman priests carrying the sacred images; and an immense retinue of attendants, with banners, flags, symbols of various kinds, palankeens and carriages, and all that can add pomp or state to the brilliant and imposing ceremonial. Multitudes of people from town and country are in attendance as spectators.

The whole of the road from the fort to the sea having been previously strewn with a quantity of fine white sand, the Rajah marches on foot, dressed in the native "uniform" —a single piece of white cloth fastened round the loins—and wearing a handsome cap of blue velvet, embroidered with a representation of the golden foot of Patmanābhan. His Highness carries a naked sword and a shield, and, accompanied by the first Prince, precedes the images as their servant and guardian. Behind the Rajah are the images of Patmanābhan, Narasimha, and Krishna (the first of gold, the last two of silver), borne on the shoulders of Nambúri priests, surrounded by a crowd of other Brahmans, as an additional guard and security. Several images of brass, belonging to temples in the suburbs, then follow. Behind, the prime minister and other great officers of state, all dressed in the simplest possible garb, follow in the procession. Every fifty or a hundred yards the procession halts, and the Rajah turns round and makes a lowly obeisance to the idol, which in these days of enlightenment and education he cannot but know is a helpless and lifeless piece of metal (Psa. cxv. 4—7).

On reaching the sea-shore, offerings are first made by the Rajah at the adjoining temple. The images are then placed within temporary sheds erected for the purpose on the sea-beach, and prettily decorated in native style. Other prayers are repeated, and garlands of flowers presented. Three times the priests enter the sea with offerings, which they cast into the waters; the third time carrying with them the whole of the images. Thrice the priests, holding the images in their hands, plunge into the water. But the waves, more powerful than the very gods so highly honoured, often strike down both priests and images, so that the latter are only rescued with considerable difficulty. The Rajah also bathes at the same time in the sea; and the festival closes the same evening, with the return of the images to the sanctuaries.

Another ceremony in connection with these festivals is called "Palli Vetta," or "Royal Hunting." The Maharajah goes in similar procession to another part of the suburbs. Two or three soft unripe cocoa-nuts being placed at the foot of a tree, his Highness takes a bow, and fitting an arrow in it, shoots three times into the nuts. This is probably a relic of great hunting expeditions, in which the sovereigns of the country were wont to indulge in former times.

Another festival, regarded as of very special importance, and celebrated at great cost, is that called "Murajabam," or "customary prayer." This occurs at intervals of six years, and is supposed to be eminently conducive to the defence of the kingdom and people, the procuring of a regular supply of rain, and the general safety and prosperity of the country. It is designed also to atone for any imperfection, or sins of ignorance and omission, in other religious observances.

This festival occupies eight weeks, usually in the months of November and December. The chief priest of the Nambúris, a kind of Hindu Pontiff, travels from the Cochin country to Trevandrum in great state, to preside at and celebrate the various solemnities of the festival. On his way he is accompanied from district to district by numerous followers, and is attended by the local officials of government. Loud cries of "Hari Rāmā," "Hari Rāmā," are uttered by his bearers, the sacred shell is blown to announce his approach, and all persons of inferior caste are warned and driven off to the prescribed distance.

When nearing the palace, the sacred procession is met by

the Maharajah, who, in token of humility and reverence, officiates for a short time as one of the bearers of the sacerdotal palankeen. On the high priest's alighting, the Rajah pays obeisance to his Holiness by humble prostrations at his feet. He immediately conducts the Nambúri to the apartment set apart and purified for his reception, places him on a golden seat, and washes his feet. A small quantity of the sacred and purifying water used in this ablution is drunk by the Rajah, and the remainder he pours over his head.

During the continuance of this festival the Brahmans are supposed to be constantly engaged in offering special prayers for the sovereign and the kingdom at large. From six to nine o'clock in the morning, from one to three in the afternoon, and in the evening from six to eight o'clock, about a hundred of the priests stand immersed in water up to the waist, performing religious ablutions and repeating "Mantras" and prayers in the sacred Sanskrit language. It is pretended that the water miraculously rises when the Brahmans enter, and decreases in height when they retire—which of course, in the natural order of things, must necessarily occur. This long exposure to the water is often the cause of pain and disease to the unfortunate and superstitious priests.

It is calculated that about 60,000 persons attend the Murajabam from all parts of Travancore, and some from more distant countries. The native Government provides for them food and lodging, beds, mats, &c., in extensive temporary booths erected for the occasion; large presents of money are also distributed amongst them. The cost of the Murajabam feast in 1863 was £16,361, besides about £3,000 (and other sums) spent in preparations; this is said to have been less than had been expended on previous occasions. Much evil arises from the gluttony, disorder, and vice incidental upon the attendance of these crowds of sensual idolaters.

Another remarkable ceremony, called "Hiranya Garbham," "the golden womb," or "Patma Garbha Dānam," "the lotus womb-gift," is celebrated only by native kings and princes in India at enormous expense.

The Maharajah of Travancore, as we have already mentioned, is not by birth of the Brahman caste, but a Súdra; or, rather, he is of mixed race, the husbands of the Travancore Rānees, or princesses, being usually Chatriyas of the class called Tirumulpād. From the earliest period of its history the Brahmans have, as we have seen, possessed very considerable influence and dignity in Travancore. The country is still noted throughout India for its marked devotion to the worship of the gods, its rigid conservatism of caste and other institutions of Hinduism, and its profuse liberality in the support of the popular faith. The distinctions of Brahmanical caste therefore are greatly prized by the higher classes of the natives.

The object of the "Hiranya Garbham" rite is to raise the Rajah from the ranks of the Súdra caste, to which he properly belongs, to the position and dignity of a Brahman, or as near this as it is possible for him to become. The Brahmans are the "twice-born" and holy caste. This ceremony constitutes the *second* birth of the Súdra prince, and the title of it might therefore fairly be translated "The Regeneration Gift." After its celebration his Highness can no longer partake of food along with the members of his own family, to whom he is now superior in caste as well as in rank. He is admitted to the high privilege of being present when the Brahmans are enjoying their meals, and of eating in their presence. He wins also their admiration for piety, devotion, and generosity, and earns in addition to his other royal titles, the valued one of "Kulaseghara Perumāl."

This extraordinary ceremony was observed in July, 1854, by H.H. the late Rajah Martānda Vurmah. In the following account of this festival, the statistics and details are derived from a description written at the time by a native writer, Sreenevāsa Row.

Throughout India the cow is a sacred animal. To die while holding the tail of a cow, and presenting the animal to a Brahman, is supposed to insure heavenly felicity. Killing a cow is still, in theory, according to the ancient laws of Travancore, an act of murder. To be born of a cow in a future birth is a high honour and privilege. The five products of the cow are the elements of a composition the most efficacious for purification known to the Hindus. The new birth of the Rajah then must be either from a golden cow, or a lotus flower. Formerly the form of the sacred cow was made in gold, with a hollow body, through which the Rajah crept, and was then regarded as twice-born, and holy. The flower of the sacred lotus, or water-lily, was, however, the form selected on this occasion. This is required to be composed of a quantity of gold exactly equal to the weight of the Rajah himself, who is therefore placed in scales, and weighed against the gold for this purpose. This part of the ceremonial is called Tulābhāram—balance weighing. The golden lotus is afterwards broken up and distributed, in fixed proportions, amongst his Highness's personal attendants and the Brahmans and others present at the festival, and to the treasury of Patmanābhan. The total weight of gold used on this occasion in the construction of the golden lotus and for other purposes amounted to 9,070 kalanja of about 78 grains each—equal to nearly 124 pounds troy, and valued at about £6,000 sterling.

The gold having been duly procured from Bombay, an auspicious day was appointed for the melting of the metal and the casting of the golden vessel. This was cylindrical in form, about six feet in height and four feet and a half in diameter. The cover was lotus-shaped, with a crown on the top, richly ornamented with precious stones. After its completion, the sacred vessel was carried in procession around the palace and the great temple, in an open hall of which—the Hall of Ceremonies, massive with pillars of sculptured stone, and dazzling with decorations of silk cloths, glittering ornaments, and garlands of fragrant flowers—it was then placed in readiness for the subsequent ceremonies.

A week before the day appointed for the principal ceremony, the Rajah retired from his ordinary residence into a separate and consecrated building, secluding himself from his attendants of the Súdra caste, abstaining from the use of betel and other indulgences, and abstracting himself as much as possible from the ordinary duties of state. Here he was occupied in private devotions and in prayers to his tutelary deity for long life, happiness, and prosperity.

On the morning of the great day of the festival, the Rajah in state procession visited the temple, and having presented to the idol munificent offerings of gold coins and jewelry, proceeded to the sacred hall. Inside the golden vessel there had been placed a small quantity of the consecrated mixture, composed of the five products of the cow (milk, curd, butter, urine, and dung). His Highness entered the vessel and remained there for the prescribed period, during which the officiating priests repeated prayers appropriate to the occasion. Immediately on emerging from the vessel, the Rajah presented to the chief priest the whole of the rich jewels and ornaments which he had worn while undergoing the ceremony. At the same time a royal salute was fired by the Nair Brigade, drawn up in front of the temple. The European officers of the brigade were required to attend on the occasion of these idolatrous festivals, but they have since been relieved from all such unchristian compliances.

After the completion of the ceremony, the Rajah decorated himself with a new set of jewels, and walked in solemn procession around the temple, accompanied by the members of the Royal Family and all the great officers of state. Again, approaching the idol, he offered adoration and prostrated himself on the ground before the altar. The high priest then brought forth the magnificent crown, and placed it on the head of the Rajah, proclaiming aloud three times the royal titles,—"Kulaseghara" (head of the tribe), and "Perumāl" (a name of Vishnu).

Again the brilliant procession wended its way around the temple, the Rajah wearing the crown and carrying the sword of state, and again he entered the sacred hall; this time to be bathed in pure water. Once more the procession encompassed the pagoda, and then returned to the palace, where it was received with another royal salute of artillery and musketry.

These ceremonies were attended by several minor rajahs and their followers, by noted Gurus and expounders of the Vedas and Purānas, and by about 22,000 Brahmans from various parts of the kingdom. For the reception and accommodation of all these, liberal provision was made at the expense of the Rajah. Large presents were made to all the nobles and Brahmans present at the festival, and the whole of the gold of which the vessel was made was afterwards made into coins of various sizes, and distributed amongst them. To this fact the word Dānam (gift or bounty) refers.

On the following day the Rajah again proceeded with a magnificent retinue to the pagoda, and offered costly gifts (including a fine elephant) to the idol. The Dewān also received from him a state palankeen and a pair of handsome shawls. The procession then traversed once round the public streets of the fort.

After this the Rajah left Trevandrum to pay a state visit to the sacred shrine at Tirupāppúr, about ten miles distant, where he presented valuable offerings, according to custom.

Thence he went on to A'ttungal, the original seat of the Royal Family. The idol there is regarded as their guardian deity, and is the object of assiduous worship. From A'ttungal the Rajah returned to Trevandrum, where he was again received with due honours and demonstrations of popular esteem. Thus ended this notable and costly ceremonial, an extraordinary and vain attempt to invent "a royal road" to regeneration.

It is remarkable, that even in a rite so absurd and idolatrous in itself as that which we have described, there is a distinct recognition of the necessity to sinful man of some great change—some marked advance in holiness and purity. The people of Travancore view this change under the emblem of a new birth of the body from the golden cow or the sacred lily. The Holy Scriptures also speak of a new birth, not of the body, but of the soul, by the Holy Spirit. May the present kind and amiable Maharajah of Travancore feel the need of that regenerating grace from the one true and living God, and be led to come to Him in simple faith on the Lord Jesus Christ, through whom alone he can become truly regenerate,—twice-born in the true sense, an heir of the kingdom of heaven.*

The Tulābhāram, or balance-weighing, a part of the ceremonies just described, was recently performed by the present Maharajah. This is not in general performed immediately on the accession of a sovereign. Some people archly affirm that the delay is to allow his Highness to grow stout, and weigh as heavy as possible, for the profit of the priests. In the present case, the delay of nine years since the accession of the Maharajah arose principally from his natural hesitation to expend such a vast sum of public money solely for the benefit of the small population of Brahmans, in the face

* This account of the "Hiranya Garbham" ceremony appeared in the *Sunday at Home* for July 1, 1870.

of the expostulations and moral dissuasion brought to bear upon such an observance in the present age. A decision was at last come to, and towards the conclusion of 1869, the Bathing Festival, the Murajabam and Feast of Lights, and, on the 14th January, 1870, the Weighing ceremony, followed one another in quick succession; over three months being thus occupied in costly and idolatrous festivities.

Multitudes of Brahmans visited the capital to witness the performances; whole boat-loads of vegetables, rice, butter, and condiments for the guests were daily landed from the interior, and great boat-shaped wooden vessels, scooped out of large trees, served as rice and curry dishes. The prices of all the necessaries of life rose fearfully, and extra precautions against accident and crime were taken. Police were stationed, in different localities, in sheds erected for their accommodation by the road-side, to prevent low-caste people from entering or approaching the fort.

Gold in bars, to the value of over 120,000 Rs. (£12,000), having been procured from Calcutta, the greater portion was struck into coins in preparation for the great ceremony. Preparatory religious ceremonies, including repeated bathings and purifications, anointings and sprinklings of holy water, the worship of golden images and of the sacred scales, the feeding of Brahmans, gifts to them, and offerings of flowers, jewels, silks, and an elephant, were performed for eight days. On the last day the Maharajah, wearing magnificent jewels, specially made for the occasion, and holding the state sword in his right hand, and the state shield of black leopard's skin and a scimitar in his left, walked thrice round the scales, again prostrated himself before them, prayed, and then mounted the scale. The sword and shield were placed in his lap; then the gold, in coins and ingots, was put in the other scale till it touched the ground. The whole quantity of gold placed in the scale was 204 lbs.

avoirdupois, being rather more than the quantity specially purchased for the purpose.

In the distribution of the gold, the head priest's share amounted to nearly 11,000 rupees; other Nambúris received from about 680 rupees to about seventeen shillings, which was the amount bestowed upon all ordinary Nambúris. Over 43,000 coins were struck and distributed. They were of four sizes, the largest being worth about 13s. 8d.; the others being respectively one-half, one-fourth, and one-eighth of this sum. The device consisted of the legend "Holy Patmanābhan" on one side, and on the other the national conch-shell, each being encircled with a wreath. The largest sized coins were distributed to Canarese Brahmans, one to each adult; the third size to all Tamil Brahmans; and the smallest to the women and children of the latter.

The total expense of this weighing ceremony amounted to about 160,000 rupees; but the "Hiranya Garbha" ceremony, which will probably cost at least 140,000 rupees more, is still to be performed before the Maharajah's coronation.

CHAPTER XIII.

HINDUISM (CONTINUED).

Hindu Temples in Travancore—Car Festival—Interior Economy of Temples—Free Inns for Brahmans—Cost of Ecclesiastical Establishment—Evils of this Waste—Ordinary Annual Festivals.

THE number of heathen temples in Travancore is estimated at 3,817. Sacred places, however, such as the remains of ancient temples and idols, consecrated groves and holy wells, and solitary images or symbols of various kinds, everywhere abound. Many of the minor temples are falling to ruin, while others are still famous for their extensive tanks, ancient buildings, legendary associations, or some other marked peculiarities.

Of these the temple at Suchindram, seven or eight miles from Cape Comorin, is said to be the largest in the country. It is dedicated to Tanu-mal-āyan—Siva, Vishnu, and Brahma united in one,—and a long legend, in the usual Hindu style, is related of the miraculous origin of the local worship. About 32,851 rupees are annually expended on the maintenance of this temple, and it is occasionally visited by the Rajah in person.

The annual festival in December is largely attended by excited crowds of worshippers from all parts of the country, "mad upon their idols." The ceremonies on this occasion cost the native Government about 6,000 rupees. The festival is maintained for ten days, on the last of which the huge cars are drawn in procession around the temple by men, assisted, when necessary, by elephants. The chief Minister of State superintends this operation, and heathens of high caste are under legal obligation to the Government to attend the feast, for the purpose of making offerings and dragging the cars. The Government officials commence by pulling for a short time the ropes attached to the cars, and their example is followed by the vast multitude of people assembled. Government peons may be seen standing along the columns of men drawing at the ropes, with rods lifted up ready to point out and punish the dilatory or lazy. The cars are in themselves very heavy, and their weight is increased by a large number of idle Brahmans and musicians seated upon them. But eager efforts are made;—

> "A thousand pilgrims strain
> Arm, shoulder, breast, and thigh, with might and main,
> To drag that sacred wain,
> And scarce can draw along the enormous load."

Their fanaticism is stimulated and increased by all the accessories of the festival, and deafening shouts and cries of praise to the god are uttered all day long.

The car-drawing at Suchindram is regarded as of so great importance to the welfare of the state, that the Rajah himself is required to fast on that day until the due completion of the ceremony is announced to him at Trevandrum, a distance of above forty miles. The important (and under the circumstances necessarily very gratifying) message was formerly conveyed by mounted troopers. Afterwards cannon were stationed at intervals along the road and fired as signals. But since the completion of the electric telegraph from Nāgercoil to Trevandrum, the intelligence has been communicated from Suchindram to the telegraph station at Nāgercoil by the report of cannons, and thence by telegraph to his Highness at Trevandrum. How singular the contrast between the grovelling superstitions of ancient Hinduism on the one hand and the achievements of European science and civilization on the other! and what an anomaly and anachronism that intelligent and educated Hindus should use the electric telegraph to facilitate the worship of the stone idol at Suchindram!

A Vaishnavite temple, of great reputed sanctity, is that at Tiruvattār, about halfway between Cape Comorin and Trevandrum, to which also the Rajah pays occasional state visits. Vishnu is here worshipped under the cognomen of A'thi Kesavan. The natives believe this shrine to have been built in the mythological period, before the incarnation of Parasu Rāmen. The great granite walls of this temple are 18 or 20 feet in height, handsomely ornamented with carved work; and the edifice itself, with its magnificent flights of stone steps leading from the river to the temple, is unusually imposing in appearance.' Numerous Brahmans reside here. The annual expenditure of the temple amounts to 21,854 rupees.

Another sanctuary of considerable celebrity is that at Cape Comorin, which contains some handsome stone carvings of animals. The yearly maintenance of it costs 10,723 rupees. The proper name of the Cape is Kanyā Kumari, "the virgin daughter," a title of the goddess Doorga here worshipped. A curious kind of white sand, the grains of which are as large as those of rice, and which is therefore called "rice sand," is found here. A singular legend is related of the origin of this sand. "The youngest daughter of the King of Pāndi, named Kanyā Kumari, was sought in marriage by a foreign giant, named Vanasaram. She accepted his suit and agreed to marry him on one condition, which she hoped he could never fulfil, namely, that he should on the wedding day give the guests *rice* to eat which had been sown, grown, cut, winnowed, and cooked upon that very day. Much to her astonishment the ugly monster performed the task. Greatly enraged she cursed the rice, which became stones; she cursed the chaff, which became sand; she broke down a bridge which the giant had placed there for his convenience, and finally slew the giant himself."*

Tiruvallā, about twenty miles S.E. of Allepey, is celebrated for its richly endowed and antique pagoda, traditionally said to have been founded eighty-three years before the Christian era. The large temple, encompassed by a high wall nearly one furlong square, forms the centre of an extensive and tolerably regular town, inhabited principally by Brahmans and Súdras. The bathing tank is faced with stone, having bathing apartments jutting out into the water on the four sides. This pagoda costs 9,356 rupees per annum.

Many other strongholds of idolatry in Travancore might well be specified, such as the temple at Varkkala, famous for a remarkable tank, and a resort of pilgrims from distant countries; that at Kulattúr, oaths taken at which are regarded as of peculiar sacredness; the celebrated and handsome temple at Yettumānur, dedicated to Vishnu, of which the annual festival and fair are attended by great crowds of worshippers; the famous Saivite pagoda at Vaikkam, on the borders of the lake, the annual festivals of which are very largely attended by visitors from all parts of the country; and many others possessed of respective features of interest and celebrity.

The principal temples of Travancore, numbering 378, are under the immediate control of the Sirkar, or native Government. The property, in landed estates and other endowments, belonging to these temples, yielding an annual revenue of about three lacs of rupees (£30,000 sterling), was assumed, with their management, by the Sirkar in 1811. In each temple there are two officiating priests, or Shānthis, receiving

* Mullen's "Missions in South India," p. 94.

monthly allowances in money and grain. These priests are employed for six years only in some temples, and for three years in others; after which they are generally transferred to another. Some, however, are hereditary priests.

"The office of the Shānthis consists in performing self-ablution every morning very early, and in going immediately afterwards to the pagoda to open the doors of the rooms in which the images are kept; to remove the faded flowers, &c., with which those images had been adorned on the preceding night; to clean the place and adore the image after purifying themselves; and then to commence the daily ceremonies, according to the established ritual. The Shānthis must abstain from all intercourse with women, and are prohibited even from speaking to them during their period of office; and when they come out of the pagoda, people must retire to a distance to avoid polluting them."*

Each temple has its manager, accountant, cashier, and storekeeper, besides inferior attendants employed as sweepers, lamplighters, &c. In the temples in South Travancore dancing girls and musicians attend several times daily. In North Travancore only two or three men with drums are employed in each temple, except in a few instances, where musicians perform on the conch-shell, drums, flageolet, and cymbals, for the delectation of the god and his worshippers.

Presents or offerings of silk, money, gold and silver images of snakes, and jewels, are made by the inhabitants to the pagodas. In some of these there are treasure-boxes for offerings, placed in front of the inner shrine, which are not opened till they are filled to the very brim. Most of the temples have flower-gardens for the cultivation of oleander, jasmine, sweet basil, and other sacred flowers used in the preparation of garlands for the idols. To some pagodas

* "Records of Travancore," No. III., pp. 3, 4.

elephants, richly caparisoned, are attached for use in the processions and festivals.

The temple at Trevandrum is under the management of a committee, of which the Maharajah is a member. The treasury is immensely rich, containing money, gold, images, jewels, precious stones, &c.; so that the managers were able to lend to the Government, some time ago, the large sum of five lacs of rupees (£50,000 sterling). Besides the temples in Travancore, the native Government maintains about twenty-three temples in other parts of India, including Cochin, Chellumbram, Rāmeswaram, and Madura, and one as far distant even as Benares.

Ootooperahs, or Free Inns for Brahmans, are another peculiar religious institution of Travancore. These inns are about forty-two in number, and were originally established by the celebrated statesman, Rāmāyen Dalavāyi, about a century ago. They are situated at convenient stages throughout the country, mostly in connection with the principal temples. In them Brahmans are fed at the expense of the Government with curry and rice, rice boiled in water, chutney, curd, milk, fruits, &c. Neither travelling nor resident Brahmans, however, are allowed to remain in the same Ootooperah longer than two days; unless sickness or other unavoidable cause prevents their leaving the place. In some of these houses only one meal a day is allowed, while in others meals are provided both morning and evening. A small quantity of boiled rice is distributed to poor Súdras daily at noon, and in two or three instances this is given to all castes indiscriminately.

The great Ootooperah is at the temple of Patmanābhan at Trevandrum. All Brahmans resorting hither, and all those resident at the capital, are at liberty to take their meals here both day and night. They are fed in several rows round the porch of the pagoda. In another of the buildings, more abundant and expensive preparations are made for the meals of more favoured guests, and of the Brahman servants of the palace and the prime minister's court.

The average annual cost of the Ecclesiastical Establishment or "Devassam," is fully five lacs of rupees, and the Ootooperahs take in addition three lacs; the whole being equal to a sum of £80,000 sterling—no less than one-fifth of the whole annual revenue of the state.

Is this expenditure true "dharmma" *piety*, or is it not rather wicked and sinful in the sight of God? The providential gifts of God to man, so liberally bestowed in that rich and beautiful country, are desecrated to the service of useless and abominable idols. Well may the Almighty reprove this people as He did the Jews of old, "Thou hast taken thy fair jewels of *My* gold and *My* silver, which *I* had given thee, and madest to thyself images of men. *My* meat also which *I* gave thee, even flour, and oil, and honey, wherewith I fed thee, thou hast even set it before them for a sweet savour" (Ezek. xvi. 17—19). The almighty Creator and Giver of all is thus dishonoured through the very gifts which He has bountifully imparted—all abused as they are to idolatrous and profane worship.

Is this true "dharmma" *charity*, or is it not rather immense waste and injury to the moral and social well-being of the community, in thus squandering so large a proportion of the national income on such profitless and demoralizing objects? This sum of money would within ten years suffice to cover the whole face of the country with good roads, well-built bridges, fertile clearings, and reproductive works of irrigation for the prevention of sudden dearth and desolating famines. Within twenty years the benefits of primary instruction might be extended to the lowest strata of the population (a consummation, however, which most of the higher classes have shown that they are far from desiring); or anyo taer great schemes for the production of material wealth, or for social improvement, might, with these squandered riches, be carried out.

As it is, crowds of sensual and dissolute Brahmans are maintained in idleness, their intellectual and manual labour is lost to the community, and they are encouraged to continue to regard themselves as quite a different species of men from the wretched, down-trodden, low caste population. The latter contribute their little share to the general revenue and productiveness of the country, but receive absolutely nothing in return; not even the privilege of free access to the courts of justice. Ignorance and superstition are privileged, endowed, and perpetuated in the country so long as this system continues in operation. Immorality, peculation, and the separation and rivalry of class interests, find everywhere abundant scope; and a mighty obstruction to the progress of truth and right is thus established. Whatever may be the various and opposing views entertained of "disestablishment and disendowment" at home, all must agree that some such operation is urgently required in Travancore, and eminently deserves to be carried out in its most stringent form and to the fullest extent.

In addition to the special ceremonies occurring at occasional intervals, to which we have already referred, periodic festivals (rarely fasts) are observed at least once a year in connection with almost every temple, and are regarded as an essential part of Hindu worship; much merit being attributed to their bountiful and punctual celebration. Many of these are of merely local interest; every temple, in fact, has its anniversary celebration, while others are of national importance.

The religious festivals of India are closely connected with the systems of astronomy and chronology by which their periods are determined. But, as most of them are reckoned by *lunar* time (like our Easter), they generally fall at different dates each year; and as these calculations depend upon the particular data and mode of reckoning that may be adopted, the times of certain festivals differ in various parts of India,—just as Easter is kept at different dates by the members of the Greek and Latin Churches. Hence the high estimation in which almanacks are held by the Hindus.

The Hindu holidays are numerous, requiring at least thirty-five days in the year; but were all of them observed, some fifty or sixty days, or even more, would be thus spent.

The leading annual festivals generally observed in Travancore are ten in number. We commence the list, for convenience, with the month of January, though the Hindu civil year begins in August, and the astronomical year in April; native calendars, Government reports, &c., embracing a period of twelve months from 15th August, the Malabar new year.

1. "*Pongul.*"—"The Boiled Rice Feast" or "Cattle Festival," as it is called, occupies about three days, from the 12th to the 14th of January. In former ages, when the Sanskrit people inhabited the regions north of the tropics, this was their new year, and celebrated the sun's reaching the tropic of Capricorn, which actually occurs on the 21st or 22nd December, but according to the Hindu computations about the 11th of January. This festival is observed with great rejoicings. Rice is boiled in cow's milk, as an emblem of abounding prosperity, and offered to the sun. Complimentary visits are paid, mutual good wishes expressed, and sweetmeats distributed. Cattle are gathered together with music, washed, adorned with garlands, and *worshipped*, to insure their fecundity and welfare throughout the year.

The 6th of January is called "Opening of the Gate of Heaven," as the righteous who die during the lucky period from January to June are supposed to obtain immediate entrance to felicity, while those passing away at other times must wait without the gates till this period commences.

2. "*Shrāddha,*" or "Funeral Offerings" to deceased ancestors, are performed for several days after their death, and thenceforward annually; presents being at the same time made to Brahmans. The souls of the dead are supposed to be greatly benefited and their happiness promoted by the due observance of the funeral rites and offerings, the favourable days for which are the new moons from August to January.

3. "*Siva Rātri*"—"Siva's Watch Night"—occurs in February or March, and is, throughout India, regarded as of the first importannce, especially amongst the Saivites. The whole of this night is spent in strict fasting and vigils, adoring the lingam image, repeating prayers, bathing, and many frivolous acts of worship. All sins are thereby expiated, and all blessings are secured.

To illustrate the merit gained by observing this night, an absurd story is told as follows:—

Once on a time a wicked and licentious archer on this day went into the forest, and in the evening, being benighted, he climbed a Bael tree for security from wild beasts. Fearing he might sleep and tumble off the tree, he began to pluck the leaves one by one and throw them down from the tree to keep himself awake. There happened to be a lingam (emblem of Siva) at the foot of the tree, and the leaves being sacred to this deity, the god was so much pleased with the hunter's offering, though accidental, that he forthwith sent a heavenly chariot and took him to his own celestial abode.

4. *Bharani*, in March or the beginning of April, is in honour of the goddess Kāli, wife of Siva. In Bengal it is called "Holi," or "Swinging Festival," and enjoyed as a season of carnival. In Travancore cocks are offered by Nairs, who generally slaughter them before the door of the temple of Kāli, or Bhāgavathi, sprinkling the earth with their blood and soliciting immunity from disease during

the year. Drunkenness, fighting, and disorder frequently characterize this festival.

This was originally a feast in honour of spring, and may perhaps correspond to the "April Fools" and "Carnivals" of European nations.

5. *Sri Rāma Navami*, "the ninth day of the god Rāma," is observed at the end of March or early in April, chiefly by Vishnuites, and commemorates the birthday of Rāma. The image of the hero is set up, adorned, and worshipped; and portions of the "Rāmāyanam" or poetical history of Rāma, his romantic adventures in search of his beloved wife, and his glorious success in rescuing her from the power of the giants who had carried her off, are sung to the delight of large audiences. This feast is regarded as most sacred and beneficial.

6. "*Vishu*" (a tropic or solstice), about the 12th of April, is the astronomical new year, and one of the most popular festivals of Malabar. Subjects present New Year offerings to the Rajah, merchants settle their accounts, and great rejoicing, with the deafening din of music in the temple and fireworks, and the firing of guns in the streets, everywhere prevails.

7. "*Vināyaga Chathurti*," "Ganesha's fourteenth day," about the 21st of August, celebrates the birth of the god of Wisdom and Fortune. Clay images of this deity, with his elephant's head, and short, stout body and legs, riding upon the back of a rat, are made, duly consecrated, and worshipped in houses and families; they are afterwards cast into a river or tank.

8. "*Onam*," in August or September, is a great national festival in Malabar, more generally observed even than the Vishu festival. Everything is now fresh and green after the rains, so that this almost amounts to a second spring feast. Houses are decorated with flowers, lamps kept burn-

ing, new clothes and earthenware purchased and the old thrown away, swings are in general requisition, and a jubilee is kept by all ranks and conditions of the people.

The legend on which the obligation of this festival is made to rest, is to the effect that a great king, Mahā Bali, by his religious ceremonies and observances, had obtained such extraordinary merit and authority as to alarm the gods themselves, and cause them to tremble for their supremacy. Vishnu, therefore, taking the form of a dwarf, asked of the king as much land as he could measure out by three steps. The request was granted. Immediately, expanding to a gigantic size, the god took one step half round the world, another step completed the circuit, and the third was taken by placing his foot on the head of the unfortunate king and crushing him down to the infernal regions, where, however, he was permitted to exercise sovereignty. Once a year, on this night, he returns to earth, and wanders about to see if his people are thriving. They endeavour therefore to appear as joyful and happy as possible.

> "This is the appointed night,
> The night of joy and consecrated mirth,
> When, from his judgment-seat in Padalon,
> By Yamen's throne,
> Baly goes forth, that he may walk the earth
> Unseen, and hear his name
> Still hymned and honoured by the grateful voice
> Of humankind, and in his fame rejoice." *

9. "*Dussera*," "the Ten Days Feast," relates to the autumnal equinox—though it is now supposed to commemorate a victory obtained by Doorga, the wife of Siva, over a wicked and ferocious monster. It falls at the end of September or the beginning of October. During this festival, which corresponds to the "Doorga Poojah" of Bengal, artisans worship their tools and implements; scholars their books, almanack, and

* Southey's "Curse of Kehama."

pens; and kings their swords and weapons. Public shows are also given.

It is at this time that the October "A'rāttu" or "Bathing Festival" (p. 165), and the "Royal Hunting," are celebrated by the Maharajah and his officers of state.

10. "*Deepāvali*," the "Feast of Lights," occurs in October or November. It commemorates the killing of a demon by Vishnu, who had not time to perform his ablutions by daylight, and was therefore compelled to do so, contrary to rule, at night. This is done by the Brahmans on this day. Bonfires are lit everywhere, and nocturnal illuminations are general in the temples, houses, and fields. The *dunghill* is worshipped with offerings of fruits, &c., and lamps are lit and set before it. The crows are also fed as an act of charity. This observance is probably a relic of the worship of the element of fire.

Other minor festivals are held in honour of the several incarnations of Vishnu; the commencement of the four great Ages, and of the Seasons; in remembrance of famous heroes and demigods, &c.,—but upon these it is not necessary to dwell.

CHAPTER XIV.

DEVIL-WORSHIP.

Alluded to in Scripture—Distinct from Image-Worship—Its Prevalence, Origin, and Resemblance to Western Superstitions—Names and Character of Demons—Mādan, Mallan, Sāttan—Female Demons—Human Sacrifices—Pattirakali, Ammen, Isakki—Instances and Illustrations of this Worship—Spirits of Wicked Men and others worshipped—The Devil-tree cut down—Minor Superstitions—Witchcraft, Magic, and Incantations—Dread of them.

In the Sacred Scriptures we find occasional allusion made to the worship of "devils"—as in Deut. xxxii. 17, "They sacrificed to devils, not to God;" so also Psa. cvi. 37. Whether the word here translated "devils" (literally "lords") refers merely to *idols* and the worship paid to them, or to the worship of *evil spirits* as such, it is not easy to determine.

On the one hand, idols and false gods may be, and in popular language often are, called devils, as a term of reproach justly deserved by those who usurp the place of the Most High in the hearts and outward adoration of His rational and accountable creatures. Or the term may be used of idolatry, on the principle that if the images of the heathen are aught but blocks of wood and stone; if they are animated and inhabited by any spirits whatever; those must be evil spirits, which delight to lead men astray and encourage idolatry and other crimes. So we are taught, in Ephes. vi. 12, that there are higher powers and wicked, hellish agencies—"the managers of the spiritual opposition to the kingdom of God,"—earnestly working to support evil and counteract good. Satan, indeed, appears to have caused himself to be worshipped by means of idolatry. He instigates and appropriates the worship paid by heathens to false gods; so that in this sense those words in 1 Cor. x. 20 are very striking:—"The things which the Gentiles sacrifice they sacrifice *to devils*, and not to God." In accordance with this view the poet says of Satan,—

> "What best pleased him, for in show he seemed
> Then likest God; whole nations, bowing, fell
> Before him worshipping, and from his lips
> Entreated oracles."

But, on the other hand, the "devils" spoken of in Scripture as adored by the heathen may refer, in some instances, to evil and malignant spirits, such as are systematically worshipped to the present day by many of the natives of Southern India.

This worship of wicked spirits, or demons, to deprecate their wrath or appease their anger, is altogether distinct from that of idols; which are supposed to represent more or less benevolent deities, and minor or mediatorial gods. It is a very ancient and wide-spread superstition, and appears to underlie many of the more elaborate and complex systems of paganism. In Africa fetish-worship is constantly practised to deprecate the wrath of departed souls, and avert the evils of witchcraft. In Mongolia, Tartary, and China * a remnant of devil-worship still lingers. In Madagascar, also, I suspect that the national superstitions—now, thank God, rapidly perishing before the power of the Gospel—are of this character; consisting rather in the worship of departed spirits, and the use of magical charms, than in the adoration of representative and symbolical images, like those of the

* Medhurst's "China; its State and Prospects," p. 203.

Hindus. In Siberia a system of demonolatry called "Shamanism" prevails. This was the old religion of the whole Tartar race before Buddhism and Mohammedanism were disseminated amongst them. The Shamanites acknowledge the existence of a Supreme God, but offer Him no worship. The objects of their worship are demons, which are supposed to be cruel, revengeful, and capricious, and the worship consists in bloody sacrifices and frantic dances.*

Very similar to this superstition is the demon-worship which prevails in various parts of India and Ceylon. This is practised by the aboriginal tribes, of whom there are, perhaps, eight or nine millions—chiefly in the hills, and in the South of India. These have some vague idea of the existence of God, but do not believe that He will injure them, or requires their worship. On the other hand, they fancy that there are hosts of—

"Demons of the air,
Wicked and wanton spirits, who, where they will,
Wander abroad, still seeking to do ill;"

flitting through the air, lurking by the road-side, dancing on the surface of the water, haunting houses and burial-grounds, dwelling in trees, going to and fro through the earth, and ever seeking to injure and torment and destroy mankind. These demons, they imagine, it is necessary to appease or pacify by offerings and worship. The first principle of their religion might be expressed in the words of an old English proverb, "Keep friends with the devil, and honest men will do you no harm." They say, "Keep friends with the demons, offer to them your property, your blood, your service, and you need not care about God; He will not harm you."

The origin of this vile and debasing worship is probably to be discovered in the dense ignorance and superstition of

* "Dravidian Comparative Grammar," p. 520.

early ages. Men were conscious of the fact that sin, pain, and suffering everywhere abounded; and the question of the origin of evil presented itself, as it must to every thinking mind. "If the Creator be good," they asked, "why so much suffering in the world? Whence, and from whom, does this spring?" The question has puzzled greater minds than those of the poor Hindus. Some such attempt to account for the origin of evil appears to have led to the famous heresy of the Manichæans in the third century of the Christian era. Perhaps the system of Parseeism, acknowledging two great principles—the one the author of good, the other of evil—also sprung from an attempt to solve this difficult problem. The existence and prevalence of disease and suffering of every kind were, by the original inhabitants of India, ascribed to the agency of wicked spirits, and these spirits they thought it wise to propitiate by whatever offerings and acts of worship appeared to them calculated to effect this purpose. Probably an instinctive fear of departed souls is also one element of this worship.

Ignorance, too, of the facts and operations of nature led to erroneous deductions, which seemed to corroborate these early guesses as to the existence of mischievous and malignant devils. How sudden and mysterious attacks of such diseases as cholera, small-pox, convulsions, and paralysis could, in the established order of things, occur, they knew not. Dwelling, as many of the early inhabitants of India did, in the midst of dense forests, and surrounded by innumerable living creatures, with the forms, sounds, and habits of many of which they were unacquainted, fearful phantoms were conjured up in the dim twilight, or in the darkness of night, by the excited and untutored imagination of the timid inhabitants, which were easily magnified into the forms and cries of demons. With this agrees a Tamil proverb "Marundavan kannukku irundathellām pey," "He who is bewildered (or frightened) thinks every dark object to be a devil." Everything that appeared supernatural, painfully sudden, or inexplicable, was thus accounted for; while the beneficent gifts of Providence, and the course of nature, were expected to continue as matters of course, without requiring solicitude or acknowledgment on the part of their recipients.

The great *resemblance* which may be traced between the general aspects and many particulars of the superstitions connected with demon-worship and those of our own forefathers in Britain, with respect to fairies, pixies, brownies, and boggarts; ghosts, apparitions, and fiends; witchcraft and magic (with which music and dancing are associated in our popular superstitions); good and ill fortune; lucky and unlucky days; the evil eye, omens, auspices, &c., has often struck me, and is very remarkable indeed. Happily, these absurd notions are fast disappearing from our own land. As the old Lancashire man shrewdly observed, "Owd Ned [the steam-engine] an' lung chimblies 'ev driven 'em away—fact'ry folk havin' summat else t'mind nur wanderin' ghosts un' rollickin' sperrits. There's no boggarts neaw, an' iv there were folk 'ev grown so wacken they'd soon catch 'em." The subject of the resemblances alluded to might prove worthy of fuller and more detailed investigation.

We proceed to give a brief account of the characters and attributes of the demons worshipped in Travancore, and of the superstitions connected with them.

There are in Tamil three words ordinarily used to express the general idea of demon or devil. These are "*pey*," a Dravidian word which bears some resemblance to our English word "fay," or "fairy;" another term is "*púthamn*," goblin or fiend; the third is "*pisāsu*," derived from the Sanskrit language, and of synonymous import. Those spirits called "púthamn" are spoken of as haunting the places where dead bodies are burnt or buried. Companies of them attend Siva, Ganesha, and other deities. They are described as dwarfs of ugly appearance, with huge potbellies and very small legs.

One of the principal objects of superstitious dread is the demon called "Mādan," a word signifying "he who is like a cow." He is supposed to be very large and tall, his body being of a black colour and covered with hair, like that of a cow.* Images of Mādan are never made. He is said to strike men and oxen with sudden illnesses, and is in consequence greatly feared.

There are numerous forms of Mādan, to which many mischievous acts are ascribed. "Chúla Mādan," or "Furnace devil," is worshipped by potters, who dread his breaking their pottery while it is being burnt in the kiln; "Kumili Mādan," or "Bubble devil," dances on the surface of the water; "Poruthu Mādan" is the "Fighting devil" (too well known amongst ourselves); "Neesa Mādan" is the "Wicked devil."

"Chudala Mādan," or "Graveyard demon," dwells in places where corpses have been buried or burnt. A silly fable, in the usual style, is related of this demon as appearing dancing in a flame with a turban, cloth, short drawers, bracelets, trident, javelin, bow, and a large club varnished with vermilion; which articles are still found in temples dedicated to his worship. "He received from Siva many privileges, such as to be worshipped by all persons living between Trevandrum and Madura, to receive human and animal sacrifices, to afflict virgins, to burn down cities, to break iron castles, to assume any shape his fancy might suggest at any time, and to play in deep waters like fishes. The people, therefore, through fear worship him to the

* Compare Lev. xvii. 7; literally, "hairy ones,—he-goats." In our popular superstitions, the cloven foot of an *ox* is attributed to Satan.

present day, and present to him offerings of fowls, goats, fruits, and flowers."

Many children are named after this and other demons, to whom they are dedicated to save them from infantile diseases. In some families the eldest son is named after the demon worshipped by the father's family, and the eldest daughter after that of the mother's family. Naturally, therefore, "a new name" (Hos. ii. 17) is given to these devil-worshippers, on their solemn and public profession of Christianity in the ordinance of baptism.

Another popular demon is Mallan, "the Giant," revered especially by the tribes who inhabit the mountains of Travancore, and who are supposed to possess great influence over the demons. Sometimes it is said that two of these gigantic fiends, sixteen or seventeen feet high, with terrible countenances and enormous projecting tusks, are seen fighting together and throwing lighted brands at each other. The engraving (page 196) gives an accurate representation of the common clay images of Mallan and his wife, Karunkāli, or "Black Kali," who is represented on his right.

"Kutti Sāttan," "little Sattan," is a familiar spirit invoked in performing juggling tricks. The name is almost the same as the Hebrew word Satan, though there does not appear to be any philological connection between the two. If invoked, Sāttan is supposed to be willing to place his powers at the service of his devotees, to effect whatever they desire, to supply them with whatever they may wish for, and to enable them to take revenge on their enemies by various spiteful means—such as throwing stones on their houses, breaking their doors, and putting dirt and clay into their food. I have heard many ridiculous and absurd tales of the tricks ascribed to Sāttan, and have been unable to persuade even intelligent Hindus that these must have been either accidental or managed by human agency, in trickery or through spite. On one occasion it was said that stones, cocoa-nut shells, and earth were thrown on the roof of a catechist's house, while several of his friends were on the watch; and that they were unable to detect any human

KARUNKALI AND MALLAN.

agency in the affair. In a town called Puthukadei stones were said to be continually falling down on one of the houses through the tricks of a demon.

There is now, in connection with the Trevandrum Mission,

an excellent old Christian, who was eminent some years ago as a native physician, especially in cases of poison, and as a professed exorcist, magician, and devil-priest. He was a worshipper of Sāttan, in whose honour he had built and maintained at his own expense two temples, in which he performed daily rites and offered sacrifices on stated occasions. His elder brother had cherished Sāttan as his familiar spirit, but afterwards professed to transfer the demon to this man, who continued to invoke him for twelve years until his conversion.

Doctor Krishnan, as he was called, stated, and I believe really imagined, that he had often seen this demon in human form, though only about two and a half feet high, with two tusks like those of an elephant, covered with hair like a cow, and with a sling and stones in his hand.

Another demon is called "Muchandei Múppan"—"the old man of the three roads." He is said to lurk at places where several roads meet, watching his opportunity to frighten and injure the passers by.

The demons worshipped in South India are supposed to be of both sexes, but the female demons appear to be still more malicious and cruel than those already noticed. Some of these are forms of Kāli, a goddess worshipped under various names and representations throughout the whole of India. She is fabled to be the wife of Siva, the god of destruction and lord of demons. She delights in blood, cruelty and lust. Human as well as animal sacrifices were offered to her. It is in honour of Kāli that Hindu ascetics cut, pierce, and torture their bodies, or are swung on hooks attached to a lofty rotating beam. She is represented as being pleased for a thousand years with the blood of a human being.

One of the Mackenzie Manuscripts states that an annual human sacrifice of peculiar atrocity was accustomed to be offered in former times at a fane of Bhāgavathi, or Kāli, in the Tiruvallā district. A young woman, pregnant with her first child, was selected, and brought in front of the

PATTIRAKĀLI.

shrine. She was then beheaded with one blow of a sword, so that the head rolled up in front of the image, on which the blood of the victim was also sprinkled. A similar sacrifice is said to have been offered till A.D. 1744. In the year following a possession of the goddess came upon a bystander, when the sacrifice was about to take place, directing that it should be discontinued. Since then it has been wholly set aside.

VEERAPATRAN.

The posterity of the woman and child spared on this last occasion are now called "Adichamar," and live together in a small community of forty or fifty souls. They receive the offerings made to the shrine, and are exempted from Government taxes. A public sacrifice of a sheep is now annually offered.

In Southern India this goddess is represented as the queen of the demons, and is called Pattirakāli, as being the wife of Patran or Siva. It is obvious that in this, as in other instances, a portion of the Brahmanical mythology has been mixed up and incorporated with the aboriginal demon-worship. Kāli is properly a Brahmanical goddess, but has been adopted in the system of demonism as a principal object of worship. Kāli signifies "black," and she is represented in Bengal as of a black, or dark blue colour. Images of Pattirakāli are usually made and placed in the devil temples. She is often represented by the hideous figure of a woman with an infant in her hand, which she is in the act of devouring and crushing between her teeth. This terrible image is habitually worshipped by thousands of poor ignorant mothers of India. She is also called "Ranapatra Kāli"—"goddess of war or of hatred."

The engraving on page 198 represents the image of Pattirakāli, and that on the opposite page her husband, Veerapatran, formerly worshipped together at a temple near Mandikādu,* the annual festival taking place at the same time as the Ammen-worship at that place. The temple and most of the images were destroyed, and a Christian congregation formed by Mr. Mead at the same place, in 1836.

Closely related to the worship of Pattirakāli is that of a class of female demons called "Ammen," or "mother,"—awful desecration of the sacred term! The principal Ammen appears to be a personification of the small-pox, the seeds of which she is said to sow upon the bodies of human beings; she is hence called "Muttaramma," "the mother of pearls." When small-pox prevails, unceasing worship is offered to the

* *Missionary Chronicle*, September, 1837.

Ammen. Her ignorant and fanatical worshippers object to take medicines, or use any means for the cure of small-pox, imagining she will be excited to greater vengeance if deprived of her expected prey.

In the village of Tiruvaram, in Trevandrum district, there were two demon temples. One was dedicated to Mādan, and contained no image, but only the painted sticks with iron rattles at either end, used in devil-dancing. Once or twice a year, or oftener in case of sickness or distress, sacrifices were made to propitiate the demon. The other temple was dedicated to Eenā Etchi, a female demon who was supposed to molest and kill women during the period of pregnancy, and was therefore worshipped by them especially, in order to conciliate her. When I visited this temple, after the people had commenced attendance at one of our chapels, there were in it earthenware images of the demon and her three children—one on either side and one in her arms. As soon as a woman thought she was in danger of being injured by Eenā Etchi, she made the usual offerings of sheep, fowls, &c. Once or twice a year a female officiated as priestess, dancing before the idols. The idols, with the exception of one which I have in my possession, were shortly afterwards destroyed; the temples are now used, one as a shed for manure, the other as a stable for cattle. The people are diligent in their attendance on the means of grace, and are making progress in the knowledge of the Lord Jesus Christ.

Another female demon much worshipped by women is Isakki, Yekki, or Chakki. She also is supposed to possess and injure women. An instance of this superstition, and of overcoming it by Christian faith, is recorded by Rev. G. O. Newport as follows:—

"The daughter of Yesudiāl, a church member, had been married some few months, when being seized suddenly with violent pains, she was brought home to her mother's house.

The native doctors were called in, and they said that the woman had been seized by the demon Isakki. Offerings must be made, or the devil would most certainly destroy her unborn child and perhaps herself. The father of the girl, overwhelmed with grief, assented to all this, and was about to sacrifice to the devil, when the mother, with tears streaming down her cheeks, cried out, 'What! do you know no better than to consent to this devil-worship?' Then turning to her sick daughter, and stroking her hair fondly, she said, 'No, my darling, they shall not make offerings to devils, either for you or for your child. We are in God's hands; let Him do what seemeth Him good. If you die, I shall be childless; but God will be my portion, and you will be with Him.' Having said this she fell sobbing on her daughter, and the whole family cried together, so much so that the heathen doctors said one to another, 'Why do we say such things to these people? Are they not Christians? Is it not a great shame to grieve them in this way? In future we must only say these things to our own people.' Prayer was made for the sick woman, and God heard it and graciously restored her to health."

The image of Paramasattee (Heavenly Power), represented in the opposite engraving, was worshipped above thirty years ago at a village in Neyoor district.* It was committed to the flames by the people on their embracing Christianity, but was rescued by one of the missionaries. It was sent to England, and placed in the museum of the London Missionary Society, where it may now be seen. It was usually kept concealed except on great occasions, when it was brought out to be worshipped.

The image is of wood, with numerous projecting iron spoons, used as oil lamps for illuminating the idol on special occasions. Several mystic letters are graven on the front of

* *Missionary Chronicle*, October, 1837.

the figure. Though worshipped as a female demon, with dancing and other rites, this image is rather connected with the Brahmanical superstition than with the aboriginal demonolatry.

PARAMASATTER.

The spirits of wicked men, or of those who have met with a violent death by drowning, hanging, or other means, are supposed to become demons, wandering about to inflict injury in various ways upon mankind. Hence arose a strange custom in the execution of murderers by hanging. It was supposed that their spirits would haunt the place of execution and its neighbourhood, to prevent which the heels of the criminal were cut with a sword, or hamstrung, as he was thrown off. This practice was abolished by the native Government in 1862.

In numerous instances the spirits of wicked men are actually worshipped after death. A noted robber, named Palaveshum, was long the object of worship in Tinnevelly. A more extraordinary case still was the worship of an Englishman, practised till lately in a part of the same British province. His name was Pole, a captain in the British army. He was known to have been a mighty hunter, and at his tomb offerings of cigars and brandy were made by the people of the neighbourhood, to propitiate his favour and invoke his continued aid against the wild beasts.*

An instance of mothers propitiating the spirits of their daughters who died before marriage, is referred to by Rev. E. Lewis as follows:—

"The catechist conversed with a number of women on the inability of devils to save men. He said, 'Do you not perform worship to the devil Kanni [a virgin]?' they replied, 'Yes.' 'Do you not, when you get ill, make vows to offer milk, fruit and cakes, silk, and coloured cloth to Kanni, in case you recover?' 'We do,' said they. 'But are not these virgin demons your own unmarried daughters, who are now dead?' They acknowledged that it was so. Then the catechist expostulated with them, saying, 'How silly and degrading a thing it is to bow down and express your sorrows, with the hope of obtaining relief, before your own children, whom you reared, who were subject to you

* "The Tinnevelly Shanars," p. 43.

and afraid of you, and who even when alive were unable to afford you comfort when they saw you weeping! Can you think for a moment that such children have power over your lives now that they are dead, any more than when they were living?' They assented to his reasoning, and acknowledged their folly."

The following is another authentic instance of the worship of departed spirits :—

Vallavan and his wife were bigoted heathens and devil-dancers, most scrupulous in their observance of the customary sacrifices and offerings. His mother-in-law was also a devil-dancer, so that there were three in that one family. "Vallavan made annual offerings to the extent of two hundred fanams; and for this purpose he would buy a fat red goat, some large fowls, cocoa-nuts, plantains, betel, rice, and various odoriferous substances, and garlands of flowers. Having procured all these, he would make to himself a god of well-trodden clay, and on a Friday afternoon would cut open the cocoa-nuts and set them in order, with the betel, plantains, and the flower of the cocoa-nut tree* before the newly made god. In the meantime his friends would boil two large potfuls of rice, and another of water, with the pulverized odoriferous substances dissolved in it. The barbers also would beat their tom-toms, whilst the women would utter a shrill cry. Then Vallavan would jump out and dance, saying that he was inspired by the demon. He would take three handfuls of the scum rising from the boiling water and put it on his head, and afterwards take a large bunch of the cocoa-nut flower from the presence of the god, dip it in the boiling water, and shake it over his head, that the water might run down his head and body. While thus dancing he would be dressed in a fine cloth, and adorned with the jewels which had been consecrated to the

* See frontispiece.

god. The persons present would tell him their wants, and seek his miraculous aid. After this the goat and all the fowls would be sacrificed, and then consumed by the worshippers as their evening meal."

At one time Vallavan decided that his mother, who had died long previously, had become a mischievous demon, and would injure them unless propitiated. They accordingly purchased a fine cloth for her, put it in the apartment which she had occupied, and offered there cakes, plantains, betel leaves, and other things known to have been agreeable to her when living. At such seasons Patmasuri, Vallavan's wife, would enter that room, dress herself with the cloth, and dance in honour of her mother-in-law. Supposing herself possessed at the time with the spirit, she would address her husband and say, "My son, am I not your mother? Be assured that I shall make you happy." Immediately he would reply, "Yes, my mother, it is so; preserve us and bless us," and would worship her, calling on all his children and friends to do so likewise.

This family were afterwards led to accept the truth of Christianity, surrendered the instruments and emblems of demonolatry, and became consistent and earnest Christians in connection with the Sānthapuram district.

Some of the demons are supposed to reside in certain trees,* at the foot of which a rough stone is placed as an image, or emblem, on which turmeric powder is rubbed. No one will pass by these places after night. Such trees are usually very large, old, and well grown, as it is considered sacrilegious and dangerous to hew them down. In some parts of the country these trees are quite common. In one of the mountains of Travancore grew a noble timber tree which our assistant missionary, Mr. Ashton, wished to secure for use in the erection of the large chapel at Neyoor. The

* Compare Deut. xvi. 21.

trunk was so large that four men with outstretched arms could not compass it, and the branches were as thick as ordinary trees of that species. This tree was supposed to be the abode of a very powerful spirit, who exercised rule over the mountains and wild beasts, and to this circumstance its enormous growth was attributed. Several rude stones of small size were placed at the base of the tree and worshipped. It was the blood and ashes and other manure deposited there on sacrificial and festival occasions that had nourished and so wonderfully enlarged this colossal tree. Even the native Government had refrained from cutting down this monarch of the forest for their public works. While engaged in the work of felling it, the missionary and workmen saw a monstrous tiger at a short distance looking at them; but on their shouting and making a great noise he walked slowly away. Had any of the people been seized by this tiger, it would certainly have been ascribed to the wrath of the demon; but the providence of God graciously preserved them from all danger. The mountaineers firmly refused to assist in cutting down the tree, so that they had to bring Christian workmen from a considerable distance. At last the tree fell with a terrible crash, which echoed amongst the surrounding mountains, amidst the screams and cries of the heathen, who from that time seemed to listen more readily to the exhortations of the missionary. Much of the woodwork of the chapel was made of this single tree; so that what had formerly been used in the service of the devil now became subservient to the worship of the one true and living God.

The minor superstitions connected with demon-worship are well-nigh innumerable; they enter into all the feelings, and are associated with the whole life, of these people. Every disease, accident, or misfortune, is attributed to the agency of the devils, and great caution is exercised to avoid arousing their fury. We shall give a few illustrative details.

Certain hours of every day are supposed to be unlucky and dangerous. At noon, as well as at midnight (especially on Fridays), evil spirits are supposed to be roaming about, waiting to seize on those who walk out of their houses into lonely places. Iron rings on the fingers or toes, or an iron staff, are supposed to afford protection from such attacks. At night the demons are supposed to call loudly, in order to allure people out of their houses into some distant jungle, where they can slay them. Hence calls at night are never responded to until the fourth repetition, devils being supposed to call only thrice.

At the period of puberty, and after childbirth, women are supposed to be peculiarly liable to the attacks of demons—the cause of convulsions and similar disorders. Dr. Day speaks of a female patient of his, who asserted her belief that a curvature of the spine from which she suffered was caused by a demon. She was then about thirty years of age, and stated that when she was about eleven, while walking in a narrow lane after dark, the demon came behind and struck her a violent blow on the back, occasioning the curve which continued from that time. Even then, she added, unless the demon were propitiated by occasional offerings, she experienced similar attacks.

The sudden illnesses of children and adults are accounted for in a similar way. An instance occurred in a congregation under my charge. The son of the elder in this congregation accidentally trod on a poisonous thorn, which caused severe swelling and dangerous fever. His parents offered prayer for his recovery, and the catechist administered medicines to the youth. But the young man's father-in-law was a heathen, and he said that this illness was caused by a devil, and had arisen from treading on the grave of some one who had died before of a similar illness. For this he said it would be necessary to present an iron stylus ornamented with gold. But the Christian father refused to listen to such evil solicitations, saying, "Such remarks do not terrify us. Our God is able to heal all diseases." They continued in prayer to God, and in the use of suitable means; and the patient recovered, to the surprise of the heathens and the joy of the Christians, who praised God for His mercy.

Our people in Travancore imagine that occasionally persons are attacked by demons even after their reception of Christian truth. They would liken this to the last struggles of the devils before their expulsion by our blessed Lord, when they threw down the possessed and tare him. A case of illness attributed by them to this cause, is that of the head man of one of our congregations, whom I baptized a few years ago, giving him the name of Moses. This man had been a popular devil-dancer and exorciser of demons from women. The next day after his first Sunday's attendance on Christian worship, the catechist visited him and found him lying on the floor of his house, ill in body and distressed in mind. He complained of illness and of occasional insane desires to rise up and break all that was in the house, to eat clay, &c. This was attributed by his relatives to the vengeance of the demons whom he had formerly served, and they urged him to return to his old practices. But, by the grace of God, he remained firm; the catechist applied a cooling ointment to his head, and he speedily recovered. Many of his neighbours have since become Christians through the efforts of this man, and he makes himself very useful in the congregation.

Although Europeans are generally allowed to be, by their learning and strength, superior to the malignant influences of evil spirits, yet their illnesses are occasionally ascribed to this cause. Some years ago, a valued and devoted missionary, who had been labouring in India for many years, was suddenly attacked with convulsions. This was at once imputed to the power of a demon whose temple he had some time previously assisted in destroying, on the conversion of those who formerly supported that superstition.

Pretensions to witchcraft, divination, and magical skill are made by many of these demon-worshippers. Some pretend that a familiar spirit appears to them in the form of a dog or jackal. To open a communication with the demon, and to gain the power of effecting whatever they may desire by his assistance, they proceed alone, naked, at dead of night to devil temples, dense jungles and other solitary places, to offer sacrifices and perform incantations.

Serious illnesses and other afflictions are frequently referred to the malice of enemies, who are supposed to have bewitched the sufferer; and counter charms and solemn incantations are used to counteract the malignant influence supposed to be at work. I have in my possession a manuscript volume of magical incantations and spells in the Malayālim language, giving directions for effecting a great variety of purposes, such as an ambitious, avaricious, or profligate heathen might desire. Many of these are fearful in their malignity or obscenity.

Some of the least abominable are as follows:—

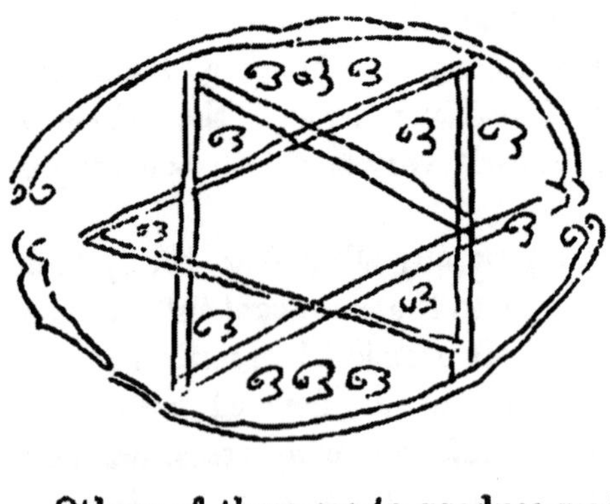

"To remove trembling arising from demoniacal possession—

"Write this figure on a plant that has milky juice, and drive a nail through it: the trembling will cease."

Others of these are to produce madness; to bring men or

women under one's power; to cause diseases—such as blindness, dumbness, paralysis, mortification, or death to an enemy. The mere perusal of such a work reveals the corrupting and debasing influence of these superstitions. Few of them are of such a nature as to allow of their publication, but here are specimens of the most innocent.

"To produce madness—write this figure and bind it on. Madness will ensue."

"To secure the favour of a king—write this figure, and tie it on the head before entering the presence of the Rajah."

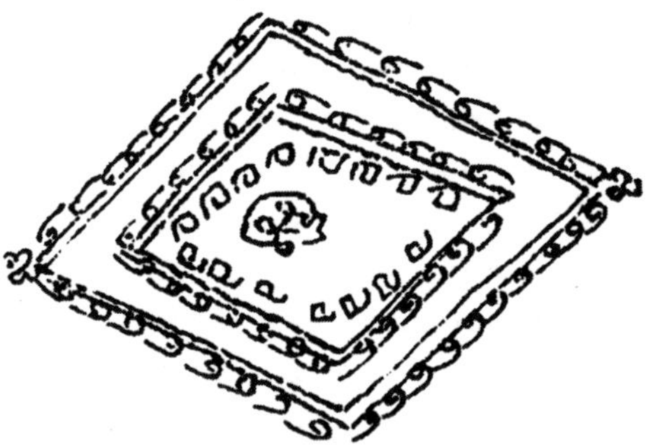

"For all diseases and counteracting enemies—writing the discus (of Vishnu) is excellent." The figure is that on the reverse of the copper *cash*, see p. 110.

Sometimes a little image of the person who is to be bewitched and destroyed is prepared; nails are driven into it at the places indicating the parts of the body to be attacked with disease, and it is then secretly buried, or deposited in the house or garden of the intended victim. It is a curious fact that similar images of clay or wax, pierced through with pins and needles, are occasionally met with in churchyards and gardens in Pendle Forest, near Burnley, where they are placed for the purpose of causing the death of the persons they represent.*

So firm and enduring a hold has the dread of being bewitched upon the minds of the people, that I have known a lamentable case of total apostasy from Christianity on this account,—the only instance of the kind, except one, which I have known on the part of a church member. Yohanan (John) had been a steady and apparently consistent member of the church, and elder in his congregation, for about twenty-five years. Most of his relatives remained in heathenism, and when he was attacked with serious illness they persuaded him that he had been bewitched, and that this illness had been caused by the devil. Notwithstanding the protestations and advices of the catechist, Yohanan consented to the celebration of the usual ceremonies, and sent for devil-priests to dig up the ground in front of his house, in search of the supposed hidden charm which had caused his illness. On hearing of this, I immediately sent two of our best native preachers to warn and exhort him, but their visit was in vain. He certainly denied having consented to the heathen rites, and assented to all that our catechists advanced, but the very next day these ceremonies were performed. The event proved that these were useless, for four days after wards he died, without giving any sign, so far as we were aware, of true repentance or of faith in Christ. The fear of the demons is the last superstition that leaves the native mind.

* "Lancashire Folk-lore," by Harland and Wilkinson.

CHAPTER XV.

DEVIL-WORSHIP (CONTINUED).

Devil Temples, Sacrifices, and Dancing—Demoniacal Possession—Mandikādu Festival—Sect of Muttukutti—Gradual Decline of Demonolatry—Its Criminality and Debasing Influence.

THE priests who officiate in the worship paid to evil spirits do not belong to any hereditary or exclusive class, like that of the Brahmans amongst the idol-worshipping Hindus. Any one, even a woman, may act as priest or devil-dancer, if he or she be but supposed to be duly possessed or inspired by the demon invoked.

"*Pey coils*," or devil temples, are very numerous throughout the country. They bear no resemblance whatever to the Brahmanical idol temples; being in general mere sheds, a few yards in length, open at one end, and mostly quite empty. Indeed, images are no essential element in demon-worship; where they are found they appear to have been adopted from the Brahmanical worship.

In front of the devil temple, or sometimes without any covered edifice, there stands a small pyramidal erection or obelisk four or five feet in height, generally built of brick and stuccoed, which is always associated with this worship, and takes the place of an image; but it is impossible to ascertain the origin or meaning of this symbol. Two of these will be observed in the frontispiece to this volume.

Inside some temples are placed the implements and symbols of demon-worship,—dancing-sticks or wands, the priest's garments, trident, &c.; and in others, one or more images of the demon to whom the temple is dedicated.

The devil-dancer's garments consist of a high conical cloth cap, with tapes hanging down at either side, probably to represent long shaggy hair; a jacket with embroidered representations of devils worked in red, to denote their bloodthirsty character; and a pair of short drawers, corresponding in style, with small bells attached to the border. A thick club and long wand, prettily painted and having iron rattles or jingling brass rings at either end, are also held in the hand while dancing; with sometimes a trident, sacrificial knife, bangles for the ankles with brass bells, and occasionally other instruments or ornaments. Most of these will be observed in the frontispiece.

The offerings usually presented to the demons are very various, and include most of the articles of food and drink that are esteemed by the people themselves. Such are cakes and sweetmeats, parched or bruised rice, roots, fruits, oil, milk, and arrack, besides flowers, &c. But it is a remarkable fact that the principal feature of their worship consists in animal sacrifices and libations of blood, to pacify the demons and secure their favour. They are represented as thirsting for human blood, but propitiated by sacrifices of the lower animals. Doubtless human sacrifices were once offered, as indeed they still secretly are in the country of the Khonds; but the custom in South India is to offer in sacrifice, on important occasions, sheep, goats, fowls, and pigs. Thus even these uninstructed heathens recognise, though in a sadly corrupted and exaggerated form, the great truth—that "without shedding of blood there is no remission of sins."

Connected with this is what is called *devil-dancing*, in which the demoniacal possession is sought. We have mentioned that certain ceremonies are at times observed in order to drive out and dispossess a devil, but on these occasions it is desired to bring him into the soul of the worshipper, who is then supposed to become his inspired oracle, and to utter prophecies, and give other information for the guidance of the assembled crowd of worshippers. These more important sacrifices and festivals are held annually, or occasionally as may be considered necessary, in times of prevalent disease, or in fulfilment of vows previously made. Funds for the necessary expenses are contributed by all interested. Night is the season chosen for the principal performances, and the festival usually continues for two or three days and nights. As devils are supposed to shrink from the presence and superior power of Europeans, and as the people also are ashamed to be seen engaged in these midnight orgies, we have rarely opportunities of witnessing the devil-dancing. I have seen it but once, and that on a small scale, and will simply relate what I then saw.

Some months after my arrival in India, I heard the sound of the tom-tom, or drum, and other instruments during the night, and went over early the next morning to a small devil temple, within half a mile of the mission bungalow, in order to observe the ceremonies. The temple had been newly painted for the occasion, and the walls ornamented with rude sketches of men, wild beasts, and flowers.

Assembled in a shed in front of the temple there were about fifty persons, including women and children—all Súdras, with one Brahman as "master of the ceremonies." South of the temple, a cocoa-leaf basket was erected upon rods, as the residence, for the time being, of the demon, and a receptacle for the offerings.

A number of those present, with whom I had been previously acquainted, approaching me, I began a conversation with them on the wickedness and folly of the worship in which they were engaged. While we were speaking together, an old grey-headed man rushed out from among the people, and ran about dancing and leaping like a madman. He was now supposed to be possessed by the demon. Those who were with me only laughed at this. The old man, after some time, went up close to the side of the temple, writhing his whole body with horrible contortions, and trembling exceedingly; during which several ran to bring the fowls* for sacrifice. These fowls were taken, one by one, by another man, and water was poured upon them. After dancing about with them for a few minutes, this man cast them upon the ground; when, if they shook the water from their wings, they were considered suitable for sacrifice, the head was cut off and the blood poured out in front of the basket. He also was then supposed to be possessed, and danced furiously round the court of the temple. To excite him still further, the drum was brought nearer and beaten still faster and more furiously, while the chanting of songs and tinkling of cymbals added to the noise. Seizing a bunch of flowers of the areca palm, and dipping it in saffron water, the wretched man sprinkled himself and the people, and then, still leaping madly, cast about the burning ashes of the fire which was used for preparing the flesh of the sacrifices. A considerable number of fowls were sacrificed; after some time the dancing ceased, and the devotee went to the neighbouring tank to bathe.

A full and graphic description of devil-dancing is given by Dr. Caldwell, in his valuable pamphlet entitled "The Tinnevelly Shānars," which contains accurate and reliable information upon the whole subject. He says:—

"The officiating priest, whoever he may happen to be, is dressed for the occasion in the vestments and ornaments appropriate to the particular devil worshipped. The object in view in donning the demon's insignia is to strike terror into the imagination of the beholders. But the particoloured dress and grotesque ornaments, the cap, trident, and jingling

* "Some cock or cat your rage must stop."—BURNS.

bells of the performer, bear so close a resemblance to the usual adjuncts of a pantomime, that a European would find it difficult to look grave. The musical instruments, or rather the instruments of noise, chiefly used in the devil-dance are the tom-tom, or ordinary Indian drum, and the horn, with occasionally the addition of a clarionet, when the parties can afford it. But the favourite instrument, because the noisiest, is that which is called 'the bow.' A series of bells of various sizes is fastened to the frame of a gigantic bow, the strings are tightened so as to emit a musical note when struck, and the bow rests on a large, empty brazen pot. The instrument is played on by a plectrum, and several musicians join in the performance. One strikes the string of the bow with the plectrum, another produces the bass by striking the brazen pot with his hand, and the third keeps time and improves the harmony by a pair of cymbals. As each musician kindles in his work, and strives to outstrip his neighbour in the rapidity of his flourishes and in the loudness of the tone with which he sings the accompaniment, the result is a tumult of frightful sounds, such as may be supposed to delight even a demon's ear.

"When the preparations are completed, and the devil-dance is about to commence, the music is at first comparatively slow, and the dancer seems impassive and sullen, and either stands still or moves about in gloomy silence. Gradually, as the music becomes quicker and louder, his excitement begins to rise. Sometimes, to help him to work himself up into a frenzy, he uses medicated draughts, cuts and lacerates his flesh till the blood flows, lashes himself with a huge whip, presses a burning torch to his breast, drinks the blood which flows from his own wounds, or drinks the blood of the sacrifice, putting the throat of the decapitated goat to his mouth.* Then, as if he had acquired new life, he begins to brandish his staff of bells, and to dance with a quick, but

* Compare Psa. xvi. 4.

wild, unsteady step. Suddenly the afflatus descends; there is no mistaking that glare, or those frantic leaps. He snorts, he stares, he gyrates. The demon has now taken bodily possession of him; and though he retains the power of utterance and of motion, both are under the demon's control, and his separate consciousness is in abeyance. The bystanders signalize the event by raising a long shout, attended with a peculiar vibratory noise, caused by the motion of th hand and tongue, or the tongue alone. The devil-dancer is now worshipped as a present deity; and every bystander consults him respecting his disease, his wants, the welfare o his absent relatives, the offerings to be made for the accomplishment of his wishes, and, in short, respecting everything for which superhuman knowledge is supposed to be available. As the devil-dancer acts to admiration the part of a maniac, it requires some experience to enable a person to interpret his dubious or unmeaning replies, his muttered voices and uncouth gestures; but the wishes of the parties who consult him help them greatly to interpret his meaning."

These ceremonies are repeated annually or oftener, especially during the prevalence of epidemics. On these occasions it was sad and distressing to hear the beating of drums all night, and the shrill and prolonged cries of the frantic worshippers; while we knew that the sick were deserted by their relatives through fear of infection, or were lying in the solitude of their own houses, perishing of painfully consuming diseases, in physical neglect, and mental and spiritual darkness and misery.

The question of the reality of any instance of professed demoniacal possession cannot readily be answered. I myself have never seen or known a case in which there was proved to be aught beyond imposture, imagination, or disease. Most of our Christian converts, who were once devil-dancers, only assert that "something came over them."

DEVIL TEMPLE AT AGASTISPURAM.

(Face page 219.)

Still, one or two learned and experienced missionaries in Tinnevelly, who have investigated the subject, have been compelled to state that they could not absolutely declare that there is, as a matter of fact, no such thing as demoniacal possession. And surely, if it is to be found in the present day, which I think not impossible,* it might be expected to prevail, if anywhere, amongst those who deliberately, knowingly, and systematically worship wicked spirits, and *seek* this infernal inspiration.

One of the principal devil temples in Travancore is that represented in the annexed engraving, situated at Agastispuram, near Cape Comorin; which is also the head-quarters of the Shānar tribe, where their Nādān, or Chieftain, resides, who was formerly allowed the privileges of having a fort, riding in a palankeen, and retaining 100 armed attendants, which he is too reduced to support now. This is a temple of Muttar Ammen, and is said to have been built in ten days by the aid of demons! The image is of silver. The rude scaffolding in front of the temple is covered with cloth, flowers, banners, and other ornaments on festival occasions.

Another of this class is the celebrated temple at Mandikādu, near Kolachal, where a great annual festival is held in March in honour of the village Ammen. To this festival a vast concourse of natives assembles from all parts of Travancore and Tinnevelly. A kind of fair is held on the occasion, at which commodities are brought for sale from different parts of India. This is one cause of attraction to the immense crowds who attend, but thousands assemble there to fulfil the vows they have made in sickness. This goddess is worshipped chiefly by Ilavars; but all castes, except Pulayars, attend the festival, and have access to the temple. Brahmans, however, cannot, consistently with their

* See a very suggestive article in *Good Words* for February, 1867.

prejudices and abhorrence of bloodshed, take part in the festival without degradation.

The festival lasts for seven days, six of which are spent in domestic ceremonies, the last and principal day at the temple.

Hook-swinging was, till recently, practised in connection with the festival at this and several similar temples in Travancore. An immense cart is made, with great wheels and a high upright pole, on the top of which a cross-beam thirty feet in length is fastened so as to turn round. Persons who are to be swung in fulfilment of vows, or in token of gratitude for recovery from sickness, (usually boys, or a man with a young child in his arms,) are not allowed for some days previously to eat fish, flesh, &c., but only boiled rice once a day, which they must cook with their own hands to avoid pollution. They bathe twice a day, and live apart from others. When about to be swung, their ears, neck, and waist are adorned with golden ornaments, and a silver belt or chain; and while swinging they carry in one hand a shield, in the other a sword.

Strong hooks of gold, silver, or iron, according to the means of the worshipper, are inserted in both sides, and are secured with cloth bandages; the devotee is then fastened to the end of the horizontal beam, and is drawn up and swung rapidly round for ten or fifteen minutes. Police attend to superintend the preparations and prevent danger from carelessness or neglect. A few years ago a poor wretch, urged by fanaticism and half intoxicated, took an infant up in his arms, but, while swinging, the spring broke, and both man and child were dashed to the ground and killed. The swinging has since been discouraged by the native Government, chiefly on the ground of the accidents which have occurred, and it has in consequence almost, if not altogether, ceased, and the attendance at the festivals has decidedly declined.

"At this festival a Brahman officiates; the native Government defray the expenses and receive the produce of the gifts presented. Outside of the pagoda on these occasions—on the roof of the temple, and hung on the surrounding trees, will be seen a large quantity of cocoa-nuts and other offerings: also a heap of wooden hands, arms, and legs, offered by those who have been restored from some injury in those members during the year. Persons who are rich present *silver* hands or legs, or *golden* ones, on such occasions; *these* are carefully put away in the inside of the temple. In one direction will be observed the swinging machine, with the victims of superstition being hoisted up by hooks inserted in the backs; other persons will be seen rolling in the dust a considerable distance round the temple, until they are exhausted by the heat and exertion which are required to perform this vow in the hottest month of the year; others, with a thin piece of cane inserted in their sides, dance along with apparent joy, while two persons in front and behind take hold of the cane, and keep step with the poor creature at a quick pace for a considerable distance. Parents and relations are seen bringing little children of both sexes to perform this cruel rite, in consequence of vows made by them on their behalf in times of sickness. On such occasions they will say, 'If this child recover, he or she shall dance before Pattera Kalee with the sides pierced.' Numerous groups of women are engaged boiling the sacrificial rice, and when the steam ascends they rend the air with shrill cries of frantic joy, and offer the rice to the idol, previously to feasting on it with their families.* Some are engaged slaying the sheep and goats; there is also a cruel custom of sacrificing a cock, by transfixing it on a sharp-pointed piece of iron placed on an altar of wood; others, with

* Compare 1 Cor. viii. 4.

considerable pain and risk, hold a pan of fire in their hands before the idol until it is consumed."*

This festival was visited by Dr. Lowe and the Rev. S. Zechariah, to preach and distribute tracts, on 4th March, 1862. The latter writes: "About 50,000 people it is believed assembled there, and were found offering goats and fowls and performing different vows to the goddess. We saw hundreds of children of both sexes, some carried in the arms and others led by their parents to perform some ceremonies, crying out and shedding tears through pain. When we went near to the pagoda, a boy was brought by several relations, with tom-toms (drums) and dancing. Then a goldsmith, who was there ready, with a large needle and small rattans, came forward and pierced through both his sides with the needle; when the boy cried aloud through pain, all the relations made a terrible noise. The smith then drew a rattan through the holes on both sides, bringing it round the back, and gave both ends of the rattan to them: they then led the boy round the pagoda."

Truly we may say, in view of these enormities perpetrated in the sacred name of religion, "The dark places of the earth are full of the habitations of cruelty."

We have not space for more than the bare mention of a curious phenomenon in the religious history of Travancore, which has appeared within the last forty years,—namely, the rise of a new sect of religionists, who have adopted an absurd medley of Hinduism and Demonolatry, with a slight tinge of the Christian element. This superstition was originated by one Muttukutti, a poor Palmyra climber, who laid claim to be an incarnation of Vishnu, and pretended to possess miraculous powers; by these means he attached to himself thousands of credulous followers. Since the death of their leader in 1848, he has been worshipped by his followers

* "Missionary Chronicle," Sept., 1837.

as a manifestation of the Supreme God; and this singular people display considerable zeal in the defence and propagation of their destructive errors.

On a candid and comprehensive review of the whole subject, however, one is happy to be able to state that devil-worship, with its accompanying superstitions, is gradually and steadily declining with the progress of enlightenment and the spread of Gospel truth. The people are compelled to see at least that the worship they pay to these imaginary demons does not insure to them immunity from sorrow, disease, and death. Many confessions to this effect might be cited.

In conversing with one of our native preachers, the chief man of a village of devil-worshippers said, "I am now about eighty years old, and the money I have spent in the service of demons knows no limit. I called the name of my eldest son, Sudalei Mādan, and he grew up an able man. The stories of the demons were his favourite study, and by his own exertions he procured all the wood and stone for the erection of this temple. I provided him with a bow with bells attached, with which he made music and sang in praise of the demons. But my wife and daughter-in-law became ill, and notwithstanding all our vows to the demons, both of them died. When I consider this, I am led to the conclusion that no good can result from the worship of demons." This old man promised soon to attend the Christian worship, and his wife and son from that time placed themselves under Christian instruction.

On another occasion, an aged magician and devil-dancer thus mournfully acknowledged :—"I see," said he, "several signs of the downfall and extinction of all the demons. Formerly, when I sang but two or three songs and uttered a few mantrams (spells), I was covered, as with a thick cloud, by a dark host of demons; but now I utter fifty mantrams, and that with more earnestness than formerly I did, without the least success. Demons now-a-days do not appear to my sight. On some occasions, it is true, I see one or two; but even then they stand afar off, and seem afraid to come near. I should think it is your religion that drives them away. I clearly see that henceforth my words will not pass current as truth among the people. We shall have no alternative left us but to embrace your religion. Your religion must prevail." God grant that these anticipations of a poor uninstructed heathen may speedily be realized, and the whole land filled with the peace and joy of the Gospel of Jesus.

Of like purport is the testimony of the missionaries at present in the field. "Nearly all the devil temples of these parts," says a recent report, "except those supported by Sircar funds, are in a deserted state; while there is no one to raise those that are fallen down, and scarcely any one who thinks of erecting a new one." Another writes, "I am encouraged by seeing here and there the village idols and their temples left entirely neglected to utter ruin by their adherents. In one place the village temple, where once stood their idol gods, is now used by the people for keeping their cows in. In another place the roof of the temple was pulled down and the implements belonging to the idols given to me. In another place stands now the prayer-house, where formerly stood several idols. These are a few instances among many similar."

We cannot well conceive any superstition more wicked and revolting in character, or more degrading and pernicious in its influence, than the baleful devil-worship which we have attempted to describe. It is, of course, in a still higher degree than idolatry, a daring crime against the God of heaven—a rejection of His authority, and a deliberate attempt to set up Satan in the throne which the Most High alone should occupy. Devil-worship is the introduction, as far as possible, of the kingdom of hell upon the earth. May it speedily and for ever disappear before the brightness and beauty of the reign of Christ amongst men.

In contemplating the moral influence of devil-worship it is evident that it hardens the heart and increases cruelty, covetousness, worldliness, and other evil passions. The bloody sacrifices, and all the associations of this superstition, cannot fail to cherish the spirit and practice of cruelty. Nor is there aught in it to cultivate the moral faculty or direct attention to the duties of morality. The inflictions of the demons are supposed to fall, not on those who are morally guilty or blameworthy, but simply according to the caprice of the demon. The great aim of the devil-worshipper is to deprecate the anger and destructive powers of evil spirits,—not to seek a blessing, but to secure relief from a curse. Consequently, he comes to think that temporal prosperity is the chief good, that material wealth, health of body and external comfort, are all that are needed. The only thought, desire, and subject of conversation among such is money and sensual enjoyment.

This vile superstition, therefore, necessarily destroys trust and hope in God, and all those finer and loftier emotions and sentiments of man's nature which are so beautifully and beneficially cultivated by Christianity. It knows no such precepts as "Thou shalt love the Lord thy God with all thy heart, and thy neighbour as thyself." Instead of looking to the Almighty for aid and support against the machinations of devils, its devotees only endeavour to appease them by offerings; thus they deprive themselves of the comforts of true religion, and increase their own wretchedness. "Their sorrows shall be multiplied that hasten after another god: their *drink offerings of blood* will I not offer, nor take up their names into my lips" (Psa. xvi. 4).

The natural result of this baneful superstition is the abasement and degradation of the human mind by superstitious fear and terror. Demon-worshippers are rendered timid and helpless in the presence of the undefined and unknown spiritual beings whom they worship. They are, it is true, naturally timorous and faint-hearted; and this is not surprising, considering the palpable evils and dangers to which they have as a people long been exposed, from the tyranny of the higher classes, from robbery, from wild beasts, from serpents and sudden disease. But all the physical and natural evils by which they are surrounded are magnified a thousandfold by vain and imaginary apprehensions of evil, from fiends and goblins, sprites, ghosts, and devils. Until this is overcome, they can never rise even to true manliness and courage.

Thus, too, is the Lord of all dishonoured, and the souls of men destroyed. Have we not reason to bless God for the converts in India who have been rescued from the power of the evil one? May multitudes of faithful soldiers be led, by the consideration of the facts which we have stated, to enlist themselves under the banner of the blessed Saviour, in His warfare against the strong man who holds in captivity so many millions of precious immortal souls.

CHAPTER XVI.

NATIVE MOHAMMEDANS.

Their Numbers—Character—Bearing towards Christianity.

THE followers of Mohammed in Travancore number, according to the last census, 62,639; or perhaps at present about 70,000. The common designations applied to them by other natives are "*Tulukkan*," a corruption of Turk; "*Māpillei*" (Moplay), literally, bridegroom (from their marrying native wives when their Arab progenitors first reached India?), or signifying perhaps "Mocha," "person;" and "*Mettan*," a word the meaning of which I have never been able to ascertain. They themselves are accustomed to say that they belong to the Fourth Religion, or revelation; acknowledging Adam, Abraham, and "Isa Nabi" (the Prophet Jesus) as the three former divinely appointed teachers and prophets—now superseded by Mohammed, the last and greatest of all.

A few are settlers of Arab or Afghan lineage, who adhere strictly to the Mussulman faith and ritual; but the larger proportion (called Lubbays) are native converts from the Hindus, or are the offspring of mixed marriages. They are an industrious and thriving people, principally engaged in trade and agriculture, and some are amongst the wealthiest of the inhabitants. The females are not secluded as in strictly Mohammedan countries. Their mosques and places of worship number 254, with apparently about 500 priests. Their chief priest, or "Tangal," resides at Ponāny. The distinctive observances of Mohammedanism are but little attended to. Being profoundly ignorant of their own doctrines and sacred writings, heathenish superstitions prevail amongst them; and they are even found joining in the performance of pagan ceremonies. Yet they are hardened against the influence of Christianity, and excited to bitter and persistent opposition by its public proclamation. Holding as they do, with more or less clearness, several cardinal truths of religion —such as the unity, personality, and almighty power of the great Creator—they regard themselves as beyond the claims and without the necessity for the gospel of Christ. Our native agents are often positively afraid to address them on the subject of Christianity, as their fierce and fanatical character sometimes leads to violence.

With a few of them, however, we have been personally on the most friendly terms, and such individuals readily hear and freely converse with us. One amiable old gentleman, possessed of large estates, who used occasionally to send us presents of native dishes, and come to drink coffee with us, generally taking a small quantity of ground coffee home with him in a paper, was on terms of almost affectionate intimacy with the writer. One day he asked in a confidential tone, "*How many* Christians do you require? I have a number of slaves," said he, "whom I should be happy to hand over to you as Christians." "Of course," added my friend, "it is no use merely talking to them; you and I can go over and give them a sound whipping, and we shall soon bring them round." I endeavoured to make him understand that we wished all men, himself included, to become Christians; but that whipping, as a means of grace, was of little esteem in our religion.

Converts from heathenism are not rarely added to the Mohammedan community. Several hundreds of the out-cast Nāiadis, of Cochin, recently joined them. They often purchase children from their parents, or adopt those who are friendless or destitute, whom they at once formally introduce into their communion. Other individuals, approving of their views of the Divine Being, or desirous of the friendship of this energetic people, embrace the profession of Islam.

It is noteworthy, that from whatever caste these proselytes have come, they at once merge into the general body, adopt their dress and manners, enjoy their privileges, and are treated accordingly by heathen and other outsiders. They secure a right of way in the public roads, and occupy, in other respects, the social status accorded to the Mohammedan community.

Now this is just what we ask for Protestant Christian converts,—that they shall be treated by the native Government simply as members of the Christian community, and be allowed to occupy a position of their own, whether high or low, quite apart from the heathen system of caste, which they have rejected. It would not, we think, be unreasonable to ask that Protestant Christians should be regarded in a light similar to that in which Mohammedans and Syrian Christians are viewed, as a body taking a separate and distinctive position of its own.

A few Mohammedan children attend our mission schools, but it is a lamentable fact that rarely do Mussulmans in South India receive the Gospel; and this state of things, I am persuaded, will continue until some appropriate special efforts are directed towards this people. Had we sufficient means at our command, one or two of our native preachers might receive a special training, and labour, with some hope of success, directly and almostly exclusively amongst this class of the population.

CHAPTER XVII.

NATIVE ROMAN CATHOLICS.

Introduction of Romanism by Xavier—Native Roman Catholics—The Schismatic Party—Romish Arguments against Protestantism—Ecclesiastical Arrangements.

THAT zealous Jesuit missionary and extraordinary man, Francis Xavier, visited India in 1542, and sought to introduce Christianity amongst the natives of the Western Coast and South India, where he laboured for about three years.

He was wholly ignorant of the language; but having first committed to memory the Lord's Prayer, the Creed, Ave Maria, and the Decalogue, he itinerated through the fishing villages, bell in hand, and taught the people to repeat these formulas, baptizing all who submitted to do so. Many, in several parts, had professed themselves Christians before his arrival; and Xavier was largely aided by the influence and *prestige* of the Portuguese Government, then all-powerful in India. Like others in his day, Xavier believed that the authority and force of the magistrate might be used to induce men to profess Christianity. According to his published letters, it appears that large sums of money were expended by the Portuguese Viceroy to secure the attendance of the natives at the sound of the bell; and doubtless there was a feeling amongst the people, that this new religion was far superior to the gloomy and unsatisfying paganism of former ages. Xavier thus founded many congregations, and built a number of churches. He said that often his hands failed through the fatigue of baptizing, for he had baptized a whole village in a single day.

Xavier was evidently, notwithstanding his doctrinal errors, a devoted, eminently pious, and self-denying man, and his letters show that he repudiated the miraculous powers attributed to him by his biographers. But, with regard to his converts, there was no questioning as to whether his words were correctly understood by the people,—there was nothing beyond the missionary's utterance of an unknown tongue, and the response in a prescribed form. Nothing was said about the Holy Scriptures, and little to exalt Christ or honour the work of the Holy Spirit.*

Xavier's former dwelling-place and principal church at Kottār, where wonderful miracles are recorded as having taken place, are the annual resort of multitudes of Roman Catholic pilgrims. Hundreds and thousands of men, women, and children from distant parts come to worship there. The embalmed remains of the saint were exhibited a few years ago at Goa, where they are enshrined and carefully preserved as relics.

The native Roman Catholic Christians are chiefly Mukkavars and Paruvars, fishermen and lime-burners. The whole coast is fringed with their churches; the fishermen everywhere being the earliest and most numerous converts.

Of the native Romanists over 80,000 are Romo-Syrians, formerly connected with the ancient Syrian church in Travancore; but who, in 1599, at the Synod of Diamper, under Archbishop Menezes, were induced by force and fraud to acknowledge the authority of the Pope, and adopt the creed of the Church of Rome. They are allowed to retain the use of the Syriac ritual and language in their public services.

A serious feud or "schism" long raged amongst the priest-

* Venn's "Life of Xavier."

hood and members of the Romish Church in India. The Portuguese Government having been the first European power in India, enjoyed the right of patronage in the appointment of bishops, which was vested in the King of Portugal in the sixteenth century. Afterwards, when both the means and the zeal of the Portuguese diminished, numerous missionaries, priests, and vicars apostolic were sent out direct by the Popes; but the bishops and priests appointed by the Portuguese, under the authority of the Archbishop of Goa, refused in some instances to render submission to the vicars apostolic, and were then pronounced schismatical. The adherents of the Portuguese See were excommunicated, and the validity of marriages and sacraments performed by them denied. A lamentable state of confusion and dissension ensued. These difficulties were healed by a Concordat, in 1857, between the Pope and the King of Portugal, by which the Pope at last reluctantly recognised the Portuguese right of patronage to Indian bishoprics, subject to his approval. The two parties now work together, with a few exceptions, on friendly terms; though there is still considerable bitterness of feeling about the conduct and failure of complete submission on the part of the Goanese priests.

The mass of the native Roman Catholics possess little solid scriptural knowledge, and this necessarily leads to superstition and error. In the Tamil language only have the Gospels and Acts (with the Authorized notes) been translated and published, and the volume is sold at what is, to an ordinary native, a high price. No portion of the Holy Scriptures has been translated into Malayālim by the Roman Catholic missionaries. Indeed, I have never actually seen a copy of the Gospels in the hands of their people, though a few no doubt possess them. Much of their literature is devotional and liturgical, or controversial in character. In a controversial catechism against Protestantism widely circulated, they charge Luther. and Calvin, and other eminent Protestants, with the most barefaced hypocrisy, profanity, licentiousness, and Satanic inspiration; the coarse and infidel statements of Cobbett are quoted as the testimony of a *Protestant* historian, and it is actually asserted that in countries where Popery prevails, there science and arts flourish, popular education stands higher, and learning spreads, by the benign influence of the Church of Rome, to a far higher degree than in Protestant lands!

They ingeniously interpret the English word "protestant" as "objector," and show that thus, according to our own account, we are mere deniers of the truth, instead of protesters against corruption and error. And, taking advantage of the careless and inaccurate use of the word "catholic," as applied by many Protestants to the Church of Rome, it is argued that they are acknowledged, even by their opponents, to be the *Catholic*, the universal and true Christian Church. Protestants are also charged with despising and calumniating the Blessed Virgin and the saints of God, and are generally designated by such terms as "Vetha purattar," "Bible twisters" or "falsifiers," and "Pathithar," "apostates" or "traitors." In this catechism, the use of images in religious worship, the veneration of relics, and all the other corrupt doctrines and practices of the Church of Rome, are warmly and zealously defended.

Many of these people are extremely ignorant and superstitious, and some are not far removed from heathenism; but many, we trust, possess sufficient knowledge of Christian truth to be the means of salvation to all who place their confidence in the Divine Redeemer, rather than in their own fancied merit, or in outward forms and rites.

Converts from heathenism are occasionally added to the Romish Church, though but little attention is paid to evangelizing operations amongst the heathen population. Indeed, they would have special difficulties in pursuing such a work as open air preaching, as appears from a circumstance which occurred to one of our native missionaries. A friend of his, a well-educated Roman Catholic catechist, was persuaded to accompany him one evening to preach to the heathen. Those who collected together on the occasion, struck with surprise at the sight of the new preacher, asked him, "Sir, are you also come to preach? Do you also venture to tell us that idol-worship is sinful? Did we not, some days ago, see your people carrying your idols round your church?" Confounded at their words, the poor catechist in vain attempted to show that it was not idols that they carried, but images, which are kept with a view to make a deep impression of good things on the minds of the ignorant, and that by bowing down to them they do not mean to worship them, but God only. "It is for the very same purpose," replied the heathen idolaters, "that we keep idols; what is the difference between your images and our idols? Are they not identically the same?" There was no more venturing out to preach after this.

The Romish churches directly connected with the see of Rome are distributed into two vicariates apostolic. One of these, including most of the Syro-Roman churches, is under the spiritual government of the vicar apostolic of Malabar, whose head-quarters are at Verāpoly, where a large monastic establishment of the Carmelite order exists, founded in 1673. The other is under the vicar apostolic of Quilon, who is assisted by eleven European and twelve native priests, superintending 59,350 native Christians.

Those connected with the Archbishopric of Goa are under the superintendence of the Bishop of Cochin, who resides in Quilon. Their converts number about 12,000. The total number of native Roman Catholics in Travancore, as far as I can ascertain, is probably about 140,000; and their places of worship are 196 in number.

Of late the management of the Roman Catholic Missions has much improved. A few years ago, in consequence of instructions from Rome, many of the churches were cleared of the images. The seat of the bishopric has also been removed from Quilon to Trevandrum, which is now occupied by European priests; and improved plans and increased instrumentalities for disseminating their doctrines amongst the people are coming into operation.

CHAPTER XVIII.

THE SYRIAN CHRISTIANS OF MALABAR.

Their Early History—Persecutions by the Portuguese—Synod of Diamper—Two Parties arise—Churches and Ecclesiastical Order—Doctrinal Views—The Jacobite Patriarch—Visit to a Syrian Church, and Description of the Service—Liturgy—Syriac Theological Terms—General Appearance and Character of the Syrians—Recent Party Disputes.

AMONGST the green hills and fertile valleys of North Travancore and Cochin, the venerable churches and quiet dwellings of a remarkable Christian people are found in large numbers. They have been there from a very early period of the Christian era, and have for some centuries, with more or less clearness, borne their testimony in a dark land for God and Christian truth. Like the Waldenses, they have been subjected to bitter persecution from the Church of Rome, and while many have succumbed to her power, others have retained their independence. They are a most interesting remnant of ancient Christianity long surviving in a heathen land, shut out from the aid and sympathy of the Christian world. Though fallen from the purity of scriptural doctrine and practice, reforms, both from within and from without, are beginning to appear; and there is reason to hope that the Syrian Christian Church in Malabar shall yet again arise and shine forth with primitive splendour and power. What a mighty influence for good might these Christians exert, as their forefathers once did, in Persia, India, and China, were the Syrian Church but revived, purified from error, and zealously engaged in labour for the glory of the Lord amongst the heathen in India and throughout the nations of the East!

These people are called by the Hindu natives "*Suriāni*," "Syrians," or "*Nazrāni*," "Nazarenes;" and by Europeans, "The Christians of St. Thomas," or more appropriately, "The Syrian Christians of Malabar." Their own traditions attribute their origin to the apostle Thomas, who visited India, they say, about A.D. 52, and preached the Gospel there, making numerous converts, who were joined some centuries afterwards by other Christians from Syria. The accuracy of the tradition of this apostle's visit to India and of his martyrdom there is exceedingly questionable, though there is reason to believe that the Gospel was preached in India at a very early period. It is probable that the Syrian Christians were, in the first instance, a small colony from Antioch; perhaps driven thence by violent persecutions about the middle of the fourth century.

A favourable reception was given to these early Christian colonists by the Hindu kings of the Malabar coast, on which they landed. Extensive privileges were granted them, according to the inscriptions on copper plates which are still in the possession of the Syrians, preserved in their college at Cottayam; fac-similes* of which, taken by Dr. Buchanan, I have seen in the Public Library of the Cambridge University, along with copies of similar grants to the chief of the ancient Jewish colony at Cochin. The Syrian plates are nearly ten inches in length and four in breadth, with large letters distinctly graven on both sides. The character is very ancient, and was once common to both Tamil and Malayālim. Other old copper plates and deeds of temples in Travancore are extant, of several of which I have taken copies, but have not as yet succeeded in deciphering the whole.

* Certainly not the original plates, as some have supposed.

These grants confer upon the Syrian chieftain possession of a village, with permission to use certain ornaments and musical instruments, and emblems of authority; to collect particular taxes and duties allotted to him; and to exercise jurisdiction over his own tribe. The dates of these important documents are expressed in such ambiguous language that it is difficult to determine the exact period. Different writers have assigned to them various dates, from the second to the fifth century A.D.

The Syrians proved serviceable allies to the native princes, and were therefore treated well, and attained to considerable political influence. They were allowed to bear arms, and were regarded as equal in caste to the Nairs. For some time their own chieftains ruled over them, till eventually the power passed into the hands of one of the Hindu Rajahs.

In A.D. 547, the Christian Church in Malabar was visited by Cosmas, an Egyptian merchant, who gives some account of their discipline and worship. It is also asserted, in ancient Anglo-Saxon Chronicles, that in A.D. 883, King Alfred sent Sighelm, Bishop of Sherburn, to India, to visit these Christians, and present gifts at the shrine of St. Thomas, near Madras. He is said to have successfully performed this great enterprise, and to have returned laden with gems and spices. Still it is difficult to determine whether Sighelm actually reached the South of India, or merely the countries adjacent to India on the north-west.

After the arrival of the Portuguese on the Western coast of India, early in the sixteenth century, the Romish priests soon discovered these people, and determined to effect their subjection to the papal authority. At first, measures of conciliation were pursued. In 1545 Franciscan friars were sent by the Archbishop of Goa to open a seminary for Syrian youths, who were afterwards ordained as priests; but the Syrians refused to admit these to their churches.

Resolved to effect their purpose, stronger measures were now resorted to. Plots were laid to seize Mar Joseph, the Syrian Metrān, whose influence against Rome was very great. He was made prisoner and sent to Portugal in 1558; but promising to bring over his people to the Church of Rome, he was allowed by the Queen to return to India. On his arrival, however, he threw off his disguise, and again taught the old doctrines. He was again captured and sent to Rome, where he died.

Another Metrān, Mar Simeon, who had been sent to India by the Patriarch of Mosul, was decoyed to Cochin, sent to Rome, and tried as a heretic by the Inquisition. There is every reason to believe he ended his days in the dungeons of the Inquisition in Portugal.

In 1595 Alexis de Menezes, who was about to proceed to Goa as Archbishop, received a brief from Pope Clement VIII., directing him to make strict inquiry into the faith and obedience of the Syrian bishop and his flock, and to prevent any bishops or priests from Syria from reaching Malabar. Early in 1599 Menezes, attended by Portuguese troops, reached Cochin, and summoned the Syrian Archdeacon George (the late Metrān being now dead) to appear before him. The Archdeacon at first boldly refused allegiance to the authority of the Church of Rome, but was at last tired out by the perseverance and zeal of Menezes and the threats of the Portuguese power, and induced to sign an acknowledgment of the Pope's supremacy. Menezes visited in person many of the Syrian churches, but they refused to submit to his authority; with the exception of a few whom he won over by denunciations, bribery, and fraud.

The assembling of a Council, or Synod, was now resolved on, that there might be an appearance of legality in the tyrannical and cruel proceedings of Menezes. This Synod met at Udiamperúr, or Diamper, near Cochin, on 20th June, 1599.

It was attended by the Romish Archbishop, the Syrian Archdeacon and 153 Cattanārs, many Romish priests, and some chief persons among the Portuguese. Here the Archbishop gained his own way. By most unrighteous means decrees were passed confirming the doctrines of Rome, and repudiating those which had hitherto been held and proclaimed by the Syrian Church. The Romish sacraments and celibacy were established, the ancient and invaluable records and historical documents of the Syrian Church (doubtless including copies of the Syriac Scriptures) were destroyed, and a Latin bishop was appointed. But it was found necessary to consent to the continued use of the Syriac language in public worship. Thus iniquitously were the Syrian Christians reduced to a nominal conformity to the Romish Church, and brought in reality into subjection to the Portuguese power.

This state of things continued for about fifty years, till the iron yoke of oppression ultimately became insufferable to those who still adhered to the early faith. In 1653 many of the Syrians revolted from the Romish power, excluded the Romish priests from their churches, and appointed their Archdeacon as Metrān, until they could obtain a bishop from their patriarch. When the expected bishop, Mar Attala, at last managed to reach the shores of India, he was ensnared and sent to Goa, where he was consigned to a dungeon in the Inquisition, and at last cruelly burnt as a heretic A.D. 1654.

A few years afterwards the Dutch seized upon Cranganore: thenceforward the Portuguese power declined, and the Syrians enjoyed freedom from external violence. Still many continued to adhere to the Church of Rome, while others remained under their own Metrāns connected with the patriarchate of Antioch. In this way arose the two great bodies that now exist,—the Syrians proper, who retain to a large extent the doctrine and ritual of the ancient Church, but to whom the Romish party have succeeded in attaching the title "*Puttan kúttu*,"—the *new* set; and the Romo-Syrians, who are under the authority of and directly connected with the Church of Rome, governed by the bishop of Verāpoly, and who call themselves "*Paraya kúttu*,"—the old set: after all there is something in a name!

The *Romo*-Syrians in Travancore number, according to the census of 1854, 81,886. The *Syrians* in the same province

SYRIAN CHURCH.

number 109,123, with 86 churches. They themselves state the total number of their people on the Western coast, including those in the Cochin state and about Calicut, to be 197,000, or even more; but I suspect that this estimate has been very loosely made, and is much too large. The total number of their churches is 146, with probably 800 or 900 priests.

The Syrian churches are solid, ancient-looking structures,

long and narrow, with gable ends surmounted by the cross, forming large, conspicuous objects in comparison with the native dwelling-houses near which they stand. The high walls are often supported by plain, sloping buttresses; the windows are small and few, and the roofs tiled. One peculiarity is that the external roof of the chancel is higher than the nave, instead of being lower, as with us. The *inner* ceiling of the chancel, however, is decidedly lower. Porch, pillars, pilasters, and other architectural ornaments in brick and plaster, adorn the fronts. Attached to or surrounding the central edifice are open sheds, cookhouses, and other buildings for the accommodation of the people on festive occasions, or sometimes a small chapel consecrated as a place of burial. In front of the church stands a pedestal on which a handsome stone cross is elevated; the whole being sometimes as much as twenty feet in height. The dark, ill-lighted interior is in general far from cleanly in appearance; possibly this is permitted that it may present a gratifying air of antiquity. At the western end a wooden gallery, or loft, contains a few simple articles of furniture for the accommodation of the bishop on his visits to the church, and is also used as a store-room. The church bell hangs inside to do honour to the host. Crosses or crucifixes, and sometimes curious paintings of their patron St. George, adorn the walls and chancel. In every church three altars of stone or wood are found,—one in the centre of the chancel and the others on either side. The honoured dead are buried in the floor of the church, near the entrance. A lamp is kept burning in front of the altar day and night.

The Syrian hierarchical order and ritual system bear some resemblance to that of the Copts, or native Egyptian Christians. They are governed by a "metrān," or metropolitan bishop, who is appointed by the patriarch of Antioch. The "cattanārs," or priests, perform the services of the church, celebrate marriages, bury the dead, &c. They do not receive stated pay, but derive their support from the contributions of the people on festival days, and from marriage and burial fees, &c. The "deacons" are often mere boys appointed by the bishop for the sake of the ordination fee which he receives. The ordinary dress of the priesthood is a long white coat of cotton cloth, tied or buttoned in front, and loose white trousers. The hair is shaven in the form of a tonsure, and the beard is usually worn long.

Previous to the Jesuit crusade against the Syrian church, they rejected many Papal errors and corruptions, such as the dogmas of Papal supremacy and the authority of traditions, the doctrines of transubstantiation and purgatory, &c. They had no images in their churches, nor were extreme unction or auricular confession practised by them. The sacraments they regarded as three, viz.—Baptism, Orders, and the Lord's Supper. The clergy were allowed to marry; the bread was dipped in the wine, and the communion thus administered in both kinds. But after that disastrous attack upon their faith and liberty, the Syrians were led to receive many errors which are still retained, though the authority of the Church of Rome is repudiated. Transubstantiation, the worship of the Virgin Mary, the invocation of saints, and even prayers for the dead, are now allowed. The Lord's Supper is regarded as a mass, and the prayers are offered in what is, to the generality of the laity, an unknown tongue. Still there is this important difference from the Church of Rome, that the authority of the Inspired Word is recognised, and its perusal is not opposed; so that there is now a reforming party within the Church itself, anxious for Gospel light and privileges, and earnestly opposing the superstition and formality into which the Church has fallen.

Baptism is performed by placing infants in the stone font, and pouring water over them with the hand. Adults are placed in the font, and a vessel of water poured over them. The sign of the cross is marked upon them in oil, and thrice the words are uttered, "Forsake the devil—receive Christ." A layman or deacon who has once married, and whose wife is alive, may become a priest; but when an unmarried deacon is once ordained a priest he may not get married, nor is a priest whose wife has died allowed to re-marry.*

The Syrian Christians are sometimes, though erroneously, called Nestorians; that is, the sect who maintain that Christ was two distinct persons as well as natures. It appears that this was their doctrine in the sixth and seventh centuries; but in the eighth century a Jacobite, or Monophysite, bishop came from Alexandria, and the Syrian Christians thus became dependent on the Jacobite see of Antioch. The Jacobites (so called after Jacobus Baradæus, an able opponent of Nestorianism in the sixth century) contend that in the Redeemer of the world there is but one nature, the human nature being absorbed in the divine, not, say they, like oil and water, but like water and wine, which become mingled and united; an error in the opposite extreme to that of the Nestorians. This, however, was readily adopted by the Syrians of Malabar, who thus veered round from one extreme to the other. In the Nicene Creed, which they acknowledge and receive, they reject the addition respecting the procession of the Holy Ghost, "and from the Son," which was inserted in that creed by the Latin Church, and which thus became partly the occasion of the schism between the Eastern and Western Churches.

The patriarch of Antioch, to whom the Syrians profess to render obedience, is one of the four great Catholic patriarchs, viz., of Constantinople, Alexandria, Antioch, and Jerusalem; of whom the first is supreme. There are no less than three prelates in Syria that claim the title and rank of patriarchs

* "The Syrian Christians of Malabar."

of Antioch; but the head of the Asiatic Jacobites is he who resides generally in a monastery not far from the city of Mardin in Turkey, in N. Lat. 37° 15′; E. Long. 40° 40′. His spiritual dominion is extensive. He has an associate in the government, to whose care, under the general direction of the patriarch, are entrusted the more distant eastern churches, and who resides in a monastery at Mosul in Mesopotamia, near to the ruins of Nineveh. All the patriarchs of this sect assume the name of Ignatius, and their associates that of Basil.

I have at different times visited and inspected several of the Syrian churches, and occasionally obtained permission, on week days, to preach in them. On Sunday, 23rd February, 1868, I paid a special visit, to observe the form of worship in one of their principal churches at Kunankulam in the Cochin country. Borrowing from the native magistrate a "manjeel," a square of canvas on which the traveller lies down on his back, and which is swung to a wooden pole and carried on the shoulders of two bearers behind and two in front, we started very early in the morning from Chowghaut, and passed on the way the churches at A'rthatty. The Romo-Syrian priest was standing outside his church, and I attempted to enter into conversation with him, but he seemed nervous and unfriendly. The church was built of very hard laterite bricks, not stuccoed. Close by the Romo-Syrian church stood that of the Syrians proper. It was very large and plain, with little ornament about it. Attached to the church on each side were open verandahs with rooms above. Over the chancel rose a square tower, with sloping tiled roof.

In front of the church was a large enclosure, with a good wall and a residence and outhouse in a row near the gateway. None of the people were in attendance; the service was to commence at nine o'clock.

Farther on, the country looked beautiful and well wooded, with abundance of cocoa-nut and jack trees, though nearer the coast it had been rather flat and uninteresting.

Kunankulam is a large Christian town and bazaar, with some good houses and shops, and a population of perhaps 2,000 souls. The church here is a kind of out-station or chapel to that at A'rthatty, which may be regarded as the cathedral, and with which five or six cattanārs and two deacons are connected.

Passing hastily through the town, I entered the church, and found that the morning service had not yet begun. The priest, a very respectable-looking elderly man, was standing within a railing in front of the chancel, chanting in the ordinary native style a Malayālim poem on sacred subjects. Attendants were preparing water, oil, &c. The brass lamp was burning in the centre of the railed space in front of the chancel, and here also some of the people stood during the service.

The church was not nearly filled, but the prevalence of small-pox at that time in the bazaar may have affected the attendance. There were about fifty or sixty men and twenty females present; I observed a Cattanār also in the priest's gallery at the west end of the church. The men were mostly dressed in the ordinary Hindu style. One or two more respectable persons wore a long blue cloth coat, with gold embroidered belt, and a red cap with tassels. One man retained both cap and shoes in the church, agreeing in this respect with neither Hindu nor Christian forms of reverence. The women wore neat white jackets, with long tight sleeves, some handsomely embroidered, and the ordinary cotton cloth worn round the waist by all classes of the Hindu women. A light muslin cloth is thrown over the head as a veil, and falls gracefully down the back. The chancel was elevated one or two steps, and from the arch a curtain was hung, so as at will to exclude the view of the chancel and altar from the worshippers in the church. The baptismal font consisted of a large granite basin about two and a half feet in diameter, set on a pillar, and covered with a wooden lid.

During the time of the service all the people stood, the women rather behind the men. Indeed, these buildings are not provided with seats or benches. One by one they commenced to read or repeat prayers in Malayālim, frequently crossing themselves, touching the forehead, then the shoulders from left to right.

The principal altar, or "throne," as it is called, in the centre of the chancel, was covered with a neat white cloth, and decorated with handsome carvings in wood; but no pictures or images were seen, except two or three ornamental cherubim in the plaster work. On the altar stood a cross, and another, with circular hangings beneath, at the railing in front of the chancel.

At the commencement of the service the Cattanār ascended the steps into the chancel, where he proceeded to robe himself in the various parts of his official vestments, repeating prayers suitable to each act. He put on, one after another, a pair of sandals, a long blue coat over his ordinary white cotton dress, a blue cap, a long white robe with waist-belt and cope, scarf and sleeves of embroidered silk. The shoes were again put off in certain parts of the service.

Two or three boys, in ordinary native dress, chanted the responses. The service was lengthy and highly ritualistic, including frequent genuflections, kissing and perfuming the altar, signing the cross, the ringing of bells, elevating and incensing the host, and the minute and multifarious ceremonies prescribed in the Syriac rubric. A considerable portion of the service was in Malayālim, the remainder in Syriac. The curtains were drawn down several times during the performance of the most solemn parts of the ceremonial.

At first the people seemed careless and inattentive, but afterwards, especially at the consecration of the host, the venerable appearance and dress of the priest, the loud ringing of bells, the waving fumes of the incense, and the loud and apparently earnest prayers offered by the people, appeared to me under the circumstances very affecting and impressive. No one communicated on this occasion except the priest. He pronounced the benedictions with exquisite grace.

The incense was once carried round the congregation, those who received the benefit bowing to the youth who bore the censer.

A curious ceremony called "giving the peace," probably intended to answer the same purpose as the kiss of peace in early ages, was performed before the consecration of the elements. The deacon who carried the censer took from it a double handful of the smoke, which he smelled, and then appeared to hand to the priest, who received it with both hands. Going to the people he gave it into the hands of two or three of the nearest, who put it to their faces, and then pretended to pass it on to others, till it went round the whole congregation. One of the good people came up to me where I was standing and said, "Do you want this peace, sir? This is the sign of peace." "Yes," I replied, and gave my hand, which he took in both his and slightly stroked. This I thought a very pretty observance.

After the conclusion of the service some of the people invited me to a neighbouring house, a good building with chairs, neat coloured grass mats, and a table covered with a white cloth, on which were placed bread, fruits, plates, teacups, &c., in imitation of the European style. Here the Cattanār, Jacob, shortly joined us, and we entered into conversation at breakfast respecting their church and customs.

No one, he informed me, in that part of the country preaches to the people, but only a few of the priests farther south. I procured copies of their prayer-books, and had the pleasure of preaching in Malayālim at eleven o'clock, in the mission church belonging to the Church Missionary Society, to a most attentive and interesting congregation.

The ancient liturgy in general use throughout the Syrian churches, called St. James's Order, has been translated more than once into English, and may be found entire in Hough's "History of Christianity in India." Some of the prayers are beautiful and sublime, but many include invocations of the Virgin and saints, and prayers for the dead.

The small Malayālim prayer-books' used by the Syrians contain prayers for several occasions, and short prayers to be offered in the course of the public service; but no translation of the prayers offered by the Caṭṭanār in the celebration of the mass.

Though the Syrian Christians speak and write Malayālim as their mother tongue, the style of their religious works in this language is very peculiar, being interlarded with Syriac words in a pure or modified form. Their technical and theological terms are all Syriac, and the compound of Syriac and Malayālim seems rather strange to the unaccustomed ears of a Hindu Malayāli. A few of the principal terms are as follows:—

Gospel	=	Evangelion.	Doctor	=	Rambān.
Epistle	=	Enkrattā.	Angel	=	Mā'āk.
Psalm	=	Masumúrā.	Baptism	=	Māmmōdisā.
Apostle	=	Sleehā.	Mass	=	Kurubāna.
Prophet	=	Nibyā.	Unction	=	Uprisimā.
Deacon	=	Meshamshana.	Chancel	=	Madubhā.
Priest	=	Cattanār.	Nave	=	Haykalā.
Parish Priest	=	Kashisha.	Holy Ghost	=	Rúhāda Kudisha.
Bishop	=	Mār.	Jesus Christ	=	Eeso Mashihā.
Sexton	=	Kappiāra.	Father	=	Bāwa.

There is reason to believe that in many instances very serious corruptions, and even heathenish practices, have been allowed to prevail in some of the Syrian congregations. Several of the festivals and fasts are in some places conducted in a manner little better than those of the heathen. Certain ceremonies performed for the dead are even called by the Hindu title of similar observances, and there have been instances of heathen songs having been sung in churches for the amusement of the people, besides other degrading and unchristian acts of compliance with heathen sentiments and practices.

The Syrian Christians are generally respectable in appearance and dress, and are comparatively fair in complexion. Many are engaged in trading and agricultural pursuits, and some are possessed of much wealth. Their houses are often spacious and good, with neat wood carvings and other decorations in the Malabar style. On the whole they are intelligent, and display considerable intellectual activity as well as commercial industry and capacity. Several of their number occupy good positions as English teachers, astronomers, lawyers, and clerks. One of this race translated into Malayālim, for the writer, a number of popular Tamil Christian lyrics, which have been published, and are very well received by native Christians. Another Syrian youth, connected with the Church Mission, Mr. T. C. Poonen, B.A., has been awarded the Government of India Scholarship, and is now studying in England for the bar. An able and devoted native minister in connection with the Church Mission, Rev. George Mātthan (lately deceased), published some years ago a valuable and original grammar of the Malayālim language, and was a very scholarly and accomplished man. A history of the Syrian Christians in Malayālim, a translation of Shakspere's "Comedy of Errors," besides several original poems and other works, have recently been published by various individuals connected with this interesting people.

The personal disputes and party contentions which have occurred in the more recent internal history of this remarkable church are most painful to contemplate. Rival priests have visited the distant patriarch of Antioch with their *ex-parte* statements and representations, or misrepresentations, as the case might be, afterwards returning to Malabar to carry on their jarring disputes in the very bosom of the Church. At various periods several bishops have simultaneously put forward antagonistic pretensions to primatial authority. In 1848 there were no less than five bishops in Malabar, each decrying the others as unauthorized intruders. Hence arose scandalous disputes and confusion.

At present there are two metrāns, bitter and avowed rivals. A third, Mar Joseph Coorilos (Cyril), is Bishop of Anjoor, near Calicut, where he has been for twenty years. He acknowledges his subordination, as suffragan, to Mar Athanasius.

Mar Athanasius, the recognised metropolitan of the Syrian Church in Malabar, resides at Cottayam. He has appointed his brother, Mar Thomas Athanasius, to be his suffragan and successor. A native of Travancore, Athanasius obtained a good education in the Church Mission College at Cottayam, and was one of the Syrian deacons who adhered to the missionaries at the time of the separation. He was afterwards dismissed, however, as unfit for the ministry; and then started for Antioch, and visited the patriarchs at Mosul and Mardin. Although well aware that there was a metrān in Travancore, he induced the patriarch to consecrate him, and returned to Malabar in 1843. For a long time he was not well received, but his position has gradually improved and his influence strengthened. He has been recognised by the native Government as in possession of the supreme ecclesiastical authority and of the churches belonging to the Syrians. As the result, probably, of his early connection with the Protestant missionaries, as well as of the circulation of the Scriptures in Syriac and Malayālim amongst his priests and people, this metrān favours the reforming party—who seek to have the services conducted wholly in the vernacular, partake of both elements in the sacrament, and have discontinued the invocation of saints and prayers for the dead. Great improvements have therefore taken place during the last twelve or fifteen years within the bosom of the Syrian Church. The chief stumblingblock still is communion in both kinds.

The opposing metrān is Mar Dionysius, who is at the head of a small conservative and ritualistic party. He is a native of Kunankulam in the Cochin state; his mother is a Romanist, and his own proclivities lie in this direction. He has little learning, but belongs to a wealthy and influential family.

When disputes were going on in India, Dionysius visited Antioch, where he professes to have been consecrated in 1867. Mar Athanasius, he affirms, was at the same time deposed by the Patriarch. The documents of consecration and letters patent of deposition which Dionysius produces have been subjected to official scrutiny, and pronounced to be of very doubtful genuineness. Nor does it appear that the ecclesiastical canons confer upon the Patriarch the right, thus readily and without examination, to depose Mar Athanasius. Dionysius threatens, if necessary, to carry on his litigation respecting "vested interests" before the British Parliament itself.

CHAPTER XIX.

THE CHURCH MISSION IN TRAVANCORE.

Sketch of the History of the Mission—Its Successes, and Present Position.

The Church Missionary Society commenced its operations in North Travancore in 1816, about ten years after the commencement of the London Mission in the South. Intense interest had been excited in England by Dr. C. Buchanan's glowing and unconsciously exaggerated account of his visit to the ancient Syrian churches in Malabar; and Colonel Munro, then British Resident at Travancore, applied to the Church Missionary Society for English clergymen for their instruction. Accordingly, Messrs. Bailey, Baker, and Fenn were sent out to labour amongst the Syrians, while Mr. Norton opened a mission station at the important seaport of Allepey, amongst the heathen and Roman Catholic population. For some time the Syrian metrān and priesthood worked cordially with the English missionaries, admitting them to preach in the Syrian churches, and to instruct candidates for the ministry. Considerable reforms were thus effected, and much light infused into the Syrian Church. But in 1838 a change took place. The metrān then ruling discouraged the preaching and efforts of the missionaries amongst his people, and ultimately dissolved all union with the Church missionaries. It was then decided by the missionaries that their work should be carried on as a mission of the Church of England, and that proselytes from the corrupt Syrian Church, as well as converts from heathenism, should be received into their communion.

The principal station of the Church Mission is Cottayam, which may be regarded as the head-quarters of the mission. Seven European missionaries are now earnestly and successfully prosecuting their labours in North Travancore and Cochin, in connection with whom there are thirteen ordained native ministers, and eighteen native catechists and readers.

"The Mission converts consist partly of Syrians who have renounced either the Romanist or Jacobite communions, partly of a few converts from the Nairs, Brahmans, and other castes, with a large proportion of Chogans, a class similar in standing to the Shānars, together with some increasing bodies from the slave castes and the Hill Arrians." Altogether, connected with this mission in North Travancore (including also Cochin) there are 12,092 native Christians, of whom 2,847 are communicants.

The movement towards Christianity amongst the slave castes in North Travancore commenced about 1852, and has rapidly spread. Many of these poor people have exhibited in a striking degree the renewing power of the Gospel, and have proved devout, earnest, and simple-minded believers, zealous also for the spread of knowledge and truth amongst their own people. "Sir," said the head man of a Syrian metrān to Mr. Baker, "those people of yours are wonderfully altered. Six years ago I employed clubmen to guard my paddy while being reaped. Now, for two or three years, I have left it entirely to your Christians, and they reap it, and bring it to my house. I get more grain, and I know these very men were the fellows who robbed me formerly." This was unsought-for testimony. On another occasion, in discussing with a Súdra, a native missionary was one day arguing that "if ignorance were a sufficient plea to rid men

CHURCH MISSION STATION, COTTAYAM.

of responsibility, the poor ignorant slaves who lie, cheat, steal, and —— " The Súdra at once interrupted him, saying, "Nay, the slaves don't lie or steal, or get drunk or quarrel now; they have left off all these since they learned this religion." What a noble testimony to the reality of the change from the lips of a heathen on the spot!

The remarkable work amongst the Hill Arrians, who dwell on the western slopes of the Ghauts, was commenced in 1848 by the Rev. H. Baker, jun., whom several heads of villages had invited to visit and instruct them. "You must know," said they, "that we know nothing right; will you teach us or not? We die like beasts, and are buried like dogs; ought you to neglect us?" Amidst many difficulties and dangers from deadly malaria, wild beasts, and hostility of heathens, the work was begun and carried on, and the people proved to be eager and willing learners.

The hill station of Mundakyum thus established, now numbers 893 adherents, of whom 710 are baptized Christians.

CHAPTER XX.

ESTABLISHMENT AND EARLY HISTORY OF THE LONDON MISSION IN TRAVANCORE.

Ringeltaube proceeds to India—Providential Invitation to labour in Travancore—His Operations and Success—Messrs. Mead, Mault, and Knill—Great Increase of Professing Christians—Establishment of Mission Station at Quilon—Missionary Plans—Visit of the Deputation, and Commencement of Neyoor District—Persecution; its Causes and Occasion—Oppression of Native Christians providentially overruled—Mr. Thompson's Labours at Quilon.

THE first enterprise upon which the London Missionary Society entered immediately on its establishment in 1795, was the mission to the islands of the South Seas, which have since been the scenes of glorious triumphs of the Gospel. A few years afterwards, as the means at the disposal of the directors of the Society and their experience in the work gradually augmented, they began to take into consideration the propriety of extending their efforts to the vast continent of India, at that time the field of great and exciting contests between the British forces and those of the Mysore, Mahratta, and other native powers. The original design and constant aim of the Society was, as far as means and opportunity should afford, to "preach the gospel to every creature;" and as to the particular mode of effecting this great purpose, it endeavoured to exercise a wise and enlightened judgment, seeking at the same time the guidance and direction of Divine providence.

The attention of the Missionary Society had been drawn

to the strong claims presented by the beautiful island of Ceylon, and to the necessity of endeavouring to restore and instruct the multitudes of nominal Christians there who had been induced to conform to Christianity chiefly by the political influence and patronage of the Portuguese and Dutch Governments, but were then destitute of religious instruction, and, as might be expected, were fast relapsing into heathenism. The claims of various parts of continental India were also discussed; but in those days of slow communication and defective information respecting distant lands, it seemed difficult to come to a decision in London upon so important a point as the particular localities and stations to be occupied in the establishment of new missions in India. After much thought and deliberation, the ultimate decision of this question was very wisely left to the missionaries themselves, who were placed at liberty to act as seemed best, under the advice of Christian friends on the spot, and the intimations of Divine providence.

Amongst other devoted and useful labourers raised up for the service of God in this emergency, appeared one remarkable man, William Tobias Ringeltaube. Born in 1770, at Scheidelwitz, near Brieg, in the south of Prussia, he studied at the University of Halle, and was ordained to the ministry at Wernigerodu in 1796. The Society for the Promotion of Christian Knowledge then sent out Ringeltaube as a missionary to Calcutta, but somehow he soon tired of the work there, and returned to England in 1799. This is the more surprising as he was a clever man, and was afterwards very active in the service of the London Missionary Society. While in England, Ringeltaube urged the claims of the heathen in India, associating chiefly with the Moravians, or United Brethren. In 1803, however, he accepted the invitation of the London Missionary Society to form a part of the proposed mission to India.

On the 20th of April, 1804, the missionaries for India and Ceylon, Messrs. Ringeltaube, Desgranges, Cran, Vos, Erhardt, and Palm, sailed from Copenhagen for Tranquebar in the Danish ship *King's Packet*, the only means of communication with India then open to missionaries.

They reached Tranquebar at the end of the year, and were most cordially received and encouraged by Christian friends.

Three of the brethren shortly proceeded to the island of Ceylon, and two to Vizāgapatam; while Ringeltaube remained for above a year at Tranquebar, diligently studying the Tamil language, and deliberating as to a suitable sphere of labour. In a letter written to the Society at this time, he expresses his firm trust in Providence, and his confidence in the ultimate success of his work, in the following noble words:—"The operations of Providence are slow but sure. The tooth of time seems to gnaw incessantly here as elsewhere, and God will finally lay rocks in the dust. The missionary aspect of the country is so changed since the English came into these parts, that, the Lord helping His servants, we need not despair of final success. I am one of the greatest cowards that ever went forth shod with the preparation of the Gospel, but the Lord in mercy comforts my wretched Parian heart more and more as I approach the field of action. He has indeed appeared for us; whom shall we fear? And if we fall in the heat of the battle, before success decides in favour of our beloved Leader, we shall only be sorry that we cannot die ten times for Him."

While thus diligently engaged in the work of preparation and waiting for providential openings, Ringeltaube's attention was directed to the Shānars of South Travancore. His interest in that remarkable people had been already excited, when one day, as he was sitting alone, an individual of this tribe came suddenly before him and exclaimed, "*Parabaran-ukku stottiram*," "Praise be to God." Gladly embracing the opportunity, Ringeltaube entered into conversation with the Shānar respecting his people and their customs; but was unable, he says, to get any satisfactory or sensible answers to his inquiries, owing to the stupidity of his visitor.

But the earnest cry of the people of Travancore, "Come over and help us," was soon, in the most distinct and unmistakable manner, brought to the ears of the servant of God, by a pilgrim from that country named Mahā Rāsan. He was a Pariah of some education and good character, a worshipper of Siva. Becoming dissatisfied with the worship conducted in his native village, Meilādi, he proceeded on a pilgrimage to Chillambram. Here he performed the usual ceremonies, but without obtaining the peace and satisfaction of mind that he sought. He afterwards visited Tanjore and other places. On one occasion, passing by the mission church at Tanjore, he came to the door of the church, where he stood and listened to the sermon which was then being delivered by the Rev. J. C. Kohlhoff. Recognising the man by his garb as a religious pilgrim, Mr. Kohlhoff specially addressed him in the course of his sermon; the poor man's attention was arrested and his heart touched. He remained in Tanjore for some months as an inquirer, listening attentively to the instructions of the missionaries. Then he returned to Meilādi to his friends, showed them his Christian books, and built a small hut, which he set apart for the worship of the true God.

After a few months Mahā Rāsan again visited Tanjore to endeavour to induce a European missionary to come to Travancore. No missionary could be spared; but a catechist with his wife and family accompanied the convert to Meilādi, and preached there for some time. Ringeltaube, however, heard of these circumstances, and rightly regarded them as a providential call to him to labour in the Travancore territory, whither he determined at once to direct his steps.

Col. C. Macauly was then the British Resident at the Court of Travancore, and proved a kind friend to Ringeltaube and his work. He procured a passport for the missionary, and offered personally to defray his travelling expenses. Accordingly, on the 13th of April, 1806, Ringeltaube set out for the principality, and soon reached the Southern frontier. But while the natural scenery on which he gazed was most beautiful and inviting, he was made to feel deeply the bigotry and inhospitable character of the people. "As soon," he says in his journal, "as we had entered the Ghaut, the grandest prospect of green-clad precipices, cloud-capt mountains, hills adorned with temples and castles, and other picturesque objects presented themselves. A noble avenue of immense banyan trees winding through the valley adds greatly to the beauty of the place. My timid companions, however, trembled at every step, being now on ground altogether in the power of the Brahmins, the sworn enemies of the Christian name; and, indeed, a little occurrence soon convinced us that we were no more on British territory. I lay down to rest in the caravansary appropriated for Brahmins only, when the magistrate immediately sent word for me to remove, otherwise their god would no more eat. I reluctantly obeyed, and proceeded round the southern hills to a village called Magilādy, from whence formerly two men came to Tranquebar to request me to come and see them, representing that 200 heathens at this place were desirous to embrace our religion. I lodged two days at their houses, where I preached and prayed. Some of them knew the Catechism. They begged hard for a native teacher, but declared they could not build a church, as all this country had been given by the King of Travancore to the Brahmins, in consequence of which the magistrates would not give their permission. I spent the day most uncomfortably in an Indian hut, in the midst of a noisy, gaping crowd which filled the house. I had expected to find hundreds eager to hear the word; instead of which I had difficulty to make a few families attend for an hour. On Monday a catechist from a neighbouring congregation arriving to speak with me, I committed this infant flock to his charge, and he is to come once a week to see them."

Ringeltaube reached Trevandrum on the 30th of April, 1806, and was most kindly received by the British Resident, who promised to procure permission from the Rajah for the purchase of land and the erection of a church for the Christians at Meilādi, and offered his own personal contribution towards this object.

A fortnight afterwards Ringeltaube paid a visit to the Dewān, in furtherance of his object.

"Of what religion are you?" asked the Minister.

"Of Colonel Macaulay's religion," answered the missionary.

"I never knew there was such a religion," was the reply.

Ringeltaube endeavoured to explain what it was, but with little success. The Dewān told him frankly the thing was not to be done, as it was an innovation on established customs.

Some time after this interview, the requisite permission was obtained from the Rajah through the intercession of the English friends of the mission, notwithstanding the evasions and opposition of the Dewān and the Brahmans.

Many difficulties still standing in the way of making a permanent settlement in Travancore, Ringeltaube took up his head-quarters for the time at Pālamcotta, in Tinnevelly, about sixty miles from Meilādi. In that province there were then about five thousand Christians under the care of thirty native agents, supported by the Society for the Promotion of Christian Knowledge, and a strong impression in favour of Christianity prevailed amongst several classes of the heathen population. Ringeltaube undertook the charge of these native Christians in Tinnevelly, agreeing that all the increase there should belong to the Christian Knowledge Society, for whom he acted, while the congregations in the native State should belong to the Missionary Society, with which he was more immediately connected. He travelled about from place to place, preaching the word and administering the ordinances, and writes that "he had reason to bless the Lord of the harvest that He had graciously owned his feeble labours." He rightly regarded these fields of labour as ripe with the promise of a glorious harvest.

On his second visit to Meilādi, Ringeltaube had the privilege of baptizing in one day forty persons, who had been instructed and led to the truth by the catechist whom he had left in charge of the work there. Ringeltaube made these converts promise that they would perform the accustomed Government services, and obey the king and magistrates as before. Among those baptized was Mahā Rāsan, whose name was changed to Vethamānikkam, and who was appointed catechist of Meilādi; the former teacher returning with Mr. Ringeltaube to Pālamcotta.

This first convert in Travancore continued faithful and consistent till his death many years after. During the war between the Dewān and the British in 1809, a party of Súdras, instigated by hatred and ignorance of Christianity, resolved to kill Vethamānikkam, charging him with having been the means of bringing the English into the country. A friendly Súdra, however, informed the Christian teacher of the conspiracy against his life, and advised him to flee He escaped to the mountains and concealed himself for some time, returning to his house after the excitement had subsided. His grandson, Rev. G. Māsillāmani, was ordained to the Christian ministry in 1866, and is now the respected and efficient pastor of the church at Dennispuram.

For three or four years Ringeltaube travelled diligently in

South Tinnevelly and Travancore as an itinerant missionary, preaching and teaching the word of the kingdom. In Travancore he preached regularly in six or seven villages in which he had erected chapels, distributed the Scriptures, and employed five or six schoolmasters, "for it is in vain," said he, "to print and distribute the Bible if there are none to read it." He also trained several native youths for evangelical labours, and was assisted for short periods by two country-born youths, Messrs. Fleury and Wheatly.

In 1808 Ringeltaube's labours were much interrupted by the war in Travancore; but in 1810 he settled in Oodiagerry, and in 1812 in Meilādi. The work continued to prosper, and the light of divine truth to spread around. Ringeltaube was privileged to baptize in all about 900 persons. His spirit and manner will be seen from the following extract from a letter written in 1810:—"At A'tticādu, after preaching to a considerable number under a mango tree, I baptized an old man from Covilvilei, of ninety-seven years of age, whom I called the Patriarch Jacob, and who, leaning on two of his sons, shed tears of joy for their conversion as well as his own, for they were baptized at the same time with himself. But a more interesting figure, if possible, in this group was a schoolmaster, crippled in both legs by a fall from a tree, who had been brought ten miles on men's shoulders to hear the word. 'Since,' said he, 'I lost the use of my legs, I have nothing but heaven in view.' After preaching on the latter part of the second chapter of the First Epistle of Peter, I took occasion to exhort the people to be obedient to their masters, and particularly to the magistrates, and to waive all views of temporal advantage by professing Christianity, and not to imagine they would be exempt from the cross, or discharged from the obligation of their relative duties."

But after twelve years of labour in South India, failure of

health, through incessant toil and privations, ensued; and early in 1816 Ringeltaube relinquished his connection with the mission, and went to Ceylon and the Cape of Good Hope. Various accounts are given of his subsequent history. One statement is to the effect that he went to Batavia in 1817. Another report is that he was killed on a journey into the interior of Africa before 1820. But we have no certain knowledge of the time, place, or manner of his death; there was even at one time a legend amongst some of the Christian natives, that as Enoch for his piety was translated, that he should not see death, so was Mr. Ringeltaube for his self-denying labours. He left behind him six or seven principal stations with chapels, five or six schools, 900 baptized converts and candidates for baptism,—all the fruits of his earnest and devoted efforts.

This founder of our Travancore mission was an able but eccentric man. He laboured devotedly, assiduously, and wisely for the conversion of the heathen and the edification of the Christian converts. Those whose motives appeared worldly and selfish were rejected by him, and all professing Christians were warned and instructed as to the spiritual character of the religion of Christ, and the permanent obligation of all relative and social duties. He was most generous and unselfish in regard to money, and is said to have distributed the whole of his quarter's salary almost as soon as it reached his hands. His labours were abundantly blessed, and his memory is precious and greatly honoured in connection with the foundation of this now flourishing native Christian church.

These ten years, from 1806 to 1816, may be regarded as comprising the *first* period in the history of the mission—its establishment by Mr. Ringeltaube.

In anticipation of Ringeltaube's departure, the Society had already appointed another missionary, the Rev. Charles

Mead, who has since been honoured to enjoy great success in this mission, to officiate in his stead. He embarked early in 1816 with several other missionaries, including that singularly devoted servant of Christ, Rev. Richard Knill, and reached Madras on 28th of August that year. They found that Ringeltaube had already left; but Mr. Mead was detained by illness at Madras and afterwards at Penang,

MISSION BUNGALOW, NAGERCOIL.

where the vessel in which he sailed for Travancore called, and where he lost his devoted wife. Reaching Meilādi at length in the beginning of 1818, he found that though the mission had been left vacant for about two years, the catechist left in charge by Ringeltaube had carried on the work with diligence and success, and the people had remained faithful to their Christian vocation. Mead was joined in

September, 1818, by Knill, whose health had failed in Madras, and both went to reside at Nāgercoil, about four miles from Meilādi, which henceforth became their principal station.

The British Resident at that time was Colonel Munro, a zealous and distinguished friend of missions. Colonel Munro had been the saviour of the country in the recent period of confusion and misrule, and he was therefore all-powerful in political matters. He greatly favoured the mission, and used his influence on its behalf. He procured grants from the Rānee of the bungalow at Nāgercoil, in which the missionaries resided, and 5,000 rupees for the purchase of rice-fields as an educational endowment, from the income of which the English seminary, established in 1819, has ever since been supported. Similar aid was at the same time rendered to the Syrian Christians and the Church missionaries labouring amongst that people.

A strange but well-meant experiment was tried by Colonel Munro, in procuring for Mr. Mead the appointment of civil judge at Nāgercoil, as there were then so few persons in the country who could be entrusted with such an office. The duties of this post were certainly discharged with great efficiency and much benefit to the natives, so as to excite in their minds strong sentiments of grateful esteem for Mr. Mead, and make an impression throughout the country highly favourable to the external success of the missionary cause. It was felt, however, by the Society that such a union of offices was somewhat incongruous, and Mr. Mead accordingly resigned his civil appointment after about a year.

And now the tide of popular favour flowed in upon the missionaries. Not only did their message commend itself to the consciences of the hearers, but there was doubtless in many instances a mixture of low and inferior motives in embracing the profession of Christianity. The missionaries were the friends of the Resident, and connected with the great and just British nation. Hopes were perhaps indulged that they might be willing to render aid to their converts in times of distress and oppression, or advice in circumstances of difficulty. Moreover, the temporal blessings which Christianity everywhere *of necessity* confers, in the spread of education and enlightenment, liberty, civilization, and social improvement, were exemplified to all in the case of the converts already made. The kindness of the missionaries, too, attracted multitudes who were accustomed to little but contempt and violence from the higher classes, and who could not but feel that the Christian teachers were their best and real friends. What were these to do with those who thus flocked to the profession of Christianity? Receive them to baptism and membership with the Christian Church, or recognise them as true believers, they could not and did not; but gladly did they welcome them as hearers and learners of God's word. The missionaries rejoiced to think that the influence for good which they were permitted to exert, and the *prestige* attached to the British nation in India, were providentially given them to be used for the highest and holiest purposes. They did not hesitate, therefore, to receive to Christian instruction even those who came from mixed motives, unless they were evidently hypocrites or impostors. And from time to time, as these nominal Christians, or catechumens, appeared to come under the influence of the *power* of godliness, and as the instructions afforded them appeared to issue in their true conversion and renewed character, such were, after due examination and probation, received into full communion with the Christian Church. Their children, too, came under instruction at the same time in the mission schools, and became the Christian professors and teachers of the next generation.

During the two years immediately following their arrival,

about 3,000 persons, chiefly of the Shānar caste, placed themselves under Christian instruction, casting away their images and emblems of idolatry, and each presenting a written promise declarative of his renunciation of idolatry, and determination to serve the living and true God. Some of these doubtless returned to heathenism when they understood the spiritual character and comprehensive claims of the Christian religion, but most remained faithful and increasingly attached to their new faith.

There were now about ten village stations, most of which had churches, congregations, and schools, all of them rapidly increasing. Native catechists were employed to preach and teach, and these teachers met the missionaries periodically for instruction and improvement in divine things.

These early missionaries entered upon the work (which one of them calls "De Propaganda Fide, but not without instruction") with great spirit and enterprise. A printing press was soon established. The seminary for the training of native youths was opened, and plans prayerfully laid and diligently carried out for the periodical visitation of the congregations and villages.

The congregation at Nāgercoil alone numbered now about 300, and a large chapel for occasional united meetings at the head station being urgently required, the foundation was laid by Mr. Knill on New Year's day, 1819. Striking evidence of the strong faith and hope of these early labourers is seen in the noble dimensions of the chapel, the erection of which they then commenced. It is, perhaps, the largest church in South India, measuring inside 127 feet in length by 60 feet wide, and affording accommodation for nearly 2,000 persons, seated, according to Hindu custom, on the floor. Had this fine building not been erected, we should have since grievously felt the lack of accommodation for the great aggregate missionary and other special meetings of our

Christian people, which we are now privileged to hold within its walls.

Early in 1819, a country-born youth named George Harvey Ashton, who had been carefully trained by the Rev. J. C. Kohlhoff, at Tanjore, was employed as an assistant missionary; he lived to render faithful and valuable service to the mission, in many forms, for the long period of forty-one years.

Mr. Knill's health again failing, he was compelled, after about a year's zealous and affectionate labour in Travancore, to return to England. The mission was again reinforced by the Rev. Charles Mault and Mrs. Mault, who laboured together uninterruptedly for thirty-six years.

Another missionary, the Rev. John Smith, reached Nāgercoil in May, 1820, and remained there for several months, studying the language and the details of mission work, and deliberating on various plans for the future. As the capital was not at that time open to missionary efforts, it was decided to occupy the large and important military station of Quilon, about thirty-eight miles N.W. of Trevandrum. Quilon has a population of at least 20,000. It is situated on a sandy plain, close to the sea and to one of the backwaters, with numerous ramifications, and thus has easy water communication with both North and South. The Nāgercoil missionaries had previously made tours as far as Quilon, but it was first occupied as a principal station by Mr. Smith, in February, 1821. He was accompanied and assisted for the first few months by Mr. Ashton. Smith hired a house at Tangachery, a British suburb of Quilon, and commenced the study of the Malayālim language, and educational and evangelistic operations. Substantial aid was rendered by the British Resident, Colonel Newall, and by the chaplain and several military officers resident at the station. But the results were small. No such success was experienced as in the South, and after three or four years Smith returned to England on account of ill-health. Before his departure, the Rev. William Crowe reached Quilon, but his health also failed, almost from his arrival, and he also returned to England within two years, without having been able to effect much. This mission was then left from November, 1825, in the hands of Mr. Ashton, aided by the occasional visits and general superintendence of the Nāgercoil missionaries. There were then ten schools in operation in this part of the country, with about 400 scholars, and with five catechists labouring in the surrounding district.

Meantime the work in the South, in the hands of Messrs. Mead and Mault and their helpers, was vigorously prosecuted and flourished greatly. The good hand of their God was on them for good, and constant accessions to the Christian community took place. In 1822 it was reckoned that 5,000 persons had since the commencement of the mission embraced Christianity. The congregations then numbered twenty-two, amongst whom seventeen native teachers were labouring, while twenty village schools were in operation. The next year seven additional congregations were formed, and a boarding school for girls was opened by Mrs. Mault with twenty-seven boarders. The efforts of the brethren were united, their consultations frequent and harmonious, and their plans effective and encouraging. In all their work suitable means and instrumentalities were employed, and they had reason to expect the promised blessing of God upon their prayerful and indefatigable efforts. Vernacular and itinerant preaching was systematically practised, in order to reach, as far as possible, the mass of the adult population. Native agency, the best within reach of the missionaries at the time, was availed of, while a better educated class of agents was under training in the seminary, in which they had now thirty-eight pupils. Scriptural education was afforded to the children both of Christian and heathen parents in the village day schools. Great attention was, from the first, paid to the subject of female education, for the training of schoolmistresses and furnishing suitable wives for the catechists. The manufacture of lace* was taught in the female boarding school by Mrs. Mault, and school-

LACE WORKER WITH PILLOW.

mistresses were afterwards employed to teach the girls of the village congregations. It cannot be told how much the cause of female education in Travancore owes to the devoted wives of missionaries then and since. The printing press was also in active operation. Thousands of copies of tracts, periodicals, and Christian books, on a variety of

* See page 68.

important subjects, were printed and distributed from year to year. A new version of the Tamil Scriptures being prepared by Mr. Rhenius, who had settled at Pālamcotta in 1820, the Nāgercoil missionaries largely assisted in the work of revision, and great numbers of copies of the Holy Scriptures were printed and circulated in the South of India.

In 1824 the number of congregations was nearly doubled, rising to 48, under the care of 27 native teachers, while 47 schools were in operation, with a daily attendance of 1,300 scholars. And although during the succeeding year hundreds of the people were carried off by cholera, yet others, deeply impressed by this visitation, renounced their idolatries, and placed themselves under Christian instruction.

The visit of the deputation from the Society, Messrs. Tyerman and Bennett, in August, 1827, was the occasion of an important modification in the plan of the mission. It had been felt that the Western congregations laboured under great disadvantages in consequence of being so remote from the missionaries. It was therefore decided to divide the mission into two distinct districts, each under the charge of a European missionary. Neyoor, a small village at a distance of about ten miles west of Nāgercoil, was selected as the head-quarters of the *Western division.* Though in itself an unimportant village, it was situated in the midst of a dense population, and lay close to the large towns of Iraniyal, the head-quarters of a Tahsildar, or county magistrate, and Tiruvithāngodu, an ancient but decaying capital of the kingdom, where great numbers of blacksmiths and other branches of the Súdra caste and native Mohammedans resided.

Mr. Mault remained at Nāgercoil in charge of the *Eastern division*, with the seminary, assisted by Mr. W. B. Addis, who came out from England during this year as a schoolmaster, but was ordained after about three years' useful service in Travancore, and then founded, and long and successfully laboured, in the important mission in the town and province of Coimbatoor. Mr. Mead removed to the *Western division*, taking up his temporary residence in the meantime at Mandikādu, on the coast, until the requisite buildings should be completed at Neyoor. He was assisted by the Rev. William Miller, who also arrived about this time.

The two districts were nearly equal as to the number of schools, chapels, congregations, and native teachers. Altogether there were 26 chapels, with 2,851 native Christians of all ages (of whom 535 were baptized), 33 native teachers, or catechists, 95 schoolmasters, with 1,916 children under Christian instruction. Very discriminating but encouraging testimony was borne by the Deputation to the character of the work then in progress. "We had several opportunities," they wrote, "of seeing all the native teachers, as they assemble once a week at Nāgercoil to report to the brethren their labours, and to receive instruction and seek encouragement and admonition, such as it may be deemed necessary to give. Nearly the whole, it is hoped, are pious and consistent men and efficient labourers, possessed of good common sense and a competent knowledge of theology; they appear to be much devoted to their work, and we had every reason to be satisfied with their qualifications and their labours. They are essential auxiliaries to this vast and extended mission. With them is the superintendence of the schools; they likewise assemble the people in the chapels on Lord's days and other occasions, and read and explain to them the Word of God, and go from house to house catechising men, women, and children. The schools we found in general to be in good condition. The girls' school under the care of Mrs. Mault is in an excellent state, and does her much credit. Twelve of the (forty) girls learn to make lace, some of which is exceedingly well done; the children in this school and the seminary are entirely supported, clothed, fed, and educated from the proceeds of land given for this purpose, and the sale of the lace made by the girls. The seminary contains thirty-one boys; this institution is in a good state. The printing establishment appears to be conducted with efficiency. We are most highly gratified with the general aspect of this mission. The whole is exceedingly encouraging."

But the remarkable progress of the Gospel, the increase of agencies, and the formation of new congregations and mission stations, now attracted the attention and awoke the opposition of the enemies of Christianity, and the fires of persecution soon began to rage. Throughout the whole history of the Travancore mission it has been found, that as each step of marked progress was achieved, the attention of the heathen was necessarily drawn to the fact, their jealousy and hatred were aroused, and attempts were made to put a stop, by violence and outrage, to the spread of divine truth.

The question has been asked—Why do the disturbances which have arisen in connection with the spread of *Protestant* Christianity in Travancore not occur between *Roman Catholics* and heathens? The reply seems to us obvious. There is, in the first place, less difference between Romanists and Hindus than between Protestants and Hindus. The Romanists are by no means so well instructed, either in scriptural or secular knowledge, as our people are. The native Romanists are admitted much more readily to baptism and communion with the church than are those who apply to us. In common with Hindus they practise image-worship, processions, and pompous ceremonies. They observe caste to some extent, and have often separate chapels for worshippers of different castes. Hence they do not excite the jealousy of other castes by rising in the scale of enlightenment and civilization, but have remained for nearly three hundred years stationary in these respects, while our converts have mostly escaped from the power of hard masters, and have in fifty or sixty years risen amazingly in character and position. Nor is there anything like the active converting agency at work amongst Roman Catholics that is carried on in our mission. Very few are added to their numbers from heathenism, which therefore has not much cause to fear them on this ground. The Romish congregations, too, are chiefly situated in the maritime districts, where they have existed for so long a time that they are looked on as a familiar and established class, and as an integral portion of the population.

In the early period of our mission history some of the converts were slaves, and these, at the period of which we write, were being educated and enlightened, so that it was evident to their masters that it would soon be impracticable to hold such persons longer in a condition of servitude. One of our principal catechists was a slave all his life, but somehow after his conversion his master never claimed his services. Súdra ascendency appeared to be about to diminish, and fewer opportunities and means of oppression remained to them. As the Shānar and other Christian converts advanced in education and enterprise, and improved in worldly circumstances, it was most natural that they should not so tamely, as before, endure the injustice and oppression to which they had been exposed from the higher castes. The Súdras could not brook the advancement of the inferior classes, who were now rising through education and religion to an equality with themselves. In the persecutions which followed, heathens, Romanists, and Mohammedans, all alarmed at the progress of Christianity, united against the rising Christian community. The Súdras, however, were foremost in action, the Brahmans and others standing behind the scenes and appearing but little in the matter.

Attempts, too, had recently been made by Mr. Miller to

establish a mission in Trevandrum, but permission to do so was refused by the Government. Still it was feared that this polluting Christian religion would, unless severe measures were used, ultimately find its way into the sacred capital itself.

CHRISTIAN FEMALE, WITH JACKET AND UPPER CLOTH.

The specific and ostensible subject of dispute, however, was the wearing of certain articles of dress by the Christian women. To maintain the laws of caste, it had been found necessary to enforce several arbitrary and indecent restrictions respecting dress, as well as distance and deportment; otherwise, a person of low caste, dressing and wearing ornaments like those of the high castes, might approach them nearer than was permitted, or even pass, in the courts, markets, and other places of public resort, as of the higher castes. It had therefore always been forbidden to Shānars, and others of inferior caste, to cover the bosom or to wear any clothing whatever above the waist.

But the truer and better instincts of humanity had been aroused by Christianity, and the Christian females were accustomed and taught to wear a kind of plain loose jacket with short sleeves, devised by one of the missionary ladies. This of itself was displeasing to the Súdra aristocracy. And in addition to the jacket (which is not worn by the Súdra females) some of the Christian women, without the consent of the missionaries, and even in several instances in opposition to their advice, had taken the liberty of wearing an additional cloth or scarf laid over the shoulder, called the "upper cloth," as worn by the Súdra women, and this the latter interpreted as an infringement of their peculiar and exclusive privilege.

On the whole, then, it was determined that by some means, or by any means, a stop must be put to the progress of Christianity and to the spread of the reforms and innovations already in progress and impending.

The persecution commenced about the middle of 1827, and continued till 1830. The storm raged chiefly in the Western division of the mission, although a part of its fury extended to the Eastern division. The opposition to the truth commenced in threatening language, and afterwards proceeded to overt acts of personal assault, annoyance, and public outrage. Threats were uttered that the missionaries would be assassinated, and their chapels, schoolrooms, and houses set on fire; the erection of the Neyoor mission-house, then in process of building, was forcibly hindered. It became necessary to guard the mission buildings night after night. Several chapels and school-houses were actually burnt down to the ground by incendiaries, and the erection of new ones prevented by the threats and violence of the Súdras. A native gentleman of high caste, Rāman Tambi, who had proved himself friendly to the missionaries, and had ventured to sell them the ground on which they were erecting the mission-house at Neyoor, was seized and imprisoned on false charges, and was not released for seven years. The native converts were falsely accused, thrown into prison, and sometimes removed from place to place for months, so as to conceal the place of their confinement. Heathen Shānars and Pariahs were sent, under the guise of inquirers, to act as spies and carry their report to the persecuting party. Some of the schools were interrupted, and the books torn and cast into the street. Menaces were used to deter the native Christians from attending public worship; men were seized on the Sabbath, and compelled to work on that day; women were insulted and beaten in the bazars; and alarm and terror spread amongst the timid people in every direction.

Among the Christians seized at one place were the schoolmaster and the principal man of the village, who had recently embraced Christianity; the house of the schoolmaster they first plundered and then burnt. The house of another respectable native, whom, with others, they had falsely charged with murder, they broke open, robbed, and, he himself being absent, seized his three sons. At length their outrages became so alarming and intolerable as to render it absolutely necessary to apply for military aid, which was at once afforded, and was the means of checking for the time the further violence of the assailants.

One poor man was tied to the hind leg of an elephant, and ill-treated for refusing to do forced labour without pay. Mr. Ashton had to accompany several women, who had been shamefully beaten, and whose clothing had been publicly torn off, to the Dewān, Venkata Row, who had been sent to investigate into these disturbances. They went, wrote Mr. Ashton, to a large building in the fort at Palpanābhapuram, where the Dewān held his court. The Súdra Sepoys would not allow the women to pass the gateway covered, so they had to remove their cloths and reclothe themselves after entering. They found the Dewān surrounded by a large guard in full uniform, together with the Government officials (*all* of high caste) and the head men of the Súdra villages, all filled with rage at the unfortunate Christians, and awaiting their arrival. The tumult was great, but the missionary was kindly received by the Dewān, who recommended the Christian women to place their cloths across the bosom instead of over the shoulders. After a few inquiries, he advised all to live at peace together and maintain the ancient customs without change, promising that a proclamation with regard to the use of the upper cloth should soon be issued.

This proclamation appeared on 29th February, 1829, but afforded no relief to the Christians, nor any extension of liberty as to the use of decent and convenient clothing. In it the Christians were blamed for desiring to wear the upper cloth "contrary to orders and ancient customs," and were charged with refusing to perform the Government service. The use of the upper cloth was absolutely prohibited, the jacket only being allowed. Exemption from Sunday labour and from employment in idolatrous service was granted. An appeal was made to the precepts of Christianity, as "inculcating humility and obedience to superiors;" totally ignoring the fact that the whole genius of the Christian religion leads to advancement in civilization and decency, and destroys the possibility of slavery and tyranny. The regulation as to obtaining the permission of Government for the erection of chapels, &c., was repeated, and strong hints given against the interference of the missionaries, who had sought to aid their people by constitutional means in bringing their grievances before the notice of the Government. Promises were made of redress in the courts of justice; but these were presided over at that time, almost without exception, by corrupt and partial Brahmans and Súdras, so that the poor had no access to them on just or equal terms.

But again the providence of God overruled the vile passions of man for His own purposes and the advancement of His kingdom, so that the cause of Christianity was eventually a gainer. Even while this severe persecution was going on, and the violence and cruelty were at their highest pitch, the people flocked to the Christian congregations from all directions, voluntarily demolishing with their own hands their shrines and idols, some of them bringing their gods of gold, silver, brass, and wood, and the instruments of idolatry, which they surrendered to the missionaries. "So mightily grew the word of God, and prevailed."

Meanwhile the Quilon Malayālim Mission had again been resuscitated by the Rev. J. C. Thompson, who arrived in November, 1827, and at once commenced the study of the language and established several additional village schools. Mr. Thompson continued to toil on steadily amid many trials, discouragements, and difficulties, for twenty-three years, until his death in 1850. He was joined in 1832 by Rev. William Harris, but within a short time he also was compelled, by failure of health, to return to England. During Mr. Thompson's lifetime, boarding schools for boys and girls, village schools, and the printing press were in operation. There was a gradual though slow increase of converts. In 1837 a church was formed, composed of six individuals, in reference to which event Mr. Thompson wrote in the church book, "Praised be God that even after ten years' labour in India I see a few subscribing themselves on the Lord's side." At his death there were about 200 persons under Christian instruction in the district of Quilon.

In 1834 the Rev. Charles Miller (not related to *William* Miller) arrived at Neyoor to assist Mr. Mead. Charles Miller died in 1841, after seven years' faithful labour in the service of the Lord.

The twenty years from 1817 to 1837 may be regarded as the *second* period of the history of the mission, including the labours of Messrs. Mead, Mault, and others.

PAREYCHALEY MISSION STATION.

(Face pag . 117.)

CHAPTER XXI.

EXTENSION AND PROGRESS OF THE MISSION.

Reinforcement of the Mission, and Occupation of New Stations—Description of Trevandrum—Medical Mission—Sudden Death of Mr. Leitch.

A NEW era—that of extension and rapid progress under the third set of missionaries—commenced in 1838, with the arrival of six new brethren and their wives appointed to reinforce the important and flourishing mission in Travancore. Mr. Mead had paid a visit to England, and successfully pleaded the cause of the Travancore Mission; and now returned with the Rev. Messrs. Abbs, Cox, Russell, and Pattison, missionaries, and Mr. A. Ramsay, a medical practitioner, as an assistant and medical missionary. These brethren reached their destination at the end of March, 1838. Scarcely had they landed ere the mission suffered a serious loss in the death of William Miller, of Nāgercoil, who had been suffering to some extent for nearly three years previously. Arrangements were at once made for extending operations, and increasing the number of mission districts. The district of Nāgercoil was therefore subdivided, and the eastern part of this district, including a number of congregations in Tinnevelly connected with the Travancore Mission, was placed under the charge of Mr. Russell. He erected a bungalow about nine miles east of Nāgercoil, close to the frontier, and established a Christian village which he called Jamestown. The surrounding country closely resembles that of Tinnevelly, being flat, sandy, and dry, with numerous palm forests and extensive rice-fields. Here Mr. Russell laboured with characteristic energy and affection, for the lengthened period of twenty-three years.

Mr. Abbs took up his residence for about seven years at Neyoor, but with the special charge of the north-western portion of that district. In 1845, however, he removed to the bungalow which had then been completed at Pāreychāley, about fifteen miles from Neyoor. This village thus became the head-quarters of a mission district which has prospered and increased to a marvellous extent, containing at the present time ninety-three congregations, and 10,999 native Christians under the charge of one European missionary,—probably the largest mission station in the world.

Pāreychāley is a small village on the highway from Trevandrum to the Cape. It contains a Hindu temple of some antiquity and importance. The surrounding scenery is most delightful. "The house," wrote Mr. Leitch, "is situated on the top of a hill, and overlooks one of the most lovely landscapes which I ever saw. Hill and dale enriched and variegated by the richest vegetation, the sun of the tropics pouring a flood of light on the scene, and the cooling breeze from the adjoining coast, rendering the situation of the beholder comfortable, left nothing to be conceived of as much grander or more pleasing." Here Mr. Abbs was privileged to labour incessantly and devotedly for twenty-two years. An interesting narrative of his experience during this period has recently issued from the press.*

Medical missions have long been valuable auxiliaries to missionary agency. Attracted by the benevolence and skill exercised in healing their diseases, the heathen are prepared to lend a willing ear to the truths of the gospel proclaimed

* "Twenty-two Years' Missionary Experience in Travancore." London, Snow & Co.

to them at the same time. And no form of Christian effort, perhaps, more closely approaches in spirit and character to the life-work of our blessed Lord himself. Yet, of course, this is but one of several forms of evangelistic agency, and should not be exalted to the exclusion of predicatory and educational efforts, to which it can in practice be but auxiliary. No form of Christian labour has been neglected or left untried by the London Missionary Society. Mr. Ramsay

SEMINARY AT NAGERCOIL.

opened the medical mission at Nāgercoil, and during the first three months treated upwards of 1,500 new cases. He drew up an appeal for assistance to procure medicines and erect an hospital, which was liberally responded to by the native and European communities. This work for a time seemed full of promise. "I am happy to say," wrote Mr. Ramsay, "that people of every caste, even the Brahmans, flock to me for advice. I have now free access amongst them, and have great reason to believe that much good will be done. When the people are in health it is difficult to get them at times to listen to what is good, but when laid on a bed of sickness and conceiving themselves to be dying, then I find they will listen attentively, and I have been told by several on their recovery that they have thought of what I said, and have felt anxious to know more of the Christian religion."

But, unhappily, after about two years Mr. Ramsay accepted a secular engagement, and relinquished his connection with the mission, so that this important department of effort was allowed to fall into abeyance until again renewed by Mr. Leitch in 1853. The handsome building erected by Mr. Ramsay at Nāgercoil for an hospital, is now appropriated to the use of the English seminary.

Trevandrum, the capital of Travancore, is situated in N. Lat. 8° 30′; E. Long. 76° 59′. The time at Trevandrum, therefore, is five hours eight minutes later than Greenwich time. A telegram sent in the evening from Trevandrum, if not delayed, would reach London at noon of the same day. The town lies within two miles of the sea-coast, and a little west of the Karamana river. The site is low but uneven, being much intersected by brooks and streams, with level or terraced rice-fields on either bank. Occasionally the ground rises into little eminences to the height of between one and two hundred feet above the level of the sea.

The town consists of a Fort with the houses immediately surrounding it, and several suburbs. The Fort is about half a mile square, and is surrounded by a high wall, principally of mud, and in some parts of granite, but of no strength as a defence. Its only value to the Brahmans and other high castes who reside inside the Fort is to prevent the ingress of persons of low caste, the gates being carefully guarded by Sepoys, and no low caste people allowed to pass. But the walls hinder the fresh air from circulating in the narrow streets and badly ventilated houses on the low and swampy grounds which they enclose, so that the more intelligent and wealthy classes now find it necessary to have houses in the country, to which they can retire for the benefit of the pure air and fine scenery. Within the Fort is the Palace (built partly in the European style, and richly furnished with European furniture, paintings, clocks, &c.), with its various detached dwelling-houses, outhouses, gardens, and courtyards. Here also are situated the Government offices, the official residence of the Dewān, the mint, the jail, and last, not least, the temple of Patmanābhan, with its lofty tower and sacred tank. In the streets within the Fort there are 878 houses, with a high caste population of 4,557, nearly all Brahmans.

East of the Fort and immediately adjacent lies the "*Chālei Bazar*," the centre of the native town. The principal street is formed by rows of shops, open at the front like those of greengrocers in England, in which rice and other grains, curry stuffs, roots, fruits, and provisions of every kind, cloth and ornaments, boxes, brass and tin ware, books, stationery, &c., are exposed for sale. The close and impure atmosphere is laden with vile smells of every conceivable description. Crowds of people constantly pass and repass to and from the Fort, and are engaged in making purchases and transacting business.

Manacaud, on the south, is to a large extent the Mohammedan quarter; here the royal stables are situated. The "*Pettah*," on the north-west, contains numerous houses and gardens of East Indians,—Portuguese and Dutch descendants,—most of whom are Roman Catholics, and in poor circumstances. The East Indians in Trevandrum number 458 individuals of all ages.

North-east of the Fort lies the "*Cantonment*," formerly

occupied by British troops, and now by the Nair Brigade and their European officers. Here also are situated the English church, in which the chaplain of the station officiates; the observatory, recently closed; the civil hospital, museum, and botanical gardens; and in this locality the new range of public offices has recently been erected. To the east of the cantonment, the British Residency and lines for the Sepoy guard are situated.

The public roads are now in excellent order, and within the last few years very considerable and striking improvements, in public buildings and the general appearance of the town, have been effected. Viewed from a little distance, nothing is visible except the tops of the waving cocoa-nut trees and of the jack, mango, and tamarind trees with which every house is surrounded, and perhaps the towers of the great temple and of the English church, and the roofs of some other public buildings.

Such is Trevandrum of the present day. By the census of 1865 it appears that the population is 51,718, of which 5,700 are Brahmans, 23,000 Súdras, 3,500 native Christians of all sects, 4,600 Mohammedans, 70 Europeans, and the remainder low caste Hindus.

Between the town and the sea extends a beach of white sand, about three quarters of a mile in width, dry, arid, and barren, in some parts covered with the bleached remains of the friendless and pauper dead buried in the sands, and too often dug up again and devoured by the jackals. Close to the sea is the small village of Valiatory, the port, such as it is, of Trevandrum, with a custom-house and granary. The inhabitants of this hamlet are fishermen and Shānars, mostly Romanists. But a small congregation of Protestants was formed here in the year 1823. After permission had been refused to William Miller to settle in Trevandrum itself, it was thought that a missionary might perhaps be permitted to reside at Valiatory, and thus operate ultimately on the capital. Mr. Addis had accordingly been appointed to this station, and procured a piece of ground and attempted to settle; but even this was decidedly forbidden by the native Government, which at that time opposed every effort that was made to establish a Christian mission at or near the capital.

In 1838, however, Mr. Cox succeeded, through the decided patronage of General Fraser, the British Resident, in obtaining from the Rajah a grant of a piece of waste ground on which mission premises were erected. "Mr. Cox found in the whole district about forty professing Christians, of whom two were baptized. He found also a relative of the Rajah's family, named Samuel Tumby, who was baptized by Mr. Ringeltaube, and maintained some profession of Christianity; enough to subject him to the deprivation of his property, but not enough to cause his light to shine as a decided follower of Christ. He continued to attend occasionally on the instruction of the missionary, but at last disappeared in a manner which could never be cleared up. By the end of the first year the number of professors had increased to 107."

At this station Mr. Cox laboured without intermission for twenty-three years.

Mr. Pattison joined Mr. Thompson at Quilon, where he laboured until recalled by the Directors about seven years afterwards.

Thus several new stations were opened, the mission invigorated with new life, and evangelizing operations actively carried on during the period under review.

Other missionaries, too, shared for a time in the working of the mission. Rev. J. O. Whitehouse arrived in 1842, and for fifteen years had charge of the seminary, in which he laboured with great success in the training of a native agency. Many useful and well-qualified native teachers, now in the mission, were trained by Mr. Whitehouse during this period.

In 1846, Rev. Ebenezer Lewis removed from Coimbatoor, where he had been labouring for several years previously, and undertook the charge of the western portion of the Nāgercoil district. A handsome and well-finished bungalow was built at Sānthapuram about five miles south-west of

NEYOOR DISPENSARY.

Nāgercoil, and in this district Mr. Lewis spent about sixteen years, until compelled by ill-health to return to England. He was one of the most eloquent preachers and best scholars in the Tamil language in South India.

About the middle of 1852, Rev. C. C. Leitch, M.R.C.S.E., arrived at Neyoor to recommence the medical mission established by Mr. Ramsay, and to take the superintendence of the Neyoor district. Mr. Mead having now retired from active participation in mission work, Mr. Leitch devoted some months to a preliminary study of the language and people, &c., and to the erection of a dispensary at Neyoor, which he opened in March, 1853. Here he laboured with singular zeal and unremitting energy; and was joined in the following July by Rev. Frederic Baylis, who had previously had charge of the English Institution at Madras for three years.

But in the midst of his activity and usefulness Leitch, like Spencer of Liverpool, was suddenly cut off. On the morning of 25th August, 1853, Messrs. Baylis and Leitch resolved to go down to Muttam* on the sea-coast, about six miles from Neyoor, where Mr. and Mrs. Lewis were then spending a few days. In the evening the colleagues went together to bathe in the sea, in a place where Leitch had been accustomed to bathe on former visits to the place.

"Being remarkably quick in all his movements," wrote Mr. Baylis, "he was at the place and in the water several minutes before I was ready. We were behind some rocks, so that I could not see the part of the sea where he was till I had gone out into the water myself. I then saw him for a moment among the waves a little way out, not farther than we had both been when bathing there a few weeks before. As I was hastening to join him, in passing round the corner of a rock, a strong wave rushing past from behind threw me down, and was, as I felt in a moment, carrying me out with considerable force. I immediately struck out for the shore, and gained a footing again with some difficulty. When I recovered from the wave and looked about, I could nowhere see Mr. Leitch. For a moment I fancied he might be hidden from sight by a wave, but the next moment I felt

* See vignette on title-page.

that he must have been carried out and had sunk. I knew that it would be in vain for me to attempt to do anything alone, so I ran up the beach and called to Mr. Lewis to come quickly, as I saw him coming in the distance. He was soon on the spot, and three or four fishermen coming at the same time, they immediately ran into the water, according to our directions, and dived about in the place where Leitch had been; a boat also which had been summoned came to render assistance; but though the search was kept up, as well as the force of the waves would allow, for nearly two hours, till it became dark, nothing could be found. As we returned to the little bungalow where we were staying, it was almost impossible for us to realize the fact that our dear brother who had been amongst us that day, happy himself, and striving to make others happy, was indeed taken from us. Though every means have since been used the body has not been found."

Thus was this promising and talented missionary in a moment removed by an inscrutable providence from his people and his work. During the few months from the opening of the dispensary till his death, he had attended to 2,069 patients, and performed eighty-two operations. He was greatly beloved by the natives of all classes, and long and deeply mourned by them, as a bright and sparkling gem of Divine grace, which had sunk in the depths of the sea, but which should yet rise again resplendent and glorious, to shine like a star in the kingdom of God for ever.

One of our native Christian preachers and poets wrote on the occasion an elegy in Tamil, entitled "The Diamond lost in the Sea." The following brief (not quite literal) translation of a few of the verses will give some general idea of the style of this ode:—

INTRODUCTION.

We will shed tears and mourn over the death of Mr. Leitch, saying,—

CHORUS.

Alas! alas, thou sainted and precious one!
When shall our minds be comforted, thou beautiful Pearl?

VERSES.

Leaving parents and sisters and friends in thine own happy land,
Thou didst come through the deep raging sea to be our Teacher and Friend,
Alas! alas! &c.

And we said, "Now shall prosperity come to our land."
Thou didst heal our diseases and sorrows, gavest medicine to all who came, and clothing and food to the distressed. Why dost thou now hide thyself from our sight?
Alas! alas! &c.

Thou didst build Hospitals and Almshouses:
Hadst thou, our Benefactor, lived but a few years more, our poverty would fly away and disappear.
Alas! alas! &c.

Thou didst feel the value of our souls, and speak with loving words the Doctrine of Life:—
We weep for thee, our golden Jewel.
Alas! alas! &c.

We joyed to think that thou hadst come instead of Mr. Miller, who was cut off from our midst;
But now we mourn for thee also.
Alas! alas! &c.

Thou wert beautiful in face and form, ever diligent and useful:
Hast thou been taken to heaven, like Enoch and Elijah?
Suddenly thou hast gone, and we cannot find thee, O our Treasure.
Alas! alas! &c.

If thou hadst told us the time of thy departure, we should have saluted thee with both hands and kissed thy feet;
But thou hast been removed from us for our wickedness; thou art most happy, but we mourn.
Alas! alas! &c.

Thy dear aged parents and pious sisters shall weep for thee with streaming tears!
Let us follow the exhortation and example of our holy teacher, and meet him in Heaven!
O heavenly Lord! the Source of life! do Thou send another missionary to do good to the people!

Alas! alas! &c.

Thus amid difficulties and discouragements, loss of missionaries and occasional opposition from the heathens, the Christian congregations continued to increase and spread, so that in 1858, when other important events affected the state and prosperity of the mission, there were seven principal stations, with seven European missionaries; 210 congregations, with 16,939 native professing Christians, of whom 2,195 were baptized, and 980 in full communion with the church. Amongst these, 394 native catechists and schoolmasters were at work.

CHAPTER XXII.

RECENT HISTORY OF THE MISSION.

The "Upper Cloth" Riots—Their Origin, Progress, and Settlement—Sufferings from Famine and Cholera—Movement towards Christianity amongst the Slave Castes—Resuscitation and Success of Medical Mission under Dr. Lowe—Recent Changes in the Mission—Extension of Native Pastorate—Labours of Missionary Ladies.

TOWARDS the close of 1858 the powers of darkness, error, and paganism again came into direct collision with Christian truth and social freedom. The causes of the disturbances which then occurred had been in continuous operation for many years previously, and there had been occasional and isolated outbursts of fanatical hatred towards the Christian converts. The marvellous spread of Christianity amongst the Shānars, Pariahs, Ilavars, and others excited the jealousy and envy of the higher castes, and attempts were again and again made to put a stop to the progress of the Christian religion. The missionaries had often had to complain to the native Government of the oppressions practised by the Súdras on their timid and helpless converts. Complaints were made especially in 1855, when the oppressions and lawlessness of that caste had become well-nigh intolerable. Mr. Cox brought forward the case of Devasagāyam, who, with his wife and several others, were seized and put in confinement for refusing to sign an agreement to perform certain work at the palace without pay. The unfortunate man was shockingly ill-treated, and died from the effects of the torture. His widow and the others were released after six days' confinement in the stocks.

A number of Ilavars in A'ttungal, the estate of the Rānees of Travancore, had embraced Christianity. They were therefore severely persecuted by the local officials, who declared that they would not suffer any Christians to remain there. One man, Thomas Paul, was assaulted in his house, beaten and dragged till he was insensible, and then taken to prison, where he was kept many days, and released only when he became so ill that they were afraid he would die. Another man was stopped by the persecutors one Sabbath morning while he was on his way to divine worship, reviled for being a Christian, and beaten so severely that he lay ill in the chapel for some days.

Mr. Whitehouse reported the case of Arumeināyagam, a converted slave, who was beaten by his master, Mādan Pillei, and another Súdran for attending Christian worship. Although the serious injuries inflicted on the poor man were certified in detail by the Court physician, Dr. Reed, a mere nominal fine of only five rupees each was inflicted by the magistrate on his assailants. But an appeal being made to the Madras Government, the fines were increased to seventy rupees, and the Travancore authorities were reproved for their unjust lenity.

Other cases of oppression and cruelty were represented in detail to the Government of Madras, and a petition was presented detailing facts which proved the political condition of Travancore to be deplorably bad. The police, it was shown, was an engine of iniquity and oppression. Subjects were seized and imprisoned without any specific charges being brought against them, or were detained in confinement without investigation, and perhaps eventually acquitted only after an imprisonment extending over several years. Bribes were accepted to let off culprits, and tortures inflicted to force confession. The character of the high officials was shown to be bad, some having even been before their appointment convicted as criminals. The courts themselves were corrupt. A system of forced labour for Government supplies existed, which opened a wide door for oppression. Monopolies in pepper and other articles prevented the development of free trade and the material resources of the country. These and other prevalent evils were fully exposed. Early in 1856, the Rajah was addressed upon the subject by Lord Harris, then Governor of Madras. His Highness acknowledged that there was some ground for complaint, and stated that he was endeavouring to improve matters as far as possible.

The Rajah, however, was more devoted to superstition and asceticism than to the study of political economy. Though personally kind and well meaning, he was not possessed of sufficient firmness and courage to carry out needed reforms in opposition to the obstacles which lay in his way. The Dewān, too, who died in 1858, had been a most corrupt and unscrupulous character. The British Resident, General Cullen, who had occupied this important post since 1840, though kind and courteous in manners, generous in his gifts, and scientific in his tastes, was completely under the influence of Brahman favourites, adopted their views, and saw no necessity for missionary labours, or the Christian instruction of the poor. He was thoroughly "Hindooized" by an uninterrupted residence of nearly fifty years in India.

Another element of irritation on the part of the Súdras was the liberation of the slaves in 1855. Although these have not had the spirit and courage to avail themselves of their legal rights to any considerable extent, yet those of them who had embraced Christianity necessarily became more intelligent and industrious, and generally sought their freedom.

Perhaps, too, some of the expressions in the proclamation of the Queen's supremacy and direct rule over India, declaring that "none should be in any wise favoured, none molested or disquieted by reason of their religious faith or observances," and enjoining "all those who may be in authority that they abstain from all interference with the religious belief or worship of any" of the people, were either erroneously or wilfully misinterpreted by the Súdras, as forbidding missionary efforts and the public proclamation of Christian truth.

The great questions in dispute were those connected with the Christian and Hindu religions, caste and progress, rigid conservatism and liberal reform. But, as on former occasions, the immediate and ostensible subject of dispute was that of dress, especially the use of the "upper cloth;" and on this occasion heathen and Christian Shānars were united in opinion and sentiment. A whole race of men were not for ever to be retained in such a condition of prostration and subservience as that in which the Shānars had been kept. Many of this caste in the south of Travancore emigrate with their families to the British province of Tinnevelly, in search of employment during certain seasons of the year. There their women are quite at liberty, and are accustomed to clothe themselves above the waist decently, and on their return to the native state naturally retain that covering.

About October and November, 1858, indications of the general ill-feeling of the Súdras towards the Christians became more marked. A Christian woman was assaulted in the public market at Neyyāttunkara, and her jacket torn. The case was proved in the police court, yet the offender was let off with so slight a punishment by fine that he soon afterwards committed several similar crimes. Next the Súdras gave out that an order had been issued by the Government to strip the women of their jackets, and they threatened that they would soon carry it into effect; crowds in the markets hustled the Christians, and spat and threw earth on them. But after the visit of Lord Harris, Governor of Madras, to the Rajah in the beginning of December, and the reading of the Queen's proclamation in the middle of the month, the violence of the Súdras increased. Reports were circulated to the effect that Lord Harris had given over the entire management of the kingdom into the Rajah's hands, no longer to be controlled by the British Government, and that, consequently, the Rajah would not tolerate Christianity in his territory, and that the Súdras and others would be unchecked in any opposition they might show to Christianity.

Accordingly, on the 25th December, the Athigāri, or sub-magistrate of Pāreychāley, being remonstrated with on the illegal cutting down of a tree, exclaimed that the missionary had been deprived of authority, as the country was "*no longer under the power of the Company from whom he derived his salary.*" Shortly afterwards another Athigāri went to a market near Pāreychāley, and declaring that he had authority from the Government to do so, insulted several Shānar women, and took off their cloths and jackets. These examples were followed by others. The most extravagant reports were circulated respecting the extinction of the British power, and the liberty which had been given to murder Europeans and destroy their property. The agitation continued in the Pāreychāley district for about twenty days; during which time three chapels and three smaller places for worship were set on fire and destroyed.

In the district of Neyoor, adjoining that of Pāreychāley, opportunities were taken to rob and ill-treat many of the poorer classes. Among others, one of the catechists, Gurupātham, had a large mango tree yielding fruit cut down by some of the officials, without any compensation being made. He complained to the authorities, and an inquiry was promised, but a few days after they came to cut up the tree for firewood. The son of the catechist, who happened to be present, remonstrated, and was well beaten for doing so. His cries brought his father and mother to the spot, when they were seized and beaten till they were insensible. The poor woman, who had recently been confined, long suffered from the cruelty inflicted on her, and her husband appeared to have sustained some internal injury, and has not been well since. The Tahsildar refused to attend to the case, but it was, on the representation of Mr. Baylis, taken up by the Peishcar, fully proved, and sent to the Criminal Court. Some of the guilty parties were at last fined and removed from Government employment.

On 25th December, some Government officials, with their attendants, seized four of the Christians at Kallankuli, on pretence of taking them for Sirkar work, and tied and beat them severely. The men were carried off, kept for some days in confinement, and then dismissed. Two days after, the chapel there was burnt down during the night.

A fortnight afterwards, in the Neyoor market, a number of heathens, led by the police sergeant of Iraniyal and his men, beat many men and women, plundered their goods, money, and jewels, and then bound a number of Shānars, who were peaceably engaged in their usual occupations in the market, and took them to the prison. The disturbance appears to have commenced through some *heathen* Shānar women wearing the upper cloth. Other acts of violence were committed in the Christian village at Neyoor. The police sergeant was, on examination, suspended from office, and a few of the rioters merely *fined* and bound over to keep the peace. On the same night another chapel at Vadakkankarei was burnt down, and a third a few nights afterwards.

Charges against the parties accused of burning these three chapels, and threatening to burn others, were laid before the

Criminal Court at Nāgercoil. Every effort was made by the clerks of the court to get their Súdra friends acquitted. The first judge openly sided with the accused parties. They were let out on bail, while Shānars charged with comparatively trifling offences were kept in confinement and *in fetters* before trial. The Súdras were allowed, in open court, to bully and threaten the witnesses and pleaders for the complainants. Except in one case, that of burning the Gunamkādu school-house, where the criminals were sentenced to hard labour for periods of from one to three years (half the term of sentence was afterwards remitted), the accused parties were, as might be expected, acquitted on the ground of the want of sufficient evidence, though a few were bound over to keep the peace for a year or so on suspicion.

In the Sānthapuram district the Athigāri sent police to apprehend the catechist of Kulattuvilei on Sunday, 23rd January, 1859, while the congregation were assembling for divine worship. The teacher pleaded exemption from seizure on account of the day; but, although the peons said there was no charge against him, they compelled him to accompany them to the Athigāri. This official furiously reviled the Christian teacher and the missionaries, had the clothes stripped off the catechist and torn to shreds, and then had him put in the stocks and beaten very severely. He was kept in prison for a week before he was set at liberty.

But it was in Nāgercoil district that the rage of the Súdras burst forth with the greatest violence.

On January 4th upwards of 200 Súdras and others entered the houses of the Christians at Tālakudi, armed with clubs and knives, &c., and attacked the inhabitants, stripping the jackets off the women, tearing their clothes, and cruelly beating and kicking them. They also laid plans to destroy the catechist and schoolmaster of the place, and to burn down their houses and the mission chapel. Consequently the chapel was closed for some weeks, and the village deserted by the Christians.

Three days afterwards a mob of about 500 Súdras, *headed by Government officials*, came by day to Kumārapuram, armed with clubs, swords, &c., in search of the Christians, and of the catechist and his wife. The latter had, however, made their escape; but another catechist, on a visit to his friends in the village, was seized, cruelly beaten, and sent into confinement. The mob forcibly entered the houses of the Christians, broke and pillaged the furniture, and dragged the poor defenceless women out of doors almost naked, tearing their cloths and jackets, and committing the most insulting acts.

Similar attacks were made on the Christians at A'rāmbuli and Sembanvilei. At the latter village the mob pulled down the house of the catechist, plundered the money, jewels, and furniture which they found, belonging both to the catechist and to the other Christians, tore up the books, and beat the schoolmaster and some of the people in a most cruel manner.

The next day, Sunday, the same crowd entered the chapel at Kāttuputhúr during the time of service, drove out the catechist and congregation, tore the books to pieces, and locked the chapel and took away the key. On the night of the 10th a small bungalow at Nāgercoil belonging to the Government was burnt down. Shortly afterwards several Shānar houses at Tittuvilei, and seventy-nine houses of Romanists at Kottār, were burnt down.

On the 29th a chapel near Nāgercoil, and on the 31st another chapel in one village and three houses of Shānars in another, in the Jamestown district, were burnt. Altogether nine chapels and three school-houses were destroyed. Many of the surrounding villages were now wholly deserted by the Christians. Congregations were deprived of their native teachers, and the public services therefore ceased; the roads by which the Christians went to the markets and other public places were closed against them, and terror everywhere prevailed. In all these scenes of lawless violence it was observed that the minor officials of Government and the police took a prominent part.

Again the missionaries, as the main cause of the introduction of Christianity into the country, were threatened with assassination. Gross abuse was lavished upon them even by the inferior servants of Government. Their houses were to be burnt and themselves driven out of the country. They and their families were thus kept in a state of constant alarm. They were obliged to have guards at their residences, and were unable to venture into some parts of the country to visit their people and schools. "Fifteen and a half parts out of sixteen of your religion are gone," boasted the heathen, "and the remaining portion will very soon fly off, like cotton wool at a single blow of the mouth." "Your God," said they, "has taken His flight."

On December 27th, soon after the commencement of these troubles, a proclamation was made by the Dewān in reference to the disturbances, intimating that "it is clearly wrong to violate ancient *usage* without authority," and that "whoever does so in future shall be *severely punished*. Shānars are to hear this, and act accordingly," while "Súdras and people of the higher caste are not to do anything themselves against the Shānars, or to break the peace. If they do so, it will become necessary *to inquire into* their conduct." The gross and unconcealed partiality indicated by the different expressions used in this proclamation towards the Súdras and the Shānars was carried out in the whole proceedings, as far as the minor officials and inferior courts were concerned. While the case of the Súdras, accused of the serious crimes of incendiarism, riot, and assault, was speedily disposed of, that of the Shānars, accused of "*threatening* to raise a rebellion," was protracted by various means for months, during which time they were rigorously imprisoned and fettered. And in the discussions which followed this eventful period, the native officials, and even the British Resident, endeavoured to throw the blame of what had occurred as much as possible upon the Christians themselves. It was evidently taken for granted, *à priori*, that *the Christians* must be the parties in fault.

Early in February a petition from the missionaries was presented to H. H. the Rajah, but this having produced no satisfactory result, the entire case was eventually referred to the investigation and decision of the Madras Government; and through the prompt and effectual interposition of Sir Charles Trevelyan, Governor of Madras, the right of the Shānar women to observe the rules of decency in their attire was at length partially and grudgingly recognised by the Travancore Government.

"I have seldom," wrote Sir Charles to the Resident, "met with a case in which not only truth and justice, but every feeling of our common humanity are so entirely on one side. The whole civilized world would cry shame upon us if we did not make a firm stand on such an occasion. If anything could make this line of conduct more incumbent on us, it would be the extraordinary fact that persecution of a singularly personal and delicate kind is attempted to be justified by a royal proclamation, the special object of which was to assure to her Majesty's Indian subjects liberty of thought and action so long as they did not interfere with the just rights of others. I should fail in respect to her Majesty if I attempted to describe the feelings with which she must regard the use made against her own sex of the promises of protection so graciously accorded by her."

"It will be your duty to impress these views on his Highness the Rajah, and to point out to him that such prohibitions as those contained in the Circular Order of May, 1814, or in the Proclamation of the 3rd of February, 1829, are unsuited to the present age, and unworthy of an enlightened Prince."

Thus urged, the native Government promised "to abolish all rules prohibiting the covering of the upper parts of the persons of Shānar women, with the simple restriction of the same mode of dress that appertains to the higher castes."

This concession was accepted by the Madras Government "as a practical earnest, on the part of the Rajah, of his desire to put an end to the barbarous and indecent restrictions previously existing on the dress of the Shānar women."

The long-expected Proclamation at last appeared, on 26th July, 1859. It ran as follows, translated literally:—"Inasmuch as we have been informed of the grievance occasioned by the Proclamation of the 23rd of Magaram, 1004, on the subject of the upper cloth of Shānar women, and it is our will and pleasure to treat all people, as far as we can, in such a manner as none shall feel aggrieved; we hereby proclaim that there is no objection to Shānar women either putting on a jacket, like the Christian Shānar women, or to Shānar women of all creeds dressing in *course* cloth, and tying themselves round with it as the Mukkavattigal (low caste fisherwomen) do, or to their covering their bosoms in any manner whatever; but not like women of high castes."

A similar Proclamation was in 1864 issued with respect to the females of the Ilavar and all other inferior castes. Still the necessities of the case with regard to the Christian females have been but very partially met by this regulation. The Protestant Christian community now occupies a good position in Travancore, socially and morally. Many of the women are well educated, and trained to habits of refinement and comfort. Some are wealthy and accustomed to wear good clothing, white or coloured. A number have learnt to work embroidery or beautiful lace, for which medals have been given at some of the great Exhibitions. Yet even *such* women are forbidden to wear anything but a *coarse* cloth; and this should be tied horizontally across the breasts, leaving the shoulders bare, in the fashion of the fisherwomen—a caste whom the heathen Shānars regard as several degrees beneath them. There is no probability of the Christian women consenting to adopt this unseemly dress. Such mistaken attempts on the part of a Government to regulate by law matters of dress and social economy, in the face of advancing civilization, have ever failed in practice. The restriction, too, of so large a proportion of the people to the use of coarse materials is obviously a suicidal policy in respect to the development of commerce and manufactures. The state of the law is therefore still most unsatisfactory, and there is reason to fear that contentions will not wholly cease till all classes of the community are allowed, as in Tinnevelly and all parts of British India, full liberty to follow their own inclinations and tastes in matters of dress and personal adornment and comfort.

Again was the operation of divine Providence manifest in controlling and overruling the efforts of the heathen to obstruct the onward march of Christian truth. Even during the continuance of the riots and after their cessation, large accessions were made to the numbers of the Christian community, especially in the districts of Neyoor and Pāreychāley. Mr. Baylis was visited by the head men of several villages, who requested to be received, with their people, under the spiritual care and instruction of the missionaries. Many devil temples, large and small, were demolished, the images and other symbols and implements of idolatrous worship being destroyed or surrendered to the missionaries, and new congregations formed where hitherto the Gospel had made but little progress. During that and the succeeding year about 3,000 persons shook off the trammels of heathenism, and put themselves under Christian instruction.

While the hand of man raised against the church quickly fell palsied, and no weapon formed against her was permitted to prosper, trials more directly from the hand of God himself, in sore visitations of famine and pestilence, next fell upon the people.

The rains of the S.W. monsoon in May and June, 1860, failed almost entirely, and in consequence the rice-fields were to a large extent left uncultivated; the esculent roots, pulse, and other dry crops, perished; the palmyra yielded little juice; even cocoa-nut and other palm trees withered; food became scarce and rose to famine prices. In October, also, the rains nearly failed, and when a partial crop was in promise, a black caterpillar, before unknown to the people, appeared simultaneously in all the rice-fields, and devoured nearly all the standing crops. As the year advanced the distresses of the poor increased. Strong men were reduced to mere skeletons, and became unequal, through want of food, to sustained exertion, even when employment was obtainable. They disposed by degrees of their few articles of property and household furniture, and afterwards of their tools and garments, to buy food, and were at last compelled by hunger to eat the most unwholesome substances. Many sold their children for trifling sums to Mohammedans and others, in the hope that they would thus be fed and kept alive, while otherwise they must die of starvation before the eyes of their parents.

Soon fever, dysentery, and other diseases, appeared. About the middle of August, cholera commenced; and whether on account of the want of rain, the intense heat, or other peculiar condition of the atmosphere, or the deficiency of food, it rapidly increased to an alarming and unprecedented extent. Its ravages were most severe in the Pāreychāley and Neyoor districts, though not confined to these. Within three months there were 460 deaths out of 4,500 native Christians in the Neyoor district; and 14 native teachers and 578 others out of 5,000 in the district of Pūreychāley; hundreds besides were registered in the neighbouring districts. Altogether, about 1,500 of the native Christians were cut off, notwithstanding the exertions and care of the teachers and missionaries; and probably a much larger proportion of the heathen population perished. In some villages as many as twelve or fourteen of the Christians, besides heathens, died in one day. Several of our smaller congregations were wholly extinguished. Terror everywhere prevailed; some of the villages to which we went to preach were found deserted, the people having fled, leaving several of their relations lying ill of cholera. Many of the dead were left unburied, or simply buried in holes dug in the floor of the house where they had died, so that the Christian teachers were often occupied in burying the dead; being compelled for this purpose, in some instances, to dig the grave themselves. It was no uncommon thing to see men or women lying dead or dying in market-places or by the road-side, where their remains were devoured by jackals before there was time to bury them. Thousands of widows and orphans were left desolate:—

> "In the marsh's parched and gaping soil,
> The rice roots by the searching sun were dried;
> And in lean groups, assembled at the side
> Of the empty tank, the cattle dropt and died;
> And famine wasted wide
> The wretched land, till, in the public way
> Promiscuous, where the dead and dying lay,
> Dogs fed on human bones in the open light of day."

This have I seen; I pray that I may never be called to witness such scenes again. In this emergency appeals for aid were made to the native authorities and to English friends, to which a speedy and hearty response was made. Liberal personal contributions were given by the Maharajah, Dewān, and other native officials. Cooking-houses, at which meals of boiled rice were distributed, were opened in various localities. Beneficial public works were commenced to give employment to the labouring classes, several of the missionaries undertaking to superintend the making of new roads near their stations, at which thousands of the weak as well as the strong were employed, according to their respective capacity, to provide for their immediate wants. The friends of the mission in England, India, and elsewhere, also forwarded considerable contributions for charitable purposes, by means of which food, clothing, and medicine, were supplied to those unable to work through want and disease. Multitudes of lives were thus preserved, that otherwise must have fallen victims to hunger and disease. This proof of the sympathy of the people of England with the suffering poor of Travancore was highly appreciated by all classes of the population. "Nothing," wrote the Dewān, "can be a nobler spectacle than that of a people, thousands and thousands of miles remote from India, extending their warmest sympathies so far, and contributing so liberally, to the relief of suffering here. I have heard with admiration of the munificent sums which each successive mail has been bringing out to India for the sufferers. The spectacle is as instructive as it is noble. With such sympathies pervading the world, what splendid results may not be expected!"

Again were large accessions, amounting during 1861 to above 4,000 individuals, chiefly of the Shānar caste, made to the members of the Christian community. This was traceable, in part, to the awe produced in the minds of the heathen by the hand of God, evident in the solemn visitation of cholera, and in part to the incessant labours of the catechists, and to increased prayerfulness and effort on the part of the Christians generally. Many also were attracted and led to serious reflection by the kindness and personal influence of the missionaries and native teachers in their works of faith and labours of love.

Towards the end of 1862, a movement towards Christianity amongst the slave castes, principally Pulayars and Pariahs, commenced in the Pāreychāley district. There had often appeared a general willingness on the part of these long-degraded and enslaved people to hear and receive the glad tidings of salvation. In 1862 two small congregations, and in the succeeding year six additional congregations of this class were formed. These new adherents evinced great desire to hear and understand Christianity, and though rather dull in learning the elements of religion, were nevertheless remarkably persevering and painstaking. This work culminated in 1867, when, besides the addition of above 1,000 persons of various classes in the Neyoor district, 12 new congregations, with 2,649 new adherents, were gathered in the district of Pāreychāley. The total additions from heathenism to our Christian congregations in Travancore during that one year amounted to nearly 4,000 souls. Though generally of the lowest class, these made rapid progress in learning the truths of Christianity, and in exemplifying them in their daily lives. The writer made a tour amongst these newly gathered congregations in September, 1867, and found a remarkable spirit of earnestness, diligence, and attention amongst these poor people. Scarcely had he time, on entering the chapel in each village, to partake of some necessary refreshment ere the building was filled with people ready and waiting to hear the word of life.

They had, however, to endure a great deal of petty annoyance and persecution from the higher castes. In one instance a number of Pulayar Christians, who had been attending the markets, and using the privilege of travelling on the public roads, were, along with their catechist, assaulted and beaten by a number of Sûdras and others of high caste. The latter immediately went off to the police station, and brought a formal charge of assault *against the Christians*, and being first in the field, and belonging to the dominant caste, they had eight or nine of the Christians and the catechist thrown into prison. Here they lay for a month before a decision was come to by the native courts; they were then discharged. Their enemies had gained their point and escaped without punishment or loss, while all the Christians in the surrounding congregations were for a time thoroughly terrified. They remained faithful, however, and are now making fair progress in knowledge, piety, and liberality.

The medical mission at Neyoor, which had been left vacant since the death of Leitch, was happily revived by Rev. John Lowe, M.R.C.S.E., who arrived at the station on 21st November, 1861. The mission hospital erected by Leitch was shortly after reopened, and for seven successive years Mr. Lowe was privileged to labour with much success in this interesting sphere. During those seven years, above 37,000 patients received medical and surgical aid, besides over 11,000 individuals who were vaccinated. This extensive work was conducted free of cost to the funds of the Missionary Society,—at least, as far as medicines, instruments, hospital expenses, &c., were concerned; liberal annual contributions having been given by H.H. the Maharajah and other Hindu nobles and gentlemen, besides the British Resident and other Europeans in the country.

Patients of all ranks and castes applied for relief, and were heartily welcomed. All who came received the benefit of skilful medical aid, and were lovingly addressed by the missionary and his assistants on the subject of Christianity; many prejudices were removed, inquiry was excited, and hearts were opened to the saving reception of the truth. It was often a most interesting and delightful sight to observe persons of different and antagonistic castes thus induced to come together and listen to the Gospel message. "There might have been seen from time to time, sitting side by side under the same roof, the Brahman, Súdra, Shānar, and Pariah, the devil-worshipper and the worshipper of Siva, the Mohammedan, Roman Catholic, and Protestant Christian,—men, women, and children of all castes and creeds, listening attentively to the reading of God's word and the preaching of the Gospel. Hundreds have heard the sweet story of redeeming love, who otherwise, in all human probability, would have lived and died without once having heard the glad tidings." Dr. Lowe writes again,—"There lived together in the same room in the hospital for nearly two months a young Brahman and his mother; a Súdra, his wife and brother; and a Shānar boy and his mother; besides patients of other castes who were admitted for shorter periods. The Brahman youth had a compound fracture of the right leg, and a simple fracture of the left leg; the Súdra had fracture of the skull, with a severe scalp wound; and the Shānar boy had a compound fracture of the thigh, and simple fracture of both arms, the result of a fall from a palmyra tree. For the time being, at least, broken bones levelled their caste distinctions, and created a bond of sympathy between them. They all made good recoveries, and left the hospital very thankful for the attention and kindness they had received."

In November, 1864, a class was commenced for the study of medicine and surgery, and for the training of a few native young men as medical assistants or dressers, to take charge of branch dispensaries in the mission districts. From each mission district an intelligent youth, well educated in English, was selected and sent to Neyoor, and was care-

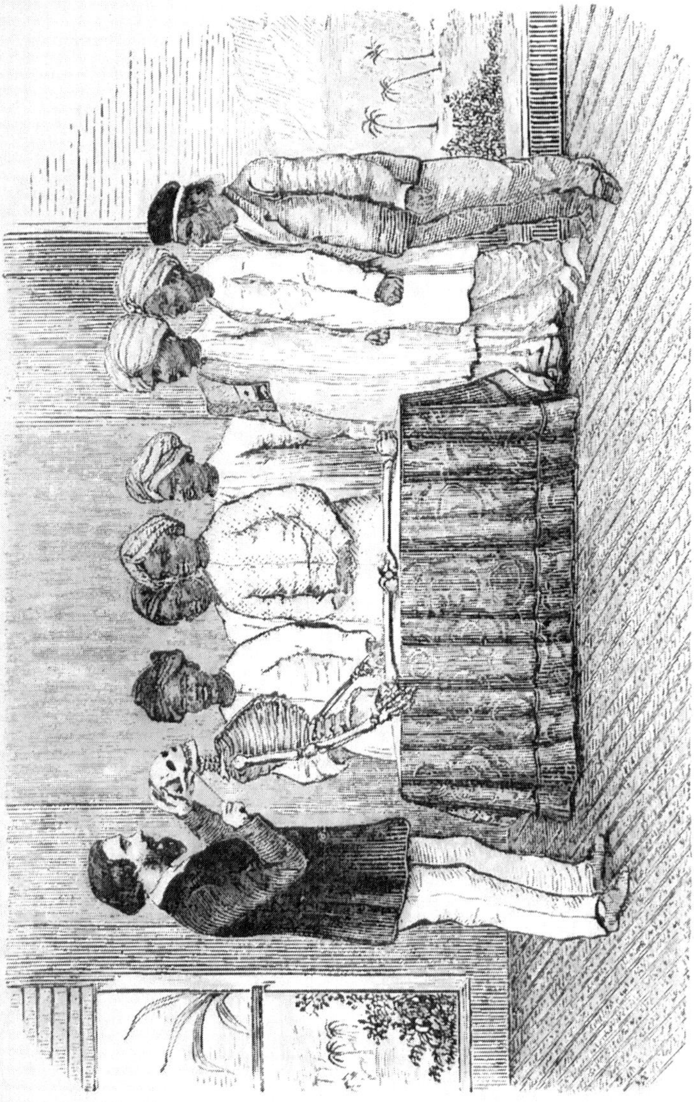

MEDICAL MISSIONARY AND STUDENTS.

fully instructed and trained for three years and a half by Dr. Lowe, assisted for some time by Mr. Baylis, in teaching Latin and chemistry. The medical students made up the prescriptions, performed minor operations, and received instruction in the various departments of medical science, so as to combine practical work with systematic study; and the scheme has proved, so far, entirely successful. Before Dr. Lowe was compelled, by the illness of his excellent wife, to leave Travancore, he opened three branch dispensaries at Agateespuram, Sānthapuram, and A'ttúr, and left the work in the hands of his native assistants.

"In order," he writes, "to test the efficiency of the dressers for the responsible duties which would devolve upon them, I gradually withdrew from the ordinary routine of dispensary work, and, for a few weeks before I left, allowed the dressers themselves to do most of the work, merely watching them, and, as opportunities were presented, making suggestions for their future guidance. The result was most gratifying. In the daily dispensary practice I saw these young men judiciously and skilfully applying the instruction they had received, often in cases of no little difficulty and danger. I saw them amputate and perform successfully serious obstetrical operations, reduce dislocations and fractures, both simple and compound, and attend to the patients till they were discharged cured. I saw them excise tumours, and perform all the minor surgical operations which are daily required in ordinary dispensary practice. I saw them going in and out among their patients, gaining their confidence by their kindness; and, while endeavouring to relieve their wounded or diseased bodies, seeking at the same time to lead sin-stricken souls to the Great Physician. I saw all this, and I felt amply repaid for my toil."

During the year 1869, these native dressers, or medical assistants, attended, in the absence of Dr. Lowe, to no less than 13,698 patients, exclusive of 3,160 who were vaccinated also during the year. We sincerely trust that this valuable and benevolent Christian Institution will continue to command the attention and support of the Society and the friends of the mission, and that a work established at such cost of labour and means may not be allowed to fall to the ground, for want either of European medical superintendence (still essential to its perpetuity) or of pecuniary assistance.

Other modifications in the staff of missionaries and the internal circumstances of the mission took place from time to time, any detailed relation of which the limits of this work forbid. We can do no more than allude to the Rev. J. J. Dennis, who was somewhat suddenly removed to the better world in 1864, after eight or nine years' residence in India. His labours, especially in the superintendence of the printing press, and the improvement of native Christian literature, were of great service to the mission. Rev. J. F. Gannaway also laboured for three years in Jamestown with much energy and encouraging success, and Rev. G. Mabbs for about a year at Nāgercoil.

We cannot omit a brief reference to the important changes in respect to native church organization which took place on the occasion of the visit to Travancore of the Rev. Dr. Mullens, in the beginning of 1866, as special deputation from the Missionary Society, before returning to England to enter upon the responsible and onerous duties of Foreign Secretary. Some of the measures then carried out had been in contemplation previously, others were decided on in the course of the consultations which took place between Dr. Mullens and the district committee.

With a view to the establishment of a native pastorate on a sound and permanent basis, four of the native evangelists were ordained, one as an assistant missionary, and three as pastors of churches which undertook the responsibility of their support. These were Messrs. C. Yesudian, the long-tried and learned head master of the seminary at Nāgercoil, Devadāsen, a Brahman convert, of singular purity of character and spirituality of mind; Zechariah, the able and devoted evangelist in charge of the Neyoor congregation; and Masillāmani, the grandson of the first Christian convert in Travancore;—all men of tried character and abilities, who had proved themselves successful preachers and evangelists during many years of steady service. These were all ordained at Nāgercoil on 13th February, 1866. Corresponding alterations were made in the geographical classification and boundaries of the mission districts. The northern portion of the Nāgercoil district, containing twelve congregations, was placed under the charge of Yesudian; while the churches of Nāgercoil, Neyoor, and Dennispuram unanimously chose as their respective pastors the other three brethren. It had been long felt by the missionaries that it was unnecessary to retain Sānthapuram, in such close proximity to Neyoor and Nāgercoil, as a separate district with a European missionary, considering the urgent claims of the populous district of Quilon, which had been left unoccupied and comparatively neglected for sixteen years after the death of Mr. Thompson. The Rev. F. Wilkinson, of Sānthapuram, accordingly consented to remove from that well-organized and flourishing, though, geographically, rather confined district, to undertake the more difficult and uphill work of resuscitating the Malayālim mission at Quilon. The congregations in the three southernmost districts were redistributed, and the boundaries rearranged, so as to require but three instead of four missionaries in the extreme South.

At Trevandrum, too, additional premises in the cantonment were purchased for the accommodation of a second missionary, long promised to this important station. Arrangements were also made for the ordination of seven other native preachers as pastors, or assistant missionaries, and this measure was carried into effect early in 1867.

It is to be regretted that our limits do not admit of dwelling at some length upon the important subject of female missionary labours,—a subject which deserves a whole volume to itself, and the discussion of which would throw much light upon one aspect of the missionary enterprise in India. The Travancore mission has been remarkable for the assiduous and fruitful efforts put forth on behalf of the females by Mrs. Mault and her daughter Mrs. Whitehouse, Mrs. Mead, Mrs. Lewis, Mrs. Abbs, Mrs. Cox and her daughters, Mrs. Baylis, and others, the periods of whose residence in the country were more brief, besides those still in the field, whose loving and praiseworthy labours are well known to the readers of our missionary reports.

An opinion has recently been strongly expressed by persons sincerely interested in missions, but for the most part destitute of practical experience in India, to the effect that it would be of great advantage to the mission work for the missionary to remain unmarried for the first few years of his course abroad; and this is urged by the consideration that several useful missionaries have from time to time been compelled to retire from the foreign field, after a few years, on account of the illness of their wives.

But, on the other hand, it should be remembered that a much larger proportion of *men* would certainly break down in health if they go out to India unmarried, without the domestic care and companionship of an affectionate and pious partner; the dangers to character and reputation in such a country as India would be infinitely increased; and certain departments of our work, such as female schools and classes, and visitation, must come to an end, so far as the unmarried missionaries are concerned.

The difficulties, too, in the way of obtaining a suitable

partner in India, and at the age of say thirty to forty, would be very considerable, and great temptations would be presented to form unequal and inconvenient unions.

Moreover, it is by no means the rule that married missionaries labour with less spirit, travel less zealously, or are more encumbered in their work, than are bachelors. All this depends rather upon the constitution and temperament of the individual, than on his domestic circumstances.

In short, our experience in Travancore is decidedly and unhesitatingly in favour of the missionaries (excepting, of course, those who deliberately and intelligently prefer a celibate life) being married. Our mission could not have been what it is but for the co-operation and effective efforts of the missionary ladies. Indeed, the wife has sometimes proved the better missionary of the two.

NOTE ON P. 34.

"RESULT OF MR. LEE'S APPEAL."

Since the first sheets of this work were printed reliable information on this point has been received. It appears that the Madras Government reviewed the whole case, and administered a just rebuke to the native Government for the inadequacy of the sentence in question, but they refrained from reversing it on the ground that Travancore is a native state, nominally independent.

The Sirkar is also severely handled for yielding so much to caste, and a statement is required *why* caste restrictions as to the use of public roads &c., should not be abolished, and *why* the native state should not conform to the customs of British India in these matters.

CHAPTER XXIII.

MISSIONARY OPERATIONS, AND THEIR INDIRECT RESULTS.

Value of General Information respecting the Mission Field—Plan and Working of the Travancore Mission—Mission Houses—Mode of Travelling—Chapels and Public Worship—Superintendence of Native Teachers—Their Duties—Character and History of Native Ministers and Catechists—Preaching to the Heathen—Stupidity—Misconceptions—Arguments—Pretended Miracles—Abuse—Difficulties of a Sincere Hindu — Wit and Humour of Native Controversialists — Indirect Results of Missionary Labour—Decline of Idolatry, and of Opposition to Christianity—Secret Believers—Position of Educated Hindus—Their Moral Enlightenment.

While we have dwelt in the preceding pages at some length on numerous topics of general interest in connection with Travancore, our main object throughout has been to seek, by supplying information which cannot properly be given in ordinary missionary reports, to excite, on the part of our readers, a thoroughly intelligent and practical interest in the great missionary enterprise carried on in that country. It is right that a Christian missionary should be acquainted with the topography, the history, the animal, vegetable, and mineral products, the ethnology, the languages and literature, and the superstitions of the country for the improvement of which he is called to labour. Such studies will often prove a needful and innocent relaxation from more severe duties, and the possession of such general information will assuredly command the respect of the natives with whom he comes in daily contact.

Without detailed and accurate information as to the various fields of missionary labour, and the circumstances of each, the friends of missions at home cannot possibly be expected to take such a deep and comprehensive interest in particular spheres of effort, nor to be able to direct their liberality and prayers to the most urgent and important objects.

But it is not, after all, these subjects that chiefly secure the attention and excite the interest of the Christian mind. It is not to obtain an acquaintance with these matters of general but minor interest that the missionaries of the Cross leave—

> "Kindred, home, and ease, and all the cultured joys,
> Conveniences, and delicate delights
> Of ripe society;"

and devote their life, their strength, their talents, to earnest and self-denying toil in distant lands. We would not sink the character of the Christian missionary in that of the mere traveller.

No, the accurate comprehension of the circumstances and general condition of a country forms but a preparation for an interest in its inhabitants, and tends to awaken our desire to benefit them in some practical way. Our deepest sympathies must centre in the people,—the sentient and immortal beings who inhabit the country, and who are there living and labouring, desiring and enjoying, struggling and achieving, suffering and rejoicing, living and dying. They are created by the same great God and for the same sublime end, are preserved by the same beneficent Providence and redeemed by the same holy Saviour as ourselves. It is, therefore, the moral and spiritual condition of the human family that excites the warmest sympathy and loving efforts of the Christian heart. In Travancore, we have idolatry and demon-worship in their worst and most corrupting forms. In that little and obscure corner of India we find above a million of heathens in dense spiritual darkness. There we find the Brahman priests and the Súdra landowners oppressing the poor cultivators, labourers, and slaves, and a large proportion of the population sunk in a condition of extreme poverty and abject wretchedness, groaning under the burdens of slavery and caste. There many of the better educated classes are proud and ungodly; the wealthy sensual and depraved; the young rising up into life without the knowledge of God and of salvation; the old hardened in the practice of sin and in hatred to divine truth; the people deceived and priest-ridden. "The prophets prophesy falsely, and the priests bear rule by their means, and the people love to have it so." There we see women superstitious, and degraded from their true social position, and multitudes of souls, saturated with superstition, suffering continual misery through the dread of demons and of magical arts. All are dead in trespasses and sins, without true peace of conscience, without the knowledge of God, without any light upon their path to the eternal and invisible world.

> "They read no promise that inspires belief;
> They seek no God that pities their complaints;
> They find no balm that gives the heart relief;
> They know no fountain when the spirit faints."

In seeking the conversion of Travancore to the Redeemer we have had, as will be evident from previous remarks, to contend not only with the natural power and love of sin in the human heart, and with the unwillingness even of many who are intellectually convinced of the truth to obey and follow it out in their lives, but also with special and peculiar local difficulties, arising from the strength and extraordinary hold of the prevalent superstitions over the minds of the people—the debasing habits and extreme degradation of many classes—the wealth and *prestige* of the ecclesiastical establishment supported by the rulers and nobles of the land—occasional outbursts of violent hostility to the progress of Christianity—and all the traditions and prescriptive usages of the system of caste arrayed against the Gospel.

But, notwithstanding all these obstructions, the Gospel has already won its conquests in that land; and is progressing, we are persuaded, to its final and universal triumph.

We shall now proceed briefly to describe THE PLAN AND WORKING of our mission in South Travancore.

The 260 congregations connected with the mission are divided, according to geographical position, into seven districts as follows, commencing from the South:—

	Congregations.	Native Teachers of all kinds.	Native Christians.
Kottāram	29	58	4,440
Nāgercoil	34	72	4,848
Tittuvilei	13	18	1,478
Neyoor	59	84	8,176
Pāreychāley	93	121	10,999
Trevandrum	29	32	2,428
Quilon	3	11	377
	260	396	32,746

Of these native teachers, 24 are schoolmistresses and 18 female assistants, or Bible women.

The Tittuvilei district is under the sole charge of a native ordained missionary, Rev. C. Yesudian; the others are superintended by the European missionaries, Rev. Messrs. Baylis, Wilkinson, Newport, Lee, and J. E. Jones; three others, Rev. J. Duthie, Rev. J. Lowe, M.R.C.S.E., and the writer, being at present in England through unavoidable circumstances.

The mission-house generally occupies a good position on a

healthy, elevated site in the centre of the district, and is surrounded by the necessary outbuildings, chapel, school-house, and separate dormitories for the boys and girls of the boarding schools. When at home, the missionary preaches in the home chapel, but as frequently as possible spends the Lord's day and one or two of the week days in his congregations, visiting daily two or three villages; so that, if he preaches in each of his chapels about once a quarter, carefully examining while on the spot into the various matters connected with the welfare and prosperity of the congregation which demand attention, this is as much as can reasonably be expected, in addition to his other work of occasional teaching, study and composition, correspondence, dispensing medicine, deciding disputes and difficult cases, preparing plans and estimates for chapels, and so forth. I have never been able to conduct more than about thirty services in a single month,—usually between that number and twenty, when in health and undisturbed by incidental interruptions.

Our means of locomotion are various, according to choice and circumstances. On the backwaters we travel about in boats or canoes, and this is exceedingly pleasant, especially on fine moonlight nights. In cases where the exposure to the sun can be borne without danger to health, riding on horseback is pleasant and speedy. Where there are no roads, palankeens are necessary; they are carried by eight to twelve men, or light palankeen chairs with cloth hoods by four to six bearers; and twenty miles is not an unusual distance for a single journey at the rate of about 3½ miles an hour. I have once gone forty-two miles during the night with a single set of bearers. Each man is paid a chuckram per mile for his work.

On the main roads, which are generally kept in good condition, we indulge in the luxury and magnificence of a "carriage and pair"—the "pair," however, it must be confessed, not graceful, high-stepping carriage horses, but stout *bullocks*, secured and driven by strong ropes running through the nostrils, instead of the conventional silver-plated harness; and the "carriage" destitute of steel springs and morocco lining—in fact, a common cart or "bandy," covered with matting for protection from sun and rain.* To compensate for the absence of springs, the bottom of the cart is filled with straw, and over this a light mattress is laid, on which

TRAVELLING CHAIR.

the traveller reclines. Bed, food, and all necessaries are carried in the cart, for our native Christians have neither accommodation nor means to receive and entertain us in their houses: at night we sleep on the mattress in a corner of the chapel, or in a small shed attached thereto. A boy to cook rice and curry, prepare tea, &c., sits at the back of the cart, the front seat being occupied by the driver, who twists

* See bullock cart in engraving opposite page 326.

the tails of the bullocks, coaxes, threatens, exhorts, and beats them, so that I have seen them *rush along* at the rate of 2½ miles an hour; 2¼, however, is the average speed.

Our chapels are very plain, unpretentious buildings—too often mere sheds,—but a few of the best are neat, well built, and commodious, and suited to the climate. We have not above a score of really good chapels of sufficient size. This is the great want of the period in the Travancore mission. The Lord has poured out a blessing which there is "not room to receive"—not room in our chapels and prayer-houses and schoolrooms for the rapidly increasing multitude of Christian inquirers and converts and their children. One sometimes longs for the grant of just as much money as has been expended on but one of the noble and graceful spires which adorn our places of worship at home—an amount which would relieve the extreme pressure on the means of our poor people, and provide for them in perpetuity fifty decent and comfortable village chapels, urgently needed as they are in many of the congregations.

The morning service commences at seven o'clock, and another service is held at eleven in the forenoon. Meetings are rarely held in the evening, on account of the discomfort of walking in the dark, the danger from snakes, and the necessity for the natives preparing food for their evening meal. Except in our town chapels, which are provided with benches, the people sit cross-legged on matting spread on the floor.

Public worship is conducted very much as in England, with singing, reading the Scriptures, and prayer. Before preaching, the people are made to repeat the text several times, and throughout the service their attention and interest are maintained by frequent questions from the preacher on the subject of discourse. Were it possible occasionally to adopt some such practice at home, would it not do much

VILLAGE CHAPEL AND SCHOOL-HOUSE IN TRAVANCORE.

(Face page 326.)

good in some congregations? A quiet doze in church is a privilege and pleasure never enjoyed by our poor native Christians, for the close questioning puts a stop to all that. After the conclusion of the service the weekly offerings are collected, the list of names of all the members of the congregation is read over, and their attendance marked, as is done in Sunday schools at home; then each is individually asked to repeat the verses of Scripture, or questions of the catechism, appointed as the lesson of the month, and the congregation is dismissed, each making his salām, or salutation, to the preacher as he leaves.

The sacraments of Baptism and of the Lord's Supper are administered by the missionary, or ordained native minister, as often as convenient. It is hardly practicable to dispense these ordinances monthly, but I endeavoured, as far as possible, to do so once a quarter in several principal congregations in different parts of my district; so that all our people might witness and be instructed by these solemn and delightful ordinances, and that aged and infirm members might be accommodated.

The instruction, superintendence, and guidance of the native preachers and teachers is, however, of at least equal, if not superior, importance to the duties of visiting and preaching to the congregations. It is upon these brethren that responsibility must eventually rest; and we deem it, therefore, better by far to train and accustom them to fulfil the work of the ministry and pastorate than that we ourselves should officiate merely as pastors of Christian congregations. In the present stage of our mission we occupy, in fact, the position of superintendents or bishops—using the word somewhat in the sense in which the term is applied in England—having our local diocese, our numerous clergy, and, for the present, necessarily, extensive powers and authority as the result of our peculiar position in reference to the European churches whose messengers we are, and to the native churches who look up to us as their fathers and founders.

The native agents of each district visit the mission-house on "report day"—generally Thursday—for the transaction of mission business of every kind, for theological and scriptural or occasional literary instruction, and to report their efforts—successes—difficulties in their various spheres of labour.

The CATECHISTS, NATIVE TEACHERS, or READERS, as they are variously denominated, conduct divine service and preach in the respective congregations to which they are appointed, visit the sick and inattentive, instruct the Christians from house to house, receive their contributions, celebrate marriages, preach to and converse with the heathen and distribute tracts, superintend repairs of chapels, and attend to the miscellaneous duties of a religious and benevolent character which constantly devolve upon them. They are practically village pastors; and, on the whole, we owe much to the labours of these devoted men; the work of the mission could not be carried on without them, and they are yearly increasing in efficiency and capacity, as the result of the careful and continuous special training bestowed upon them, as well as of the general progress of the Christian community.

It has often been remarked how God has again and again raised up extraordinary men for the service of the London Missionary Society (as well as other kindred institutions), such as Vanderkemp, Moffat, and Livingstone in Africa, Williams in the South Seas, Morrison and Medhurst in China, Ellis in Madagascar, Knill and Tidman at home, and many others who have been singularly gifted for the spheres which they have been called to occupy. In like manner we have reason to acknowledge His gracious providence in the lives and labours of many remarkable native preachers raised up at various periods for His service in Travancore. The

Nallamudian. (Patrick Thompson.) Daniel. (Oundle Teacher.) Yôvân, or John. (Ebenezer Young.)
Perinbamuttu. (Edward Cook.) Gurupâtham. (John Gwynne Hughes.) Vethamânikkam. (Thomas Rutter.) Sattianâthan. (James Macfarlane.)

PAREYCHALEY EVANGELISTS.

Face page 328.)

personal history of many of these good men strikingly exhibits the influence and operation of divine grace.

One of the most devoted, godly, and consistent ministers of the Gospel I have ever had the privilege of knowing is Rev. N. Devadāsen, pastor of the large church at Nāgercoil.* His was a remarkable conversion, and it excited much interest at the time. A brief sketch of his life, given by himself, has several times been published, but the following extracts will be read with interest :—

"I was born," he writes, "in a village in Tinnevelly, in 1815, and learned Tamil in a heathen school. At the age of seventeen, having resolved to go on pilgrimage to Benares, I stole four cloths belonging to a friend, and proceeded as far as Seringham. Tiring of the journey, however, I returned home, and concealed by various stratagems my having stolen the cloths. One day, having gone to see a mission school, my attention was arrested by the novel sight of maps hung on the wall, and children engaged in reading printed books. That was the first time I had seen or heard of Christians or their books. I conversed with the schoolmaster, who was my nephew, about the salary, and thought I should like some employment of this kind.

"Some time after I came to my father in Travancore, where I managed to obtain the situation of accountant in a pagoda. While here, I was led into much evil, and caused vexation and annoyance to many.

"Being somehow desirous of obtaining employment as a secular teacher in the mission, I applied to Rev. Mr. Miller, who kindly took me into a Preparandi class for instruction. I found it difficult to commit the appointed lessons to memory, and was on one occasion seriously reproved by Mr. Miller, who said that my mind was as hard as a piece of stone.

* Long supported, under the name of T. M. White, by friends at Morden Hall.

"After four years' training as a schoolmaster I was married to my *present* wife, then five years of age, and shortly afterwards employed by Mr. Mault to teach a village school. (At that time heathen schoolmasters of good character were occasionally employed, in default of a sufficient number of Christian teachers.) During the five years in which I held this situation I regularly worshipped the idols, performed daily ceremonies, such as reciting a Mantra in praise of Vishnu 500 times, and another in honour of Siva 250 times. To show uncommon zeal I smeared my body with the sacred ashes from head to waist, while others made merely a few marks on the forehead and breast, and wore rosaries of sacred beads around my neck and waist. Yet, in spite of the rigid performance of all these ceremonies, anger, revenge, fraud, lasciviousness, covetousness, and other vices had full sway over my sinful and corrupt heart.

"On one occasion, taking offence at the conduct of a Government messenger and his companions, who, contrary to usage, heedlessly stepped into the rest-house where I (a Brahman) was taking my meal, I instantly rose from food and went to the magistrate, addressing frequent petitions to Government until the poor man was turned out of his employment; and I was also imprisoned fifty days for my harsh and obstinate litigation.

"Soon after my release Mr. Mault again took me into my former situation, but I engaged in it with other and more tender feelings. I read in private the Christian Scriptures, and my attachment to idolatry began to decrease. My new views were strengthened by the remarks of an intelligent Brahman to the effect that the Purānas and the Rāmāyanam were but mythical legends. Daily I perused the Bible, praying to God in the words of the 119th Psalm, till at length I was resolved, by the grace of God, to embrace the Christian religion."

Fearing the consequences of making an open profession of Christianity amongst his own people, Devadāsen at first suggested that he should be sent to some other mission station, where he should be out of reach of their persecution. At last, however, he made up his mind, being unable to feel peace till he avowed his determination at all hazards to declare himself a Christian convert. Previously to his leaving his village he called his scholars and friends together in the schoolroom, and told them he intended to become a Christian; and to show them that he was in earnest he broke off the sacred string, the mark of his caste, and threw it from him, after which he knelt down and prayed with them. His friends attempted, both by persuasion and force, to hinder his profession of Christianity, but in vain. He partook of food with Mr. Mault, thus breaking caste, and shortly afterwards received Christian baptism. "Still, said he, "the conflict is not yet over. Oh, it has been hard work! Satan has tried hard to get me back. He has brought up all my old sins, and made them look so dreadful, and many that I had forgotten he has brought up against me, but I have peace now."

His conversion made a great stir in the neighbourhood. Some of the heathens said that he was mad, some that the decision he manifested was the result of deep reflection, and others that it was the work of God, and was wonderful.

As the Brahman wife to whom he had been *betrothed* when a heathen (she being then about five years of age) was not allowed by her relatives to accompany him after his conversion, though he waited a long time for her, he married a pious Christian woman of the Pariah caste, who lived happily with him for ten years till she died. Some time after her decease, the first wife sent him word that she was willing to become a Christian; he accepted her, was duly married to her in Christian form, and she is now an affectionate and pious partner in his faith and labours.

The congregation of Nāgercoil, over which he presides, now numbers 739 adherents, of whom 152 are communicants. It is entirely self-supporting, having its native deacons and church organization complete, with Bible classes, weekly prayer meetings, mothers' meetings, and local benevolent associations. A Bible woman is also supported by its funds. The contributions in 1869 amounted to 885 rupees.

REV. C. YESUDIAN.

Rev. C. Yesudian is a man of quite a different mould, culture, and temperament from Devadāsen. Born in the Christian community he has, by incessant study and the cultivation of his talents, become possessed of high literary attainments in English, and more especially in Tamil classical literature; on which subject I have heard him lecture to the admiration and delight of many learned and influential native gentlemen and students at the capital. He is also a man of independent and original mind,—a rare thing amongst Hindus. Another of our ordained native ministers is an eloquent and powerful preacher. Others have long fulfilled the practical duties of the ministry, and proved themselves efficient and successful evangelists and pastors, "workmen that need not to be ashamed," since God has been pleased to place the seal of His approbation on their earnest and prayerful efforts for the conversion of souls. In their case, fruits unite with gifts and graces in testifying their divine call to the ministry.

Two of the younger ministers in whose training it has been my privilege to take some part, I have found it necessary often to restrain from overwork, advising them to take reasonable care of their own health while zealously and earnestly engaged in the service of their Lord and Master.

Our native teachers or catechists are many of them, we confess, greatly defective in education and rhetorical power, but we seek to appoint to this office godly, earnest, intelligent men, who have at least capacity to deliver plain and suitable Scripture expositions and exhortations; and notwithstanding the comparative deficiencies of some in ability, and even in application, their co-operation is indispensable; we must work with the best tools we can secure, while we strive incessantly to improve these, and to prepare or procure better ones. The worst of these men are certainly feeble, and of little value; the best of them are noble, devoted, efficient Christian workers.

A fair and steadily increasing proportion of our native teachers have received careful and lengthened training and preparation for their duties in the boarding schools at the head stations, or in the Nāgercoil Seminary. Their wives, also, have in most cases enjoyed similar advantages in the girls' boarding schools under the care of the missionary ladies.

Some of our native preachers were once noted as religious devotees and ascetics, or devil-dancers and professed magicians. One instance must suffice.

"Meshach was a man of the Chetty caste, and originally an officiating priest in a heathen pagoda. He was very zealous in his devotions, fasted twice a week, ate, not with his hands, but by picking his food from the temple floor with his mouth, and showed himself in real earnest with his religion. While thus engaged that loathsome disease leprosy seized upon him. In his distress he called upon the goddess whom he served for relief; but none came, although he redoubled his sacrifices and services. As the heathen believe that bodily health must result from the worship of the gods, and as in his case such health did not appear, he ceased to perform his customary sacrifices, and turned his attention to Christianity, of which he had some previous knowledge. He soon made a public profession of his new faith, and grew still more zealous in it than in the old. He was admitted to the church, and employed as catechist and schoolmaster by Mr. Abbs. His disease, however, gradually undermined his constitution, and by depriving him of his toes and fingers prevented him from doing anything. Even then, however, he would creep to the road-side and preach the Gospel to the passers by. This he did even to the last. He was accompanied in this work by a blind man who had been brought to Christ by his means. The blind man and the leper sat by the wayside, and exhorted all men to believe in Christ. And when one of them was removed by death, the other was inconsolable for his loss, and soon followed. On his death-bed Meshach was asked if he were afraid to die. He replied, 'No, I have been always ready to obey the voice of Jesus in everything.' When he was spoken to of his bodily health he said that he was better off than Lazarus, who had no home, no food, and no bodily comforts. Three days before his death he invited fifteen of his Christian friends to a feast, and to pray for him, as the last token of love they could show each other in this world. In calm reliance on his Saviour he breathed his last, March 1st, 1866."*

I knew this good man well, and shall never forget his affectionate disposition, purity of character, prayerfulness, and zeal. Many other most interesting cases of a similar character might be related did space permit. Several of those who were *once devil-dancers* and devotees have become most prayerful, humble, and diligent teachers of the way of life to their fellow-countrymen.

In PREACHING TO THE HEATHEN the missionaries and native teachers come in contact with every variety of intellectual capacity and culture, of general disposition and moral character, and of religious opinion and experience. We have there, side by side, a few men of the highest literary and scientific attainments and practised talents, with others well-nigh savages, sunk in the grossest stupidity and ignorance, —unable to tell their own age or to reckon above a dozen,— hardly capable of conversing rationally and connectedly in their own language upon topics in the slightest degree above their every-day animal life.

We have, side by side, the moral and well-meaning heathen (too few, alas! in proportion to the great mass of the people) and the drunkard, the profligate, the man of lust and crime. There is the Mohammedan to whom we can appeal as a witness to the existence and unity of God, but who turns away in contempt and abhorrence from the precious name of Jesus; and the devil-worshipper, who altogether ignores the existence and authority of the Creator. We meet with some hardened

* Rev. G. O. Newport's Report for 1866.

against all religious impressions,—fools who make a mock at sin; others doubting, hesitating, trembling, half convinced, or anxiously solicitous to find the way of salvation. We have to deal with young and old, male and female, rich and poor, learned and ignorant, with their various histories, emotions, hopes, modes of life,—devotees of manifold systems of superstition and error. Well may we exclaim, "Who is sufficient for these things?" Who is able to lead all these to truth and righteousness, and to God?

We shall attempt to classify some of these cases.

1. Take the following illustration of *extreme stupidity*, existing even after enjoying some measure of Christian instruction.

"Among those who presented themselves as candidates for baptism was an old man of about sixty-five. He first placed himself under Christian instruction in the time of Mr. Ringeltaube, some fifty years ago, but afterwards dissociated himself from the Christian community for years together, without, however, relapsing into idolatry. For many years past he has again been a regular attendant; but he is one of those who are ever learning without coming to the knowledge of the truth. Among the questions put to him was, what he thought of himself as a sinner before God; to which he replied, 'I am a great sinner. I have committed every sin. I have even *beaten cows*.' Perceiving that his views of sin were still those which he held when a heathen, and not those entertained by Christians, I had no hesitation in refusing to baptize him." *

To such persons we may speak of *God*, but the hearer thinks of the sun or some local divinity; of *sin*, and some trivial or absurd breach of the ceremonial law recurs to his memory; of the *soul*, and he thinks of mere animal life; of *heaven and hell*, and ideas altogether foreign to those intended by us are suggested to the mind of the hearer. We must

* Rev. E. Lewis's Report for 1859.

therefore be continually on our guard to make sure that our meaning is rightly and fully apprehended.

2. It is only after lengthened experience that the European evangelist is prepared to calculate the probable shape which the multiform *errors* and *misconceptions* of the uninstructed heathen mind will assume. On one occasion I was preaching to a crowd in the cantonment of Trevandrum, when several Sepoys, just dismissed from drill, came up and stood to listen. One of them, a clever and talkative man, thus objected:—"Sir, you need not speak to us about becoming Christians; we cannot think of such a thing, for we should then be obliged to eat beef, and such a practice is most revolting to us." I reminded him that there is no great difference between our custom of eating the flesh of the cow, and theirs of using the milk and butter, which may in some sense be called the essence of the beef; and I endeavoured to show the spiritual nature of Christianity, which neither requires nor prohibits the use of such articles of food, and consists "not in meat or drink, but in righteousness, and peace, and joy in the Holy Ghost."

"To-day," said a Brahman on one occasion, "I have seen that Christianity is declining and losing its strength. Up to this time you were giving us large books; now you have begun to bring books of a single leaf."

"What is the use of becoming Christians?" said a heathen to a native teacher, "you also die as we do."

"Where there are so many religions," said another, "how can we know that Christianity is the true one?"

3. All kinds of specious *excuses* and arguments, sometimes rather ingenious, for refusing to embrace Christianity, are brought forward. The example and authority of the Maharajah are appealed to. "Are we wiser than his Highness? Convert him, and we shall all become Christians." The terrible consequences of loss of caste and of the means of live-

lihood are pleaded. "Each shall be saved by his own religion," says one. "Christianity is too good a religion : it is impossible to act up to its pure and strict requirements—to live without cheating and lying," exclaims another. "Idolatry is necessary to remind the vulgar and uneducated of God and of spiritual things," argues a shrewd, learned Brahman. The inconsistencies and wickedness of nominal Christians, especially of some of our countrymen in India, are cast in our teeth; and then we are heartily ashamed of those who act so little in accordance with the precepts of the holy religion they profess—who are indeed a reproach and "a curse amongst the heathen." Others lay the blame of their unbelief on fate. Daring and pantheistical objections are produced. "I am God," blasphemously declares a would-be philosopher: "God is the author and efficient agent of all things, and it is therefore He who causes me to sin or to do good."

Now-a-days a few read Colenso's and other sceptical or infidel works, and are thus becoming confirmed in their rejection of the truth by ingenious but trifling objections to the Sacred Scriptures themselves.

4. On the other hand, the *superstition* of many is sincere and intense, indeed, insuperable except by divine grace. Tales of the agency of the demons and the potency of magical arts are urged with all the natural eloquence and force which spring from honest and sincere belief in them. Pretended miracles are appealed to. "Six months ago," said a worshipper of Muttukutti or Nārāyanan, "a pot of boiled rice was presented to the god, which is still as warm and fresh as ever, and will continue so for some time to come; after which it will ferment. And there are many other miracles performed in the temple."

At a village near Nāgercoil a great image of the god Súran, about twelve feet high, is made yearly of straw and wood covered with blue cloth. A ball of mud, filled with water, mixed with red colouring matter, in imitation of blood, is inserted in the breast of the image. In the midst of the festival the priest plunges an arrow into the figure, when the hidden fluid gushes out in streams; and this is hailed with acclamations as a wonderful miracle.

Yet some of the priests and religious mendicants, on being remonstrated with on their criminal deception of the ignorant people, confessed that they only do these things "to fill the stomach." "By these means we are supported. You cannot paint," say they, "without a surface to paint upon—the body first; then only can we attend to the concerns of the soul."

5. Others, though more rarely, resort to *misrepresentation, mockery, and coarse abuse.* In one place, where many of the slaves had come to the determination to place themselves under Christian instruction, the masters spread a report among these poor people that two ships had arrived at Trevandrum, in which these slaves would be sent to England to be given as food to the tigers which the white men keep, and the demons that dig out gold for them. Our schools are sometimes emptied by foolish and lying reports of a somewhat similar character.

"If you do really desire, as you say, the good of us poor people," said some rude men to a native teacher, "why do you not give us large bungalows, a carriage and horses, and a white lady for wife?" On another occasion,—"You need not be sorry for us; soothe your sorrow by striking your heads against the trees and perishing at their foot." "Do not speak of *God* to me," said a police officer, in reply to remarks on the duty of gratitude to God for His mercies. "I cannot bear to hear the word uttered; it acts on me as if a red-hot pin were thrust into my ears. The wealth and health I have already obtained are the only heaven I desire."

6. *Pride and prejudice* appear in the self-righteous Brahmans, who contemptuously repudiate the idea of being sinners, and in the higher castes, who occasionally burst into explosions of wrath at the idea of being addressed on religious subjects by preachers of lower caste than themselves. "How dare a man of your caste," said a wealthy Súdra, "presume to speak to *me* on the subject of religion?"

And while many of the higher classes oppose Christianity, because it has freed the lower orders from their power, and is taking away their opportunities for oppression and unjust gain, some of the poorer classes also set themselves against the progress of the truth amongst their own people, when they perceive that the Gospel aims at no less than the destruction and complete abolition of their licentiousness, theft, and drunkenness, and their abominable devil-feasts.

7. The difficulties which really suggest themselves to the mind of a thoughtful Hindu are, after all, not dissimilar to those that have puzzled inquiring minds unenlightened by divine revelation in every age. This will be evident from the following list of questions, presented in writing to one of our native missionaries, in the course of a lengthened and interesting discussion at Kottār.

Questions of a Hindu.

1. Is God spirit or matter?
2. What are the properties of spirit, and what of matter?
3. If God be a spirit, how could He be capable of thought, so as to create?
4. If He has a form, what form is that?
5. Is God possessed of omnipresence, omnipotence, and omniscience?
6. Did God form His creatures when in possession of these erfections?

7. How do you account for creatures being capable of moral good and evil?

8. What is sin? and what is virtue?

9. If sin is the transgression of a command, did God know that man was capable of transgressing?

10. Are all living beings created by Him?

11. And what are their properties?

12. Are living creatures possessed of the attributes of the Creator?

13. Had God a desire to create the living creatures, to preserve, destroy, or save them?

14. And what produced that desire?

15. Who tempted the first man to sin?

16. And who created him that tempted?

17. Was God destitute of omniscience, so as not to know the nature of man and of the devil that tempted him?

18. Were there no thorns in the earth before the curse? &c., &c.

Our native teachers and Christians generally exhibit remarkable forbearance, good temper, and ingenuity in religious discussions with the heathen, overcoming violent opposition or wrath by mildness, gentleness, and polite address. *Wit and humour*, learning and poetry, are not unfrequently brought in on both sides; and I have listened with delight and admiration to the touching appeals, the quick replies, the ready wit, the apt poetical quotations and apposite illustrations of our best controversialists. When, for example, the list of questions above given was presented to the Christian teacher, he required his disputatious opponent to answer another question, viz., What other better plan might God have adopted in the creation of intelligent beings, so as not to have given room for the commission of sin? When the next meeting took place, the man sent an apology for non-attendance, with his reply in a couple of lines written on a small piece of palmyra leaf, "It would be right if God created man incapable of sin." The heathen present were of course disappointed with this reply of their champion, and were thus prepared to listen to the exposition of these weighty topics from the lips of the Christian preacher.

"A Christian weaver who frequented Kottār for the purpose of selling his cloth, used to speak about Christianity to the merchants who were dealing with him, and who, on this account, made him an object of derision wherever they met him. But the pious weaver generally succeeded in silencing them by calmly replying, 'What benefit can you derive from falling down before a dumb idol which cannot answer your petitions? what assistance can you receive from a poor bird which steals away young chickens, and robs poor women of the little fish they carry in their hands? But if you believe on Jesus, the Son of the ever-living and almighty God, you will obtain endless bliss.'

"Ashamed and vexed by such repeated defeats, they were eagerly watching for an opportunity to expose him and his religion to ridicule, when, upon a certain day, a Brahman, reputed as a great scholar in the Shāstras, and revered as a Guru, came to the town. They then took the Christian before him, and said, Here is a Vedakaran; whereupon the Shāstri asked him if he was not of the Pādre's (missionary's) Veda (Bible or religion); and being answered in the affirmative, turned to the man and said, with an air of contempt, 'Do you know, man, what is *pādre?* it is a *tree*' (punning on 'pādre,' a priest, and 'pāthiri,' the name of a large tree); 'and so is his religion.' 'You are quite right, sir,' replied the Christian. 'Our Padre is indeed a tree; he is a banyan tree,—a tree with wide-spreading branches, whose fruit feeds many, many living creatures, and under whose boughs many a weary traveller of my description finds a cooling shade.'

Struck with astonishment at this unexpected answer, the Shāstri requested him to read the little tract in his hand entitled 'The Way of Salvation.' On his cheerfully complying with his demand, the Shāstri dismissed the man, politely remarking, 'That also is one way.'" *

Besides the direct and obvious fruits of the preaching of the Gospel and other evangelical instrumentalities in the conversion of individuals, the formation of Christian congregations and churches, and the introduction of Christian life into the community, there are great and important INDIRECT RESULTS of evangelical effort, of European education, and of the general enlightenment which is being gradually diffused throughout the country,—all, we hope, unitedly contributing to prepare the way for the ultimate universal reception of the Gospel.

Heathenism itself is not what it was ten, twenty, or thirty years ago. It is daily losing ground. Its vigour is diminished, its darkness less dense, its external character less abhorrent. The influence of the Brahmans and devil-dancers, and of their superstitions, is most decidedly and manifestly on the wane. Many fundamental truths of religion and morals are now well known and freely acknowledged by heathens, and even supposed to be component parts of their own systems; but they were evidently first made known or revived in their minds solely by the efforts of missionaries and the diffusion of European Christian learning.

We meet, too, with little active opposition to Christianity, and observe a marked change in the Brahmans and others, who now receive and peruse our tracts with pleasure, instead of exhibiting disgust and hatred as formerly. Many copies of portions of Scripture are purchased from the colporteurs employed under the auspices of the Bible Society. Some who were once determined enemies to Christianity now seem rather well disposed towards us.

* Rev. C. Yesudian's Report for 1865.

Many of the people have become acquainted with the character and claims of Christianity, and readily acknowledge its surpassing excellence, and the blessings it confers on mankind. *The conviction that Christianity is true, and that it shall and must prevail, appears to be gaining ground* amongst nearly all classes. As our divine religion becomes more widely known, it is, though not practically received by all, yet regarded with increasing respect, as exhibiting a high standard of morality, setting forth in the best possible manner the duties of man to man, and authoritatively inculcating doctrines, some of which are regarded as incontestably true and supremely important.

Numerous instances might be adduced in which religious impressions are made on the minds of high caste and educated Hindus. But the good seed is choked by worldly cares or riches, or by fear of the sharp trials, persecutions, and worldly losses to which persons of respectable position would inevitably be exposed by openly embracing Christianity. "It is all true," they admit, "there is but one God, the idols are but works of men; but what can a single person do, while all his relatives and friends are still addicted to heathenism?" Still, a few are known to be, in secret, prayerful readers of the word of life, and avowed believers in the Lord Jesus Christ. Several conduct family prayers in their own houses, when they read a chapter out of the Bible, and pray to the Christians' God. Some invite the mission agents to visit their houses and pray with them; while others, not quite so bold, will visit the catechist at his own house, and there unite with him in prayer. Some have even ventured to compose verses on the folly of idolatry and in praise of Jesus, a translation of a few of which, written last year, is given by Rev. C. Yesudian.

The following was composed by a learned Súdra in the neighbourhood of Tittuvilei, who kindly permitted Mr. Yesudian to carry on religious discussion in the court of his house :—

"'Tis a fun that people should buy
Lumps of stone and brass for money,
Should name them Siva and Sakthi,
Wash and perfume them thoroughly,
Deck them with jewels and garments,
Offer them rice, cakes, and plantains,
Ring bells and burn lamps before them,
Though they are lifeless, blind, and dumb."

By the same author, on another occasion :—

"We say our gods must in water be washed;
If so, how can our sin by them be cleansed?
Or how can they make our souls meet for heaven?
Let not your minds, by folly, be driven
To self-conceit, but bow before the Truth;
Let Jesus wash our souls from sin and filth."

We add one stanza more, which is the production of another Súdra :—

"Jesus is the Ladder to ascend heaven,
To cross the sea of sin the Life-boat given,
The best Inheritance that kings can hold,—
Gracious Jesus is the finest Gold."

I have no doubt that were it not for timidity and fear, and the opposition of relatives, several hundreds of the higher classes in Travancore are ready sincerely to embrace Christianity, of the truth of which they are already in heart convinced.

Much more, however, certainly requires to be done to bring the Gospel into contact with the minds of the higher castes; and especially of the new and rapidly increasing class of natives well educated in English, intelligent and inquiring in an intellectual point of view, and exemplary in general conduct. These appear, as a rule, to have lost confidence in the national superstitions, to be ashamed of idolatry, which some even venture openly to repudiate, and to recognise the truths of natural religion and the obligation of morality, though compelled by the force of circumstances outwardly to conform to Hinduism. The work of placing the claims of the Gospel before these minds would of itself fully occupy the time, and ultimately reward the efforts, of the most learned and laborious missionary.

The minds of many of the educated native youth are in a kind of transition state. They are unable to produce satisfactory objections to Christianity, yet unwilling to be persuaded of its truth. Conscious of the errors and absurdities of Hinduism, they are yet anxious to avoid trouble and annoyance by conforming, or appearing to conform, externally to its requirements. In this dilemma they are anxious to put the question aside, as one on which it is difficult to come to a decision. They say in effect, "Our religion is good enough for us, and we shall be no worse off than others if we but follow it sincerely. And the Christian religion is very good for those who profess it. Let us avoid discussion on this perplexing subject, for we shall never come to a satisfactory conclusion. In fulfilling social duties—acting honestly, uprightly, kindly—we are doing our best, and cannot be far wrong."

Apologies are sometimes made for Hinduism, which they seek to refine of its grossness, and to represent as similar in its real essence and spiritual purport to the Christian religion. May the educated natives of India soon be enlightened by the Spirit of God to distinguish between the forms of religion and its vital power—between false religions which deceive and destroy the soul, and that which alone is true, inspired, and divine!

The indirect and unacknowledged influence of Christian European learning on the higher ranks of Hindu society, in correcting the views of moral obligation, in expanding the intellect, in dissipating the grosser prejudices, and in preparing the way, we trust, for the triumph of divine truth, is patent to all who are acquainted with the present circumstances of Travancore. Take a very striking instance of this in his Highness the First Prince, brother of the Maharajah, and heir apparent to the throne.* The Prince speaks and writes English remarkably well, has published essays on "Beneficence," &c., in his native language (Malayālim), and is an excellent Sanskrit scholar. In December, 1865, he delivered at Trevandrum a lecture, in English, on "Human Greatness," at which the British Resident, the Bishop of Madras, the Dewān, and a large assembly of Europeans and educated natives were present. We were much gratified on this occasion by the correctness of the views enunciated, and the liberality of sentiment in referring to Wilberforce, Howard, Mrs. Fry, and Livingstone as examples of truly great persons. Indeed, the lecture was almost such as a Christian might deliver.

On another occasion, in a speech delivered at the examination of the High School at Trevandrum, in the presence of the late lamented Bishop Cotton, the Prince gave utterance to the following remarks :—

"Every object in this wonderful creation of God, whether within you or around you, is calculated to afford you that knowledge which teaches humility to man, and which also bids him to love and revere his beneficent Creator. That which I would urge on you more emphatically than anything else is the necessity of *moral* culture. A refined intellect without refined moral faculties cannot but be viewed with the greatest abhorrence and disgust. The deplorable fact that in India the uneducated portion of the people is notorious for mendacity and general depravity cannot be denied.

* See portrait in engraving opposite p. 68.

It is not scholastic tuition *alone* that can remove this evil. You should view the task of your moral improvement as a most sacred one; you should sincerely feel and desire to grow in the fear of God, the love of truth, of justice, and of universal charity."

The propriety and excellence of the sentiments here expressed we claim as the result of Christian and European influences, which are arousing and educating the conscience, and spreading right views of morals amongst the leaders of advanced native opinion in India.

I have heard, too, the Dewān of Travancore, Sir Mādava Row, a singularly able and liberal-minded Brahman, lecture in English, amongst other subjects, on "Astronomy." In the course of his address he stated that he had himself gone over and verified many of the calculations connected with the European system of astronomy, and could therefore assure his audience of their accuracy, and the consequent folly and futility of the common Hindu belief in astrology with its related superstitions, which he showed to be contrary to all the investigations and conclusions of true science, and which he urged them wholly to abandon.

What a remarkable scene was that!—a man of high rank and birth—one of the ablest native statesmen in South India—actually exhorting his countrymen to renounce their belief in one of the most popular, potent, and wide-spread superstitions of India. And what a contrast does this present with the former state of things in Travancore, when Christianity was persecuted, justice administered according to the prejudices and passions of the dominant class, and every possible obstruction brought to bear against the progress of enlightenment and Christianity!

The outward and visible changes which are taking place in this State through the introduction and operation of Christian agencies and impulses are patent to all, and are the subject of wonder and admiration even to the heathen. The beneficial effects of Christianity, as exemplified in the case of our Christian people, are a most lucid and comprehensible argument in its favour. This may be illustrated by an anecdote related by Mr. Yesudian. A Súdra in his district called out to a Brahman one day, "Sir, have you at all directed your attention to a wonder of the present age?" "A wonder?" the Brahman replied; "what is it?" To which the Súdra responded, "Don't you know, sir, first that the lightning struck the temple of Palpanābhan within the royal fort, and broke the sacred lamp? Then the holy car tumbled at Palpanābhapuram, and killed the Brahman lad. Thirdly, the lightning again descended on the revered temple at Tirupathisāram, and tore off the right ear of the god Vishnu. What should I say more? Listen: the Brahman is become a dealer in oil and fish, while the Shānar, or Pariah, goes about as a Brahman or teacher of the country. The Brahman woman spends her day in cooking, eating, and sleeping; while the Shānar or Pariah women are found in the streets with their Veda in their hands, pretending to teach their neighbours. Is not this a wonder? Indeed the world is turning upside down!"

CHAPTER XXIV.

DIRECT RESULTS OF MISSIONARY LABOURS IN TRAVANCORE.

Direct Results of Missionary Labour—Character of Native Christians—History of Remarkable Conversions—Testimonies of Native and European Authorities—Liberality of Converts—Self-Support of Native Churches—Need of Further Effort—Future Prospects of Christianity in Travancore.

In South Travancore, mission chapels, prayer-houses, and village schools are now scattered over the whole country. The sound of the church-going bell at the various villages at the hours of public worship will be heard; and our Christian converts, distinguished generally by their clean cloths on Sunday, and the decent jackets of the females, may be seen hastening to their places of worship. A large measure of external prosperity, at least, is at once perceived by every visitor to have attended the efforts of the Missionary Society. Let us endeavour to estimate the exact intrinsic value of these fruits of earnest toil.

Not all those whom we have hitherto spoken of in general terms as "native Christians" can be regarded as in the highest sense "Christian believers," nor have all been baptized. Of the 32,746 native "professing Christians" or "*adherents*," but 9,910 are baptized, and only 2,568 are church members or communicants. The unbaptized adherents, or professing Christians, are members of the congregations—regular and willing hearers and learners of God's word, and attendants on our ministry; in fact, catechumens.

They have given up their heathenism and immorality, and are under regular Christian instruction and discipline. They contribute towards the maintenance of the means of grace, and their names and attendance at public worship are carefully registered from week to week; they submit in every respect to the strict rules of the mission, and are called at times to endure persecution and trials for the name of Christ.

Although a much smaller proportion of our people are baptized and admitted into communion with the church than is usual in the adjoining missions of North Travancore and Tinnevelly, this is not, I apprehend, because our people are inferior in knowledge or sincerity to those alluded to, but because we administer baptism not to mere professors or learners of Christianity, but only to those who show by their lives and conduct, as far as we can judge of them during a lengthened probation, that they are actuated by love to Christ, and are living not merely in the practice of external morality and obedience to the requirements of Christianity, but in faith and holiness as true children of God. Were we prepared to administer baptism to the same class of persons as are admitted to this rite in other missions, the mass of our people would receive this holy ordinance with respect and joy. Most of the brethren prefer, however, by the present system to maintain the purity and high standard already set up for the churches committed to our care.

As might be expected, some of our hearers actually do, even after a period of Christian instruction, apostatize or backslide, or are led astray by evil influences. Choked by the thorns of worldliness, or scorched by the sun of temptation, plants which had promised well fade away and perish. Those who fall into immorality or sin, even though they continue to attend public worship, at once cease to be recognised as professing Christians, and their names are expunged from our congregational lists. They are no longer reckoned in the statistics of the mission. We are glad to see them present at divine service, and in company with the Lord's people, where they are still in the way of receiving good, but we do not consider them, as even in the very lowest sense, Christians until they have given up all known sin, and act in accordance with the laws of Christian morality and rectitude.

There are amongst the native professing Christians in India, as in every land and age, some who, though outwardly well conducted and attentive, and sincerely convinced of the truth and excellence of Christianity, are but hearers of the word, not doers of the same; who have the form of godliness, but manifest little or none of its power; who know the truth, but do it not; grudging in gifts, wavering in zeal, unreliable in temptation, negligent of spiritual duties, litigious, apathetic, worldly. Our constant prayer and effort for such is that they may be led to Christ, renewed in heart, and saved by divine grace. We instruct them in the great and vital doctrines of repentance toward God, and faith in our Lord Jesus Christ, as well as in the necessity of holiness in heart and life; and we trust that some are being, and many shall hereafter be, turned truly from darkness to light, and from the power of Satan unto God. We use the appointed means, planting and watering the seed, and look to the Holy Spirit to send the increase.

Very diverse accounts are given by different writers of the character of the native Christian converts in India. The fact is, there are two sides to this, as to most other subjects. A very dark picture might be drawn of the worst of those who call themselves Christians. Truthfully depict the excellences of the best of the Hindu Christians, and a lovely and attractive picture will be presented.

Of course those who have more recently come under instruction, as is the case of many in Travancore, are for some time very defective in their acquaintance with Christian doctrines and privileges. They are but babes in Christianity, and too much should not be expected from them.

There are many, again, of whose spiritual condition we can speak with little certainty. It is often difficult to decide (nor, indeed, do we attempt the task) how far the heart is really under divine and saving influences. Uneducated persons, unaccustomed to mental introspection, may be unable to state their spiritual experience in distinct and intelligent terms; yet they may love the Lord, and it is not our part to reject their credible profession of faith in Christ. Some are weak and fall into various temptations, yet we would hope they have, on the whole, a little spiritual strength. They are not unlike the members of the primitive churches founded by the apostles,—often possessing great excellences, yet requiring to be warned against falling into grievous sins. We would hope the best of these classes. We would not quench the smoking flax, nor break the bruised reed. We would compare them, not with what mature Christians ought to be and might be, but with what they were but lately,—devil-worshippers and slaves to the most degrading vices; and remembering the polluted moral atmosphere in which they live, and the hindrances to their spiritual life and growth, we would gladly acknowledge the progress which they are making in knowledge, purity, and strength; and trust that the good seed may be growing in their hearts, silently and slowly, but with irrepressible vigour and life.

On the other hand, many of our people, indeed the great body of our *church members*, are persons of whose Christian experience and life and genuine conversion we can bear our testimony with confidence, and whom we regard as true believers—children of God and inheritors of eternal life,—

and as our "crown and rejoicing in the day of the Lord." Information respecting some of the modes and variety of circumstances in which the providence and grace and Spirit of God unite in leading these to the knowledge of the truth will interest our readers.

1. Many of the *young* have, while attending our *mission schools*, been trained in the knowledge of Christian truth, and led to give their hearts to the Lord.

"Supeian, a little boy of the Kāttuputhúr school, on being asked by his father to accompany him to the rice-fields to perform the annual ceremony of sowing on the day fixed upon by the Sirkar, desired to know what he himself would have to do in the matter. The father replied that he would understand it on reaching the spot. He next bade him to wear the sacred ashes. The boy refused to do so. The father then forced it on his forehead with his own hand. Instantly the boy wiped off the ashes, telling him that he did not like his forehead to be thus soiled. So they came to the field. The father, amongst other ceremonies, set up a ball of cow-dung in representation of the god Ganesa, and seriously asked the boy to bow down before it to invoke a blessing upon their future crop. 'Father,' cried the boy, should I worship this cow-dung? How could we believe that a ball of cow-dung can bless us with a plentiful crop?' The father felt sorely vexed, and finding no proper reason to punish his only boy, he stood greatly perplexed."

"In the school at Kannakuritchi there is a boy whose father is a rich Alavan, and contributes one-third of the rice and money required for making offerings in the temple adjoining the schoolroom. One day this lad, seeing the door of the inner temple left open, entered within, took up a small stone image of Pilleiyār which stood in front of the large idol, ran away with it, and threw it into the tank. The schoolmaster asked him if it was true that he had done so.

He replied, 'Yes, sir, but I was only able to throw away the little one. I cannot lift the larger one; if I could I would throw that away also.' 'Are you not afraid to act thus?' 'No, for the idol has no life, it is nothing but stone, why should I be afraid of a stone?' 'Will not the people punish you?' 'What can they do? My father scolds me a little sometimes, but he will not beat me.' 'You say you are not afraid of the god; of whom, then, are you afraid?' 'I fear the Lord only.'"

Many similar instances are known, in which the children who are instructed in the mission schools have conscientiously declined to join in idolatrous ceremonies; and often have they been the means of leading their parents to reject idolatry, and unite themselves with the people of the Lord. In some instances, where the parents are utterly ignorant and illiterate, these dear children read a short portion of the Scriptures every evening, and offer their simple prayers with the parents at the family altar. Many of the young have been led to God in our schools, and some have died expressing their love to the Saviour, who has said, "Suffer little children to come unto Me, and forbid them not: for of such is the kingdom of heaven." These are now, we are sure, in the number of that great multitude of all nations, and kindreds, and people, and tongues, who stand before the throne and before the Lamb. Others have grown up and become godly, consistent, prayerful church members, teachers, and preachers of the Gospel to their fellow-countrymen. Some of our people are the grandchildren of the early converts, and exhibit in their life and character the influence of three generations of Christian teaching and privileges.

2. We have had many instances of persons who first commenced attendance on Christian worship from *inferior or even wrong motives*, but after instruction, eventually became earnest and sincere believers. Somewhat like those

who "came to mock, but stayed to pray;" they came because invited by the preacher, or induced by their friends and relatives, or by the heads of the village, to do so; or even with some undefined hope of gain, in the form of help under trials, protection from oppression, the friendship of the missionaries, or participation in the improvement in knowledge and outward circumstances which Christianity necessarily produces. Such was the case when in former times whole villages were brought over to Christianity, but we never thought of at once baptizing these, or receiving them as true converts.

One by one, as they seemed, through the blessing of the Holy Spirit, to come under the converting power of the grace of God, and to be sincerely actuated by Christian principles, they have individually been received to the enjoyment of Christian communion and church privileges.

3. The gracious *dealings of Providence* with the souls of men in leading them to turn their attention to spiritual subjects, have often been most evident and noteworthy. Individuals have, by singular combinations of circumstances, been led to listen to Christian instruction and exhortations. Sore trials have been the effective means, in the hand of God, of subduing the prejudices and softening the hearts of heathens; and we have been compelled to feel that the wise and wonder-working providence of God was on our side, and powerfully operative on behalf of His Gospel.

A respectable man was exhorted by a native teacher to receive the Gospel. "Shall I," answered he scornfully, "learn your Vedam? No, never;" and he turned away. Three days afterwards, when on his way to consult an astrologer, he passed a river, and accidentally falling in, was drowned. After this sad event his poor wife's heart was touched, and her conscience was aroused. She came with her children to the Christian teacher, asked to be taken under instruction, and they became regular attendants at the chapel.

Porutheiyudian, of Tiruvaram, was the patriarch of the Trevandrum mission, and at the time of his death, in 1860, was about 100 years old. Formerly he was a zealous devil-dancer and devotee. On one occasion he was seized with severe illness, and lay apparently at the point of death. He ordered additional offerings and sacrifices to be presented to the demons, but in vain: no relief to his sufferings was experienced. In this state he dreamed one night that a man approached, informing him that he should not die at this time, and advising him not to call upon *many* names, but upon *one name* alone, in which he should find salvation. This he regarded as a divine message. In the morning, feeling wonderfully recovered, he rose up, related his strange dream, and made inquiries as to what was meant by the "one name." That very day Mr. Mead visited the village. Porutheiyudian sent for him, made many inquiries about the way of salvation, and at once gave up his idolatry, and put his trust in the one name of the Lord Jesus Christ. He and his wife were baptized by Mr. Miller, and for nearly twenty-five years they walked faithfully as followers of Christ, and exercised a good influence on their own connections and neighbours. At the time of his death he spoke in an animated and collected manner of going to the presence of his Saviour. One of his sons is now elder of the same congregation, and another an able evangelist in the district of Quilon.

4. Others are led by the *disappointment of their hopes and expectations* from the observance of their own superstitions to inquire into and to accept the Christian religion.

"A noted devil-dancer was much sought after by the heathen in those parts, and he received a good deal of money for his advice and for performing ceremonies. The teacher sought to instruct him in the way of salvation for a period of five or six months, but he would not agree to anything that was said. One day, the catechist, hearing that his daughter was very ill, paid him a visit. As he entered the house he found the poor man wounded and bleeding, in the act of performing some religious ceremony. The folly of this was urged, but in vain. The next morning his daughter died. Then he was made to feel the worthlessness of his foolish rites. Hastening to the teacher, he begged him to bury his daughter in the Christian manner, and confessed his error in not having given heed to the advices which had been given him. He and all his followers became Christians."

The history of a native doctor, whom I had the pleasure of baptizing in 1866, is peculiarly interesting. His heathen name was Krishnan * (after a Hindu god), changed on his baptism to Paramānandam (heavenly bliss). He was then seventy years of age. When a heathen he possessed two temples of his own, in which he daily offered prayers and performed various ceremonies. He was well skilled in native medicine and heathen learning, sorcery, and charms. At first when the teachers visited him, he paid no attention to their words. But several years ago his wife was seized with a dangerous illness; he tried every means for her recovery; invoked his gods, and made costly offerings to them. But all was in vain, and his wife died. Thus he came to feel that his deities were unable to assist him in time of need, and he lost all confidence in them. Procuring a Bible he searched it daily with care, and was at last convinced; and accepted the God of the Christians as the true God. He joined the congregation, and though aged and infirm, is always most punctual and regular in attendance at worship. He prays much, and earnestly exhorts all to serve God. His sons are

* See pp. 196-7.

clever men, and inveterate enemies of Christianity. They took possession for a long time of all his property, depriving him even of his bed. He was reduced to such want that he once declared, "Had all these troubles come upon me when I was a heathen, I should have died through vexation and distress of mind. But God's word and prayer," added he "sustain my mind, and I look for happiness and spiritual riches in heaven above." He speaks with much humility of his own unworthiness, and of his trust in the Saviour. This man's conversion was regarded by all the people as almost miraculous.

5. The *kindness and skill of the medical missionary* and his assistants have in many instances secured a favourable hearing for divine truth, which has then made a lodgment in the heart, and brought individuals and families to the knowledge of the way of salvation.

A most interesting case of this kind is related by Dr Lowe, as follows:—

"An outdoor patient, a man of much influence and respectability, having many in his employment, was seized with a severe attack of rheumatic fever, and at his request, being too ill to be carried to the hospital, I visited him at his own house. Though dangerously ill, and his case considered hopeless by his native physicians and friends, the Lord blessed the means used for his recovery, and at the same time subdued his heart, and induced him, his wife, and several of his friends, to lend a willing ear to the truths of the Gospel.

"He was soon out of all danger, and with the exception of a stiff knee joint, which has since yielded to treatment, he made a slow but satisfactory recovery, and loud, and I believe sincere, were the proofs and expressions of gratitude which the patient and his friends showered upon us; but more pleasing than all such expressions of gratitude was a message we received from the patient, inviting me, my assistant missionary, and dressers, to come to his house on a certain day to receive from him his devil ornaments, cloths, and clubs, and to demolish a devil temple which he had lately built on his property, as he had no longer any confidence in his idols, and had resolved, along with his wife and several of his relatives, to join the Christian congregation in their village.

"We of course gladly accepted this invitation, and went to our patient's house, where we met with a cordial reception. Having gathered a goodly congregation within the court, we held a short religious service, and then set to work,—bearers, dressers, assistant missionary and myself; and with pickaxes, hatchets, and spades, worked like navvies till we had the devil temple level with the ground. Many poor superstitious heathens stood around, trembling with fear, and prophesying all kinds of evil; the patient's poor wife, too, was very nervous and fearful that some dreadful calamity would befall them that very night; but her husband was very bold, and from the cot on which he lay watching our work of demolition, he denounced the foolishness and vanity of his former confidences, and expressed his determination before all, almost in the language of Joshua, that henceforth 'as for me and my house, we will serve the Lord.'"

This man has since continued, with his whole family, very stedfast, and has been a great help to the catechist of the place in his work. He and his wife, with his elder brother and his wife's father, afterwards applied for admission to the church. Except Paramānandam himself, they were somewhat deficient in knowledge, but so sincere and earnest that they were at once received, and will, there is every reason to believe, prove a blessing to many around them.

6. Direct *conversions in answer to prayer*, and through the more immediate agency, we believe, of the Holy Spirit,

are not wanting in connection with our work. The facts of one case are recorded by Rev. W. Lee as follows :—

"In the village of Santhayādi, a rich heathen Shānar was a confirmed drunkard. On one occasion, when I went to the village, as a little child of his was being educated in our school, I called to see him. I found him locked up in one of the rooms of his house with his feet in fetters to restrain him from gratifying his frightful propensity for drink. I induced his sons to knock off the fetters, and come with him to the sanctuary. His case was made a subject for special prayer by the congregation, and he was induced to make a solemn promise that he would henceforth abstain from drinking. More than a year has elapsed since then; sufficient to test the reality of his reformation, and he has not even once yielded to temptation, and has continued regularly to attend the services of the sanctuary."

Another remarkable instance of the power of prayer is eloquently narrated by Rev. J. Duthie in the *Juvenile Missionary Magazine* for February and March, 1869, to which we must refer our readers, and from which the illustration on the next page is borrowed.

One of our native pastors was out on a preaching tour, accompanied by several Christian friends, when they came unexpectedly to a new and handsome temple, perched on the summit of a high rock, and just finished for the worship of Pattirakāli. The building was unoccupied, and not yet dedicated. In simple faith the Christian believers knelt down, and offered earnest and fervent prayers that this temple might become a house of God. Next morning they met a most venerable-looking old man with whom they entered into conversation, and soon discovered that he was the owner of the devil temple in which they had offered prayer. Confessing to the old man what they had done, they expressed their desires for his salvation, preached Jesus to him, and boldly urged him to relinquish his demon-worship, and decide at once for God. The word came with power to his heart: "The words I have heard from you are wonderful," said he; "the story of Jesus is indeed good; let us dedicate this house which I have built for *Pattirakāli* to the TRUE AND LIVING GOD." At once they proceeded to the temple, of which they took possession in the name of the Lord Jesus. The old man, now ninety-eight years of age wrote a deed transferring the building, upon which he had

DEVIL TEMPLE, NOW USED AS A MISSION CHAPEL.

spent a thousand fanams, to the mission; and it is now a house of God, crowded with worshippers, "whose fear of demons has been banished, and in whose hearts is the hope of heaven through Jesus Christ."

We cannot dwell at length upon the consistent life, the resolute resistance to temptation, the faith in God, the humility and submission under trials the zeal for the salvation of others, the liberality manifested by some of these Christians, nor describe in detail their peaceful and happy deaths. While we feel that we and our people greatly need the blessed reviving, quickening, and sanctifying influences of the Holy Spirit; and while we have often to mourn over the instability, weakness, defects, and falls of Christian professors, much might also be recorded of the bright side of their character. "The fruit of the Spirit is love, joy, peace, long suffering, gentleness, goodness, faith, meekness, temperance;" and each and all of these graces might be illustrated by specific examples, drawn from the lives of these Hindu converts.

The following gratifying testimonies from two very distinct quarters will indicate the estimation in which the Christian community is held by the most right-thinking and intelligent of their own Hindu countrymen, and by Europeans capable of forming an impartial and accurate judgment; other testimonies to the same effect respecting our work in Travancore are in the possession of the writer.

In reply to an address presented to the First Prince on 31st August, 1867, on the occasion of his visit to the Nāgercoil Seminary, his Highness observed:—

"The reception that you have given me this day will, I assure you, be long and endearingly remembered by me. The class to which you belong, and which you represent, viz., that of native Christians of South Travancore, has, as a rule, been characterized for loyalty, peaceableness, and moral worth, and as such it will not fail to be viewed with interest by me.

"The progress which you have made in your studies, as manifested this day, has much gratified me, and no less so is the discipline and general good deportment which is remarkedly observable in you. Continue to make the best possible use of the valuable gift of God, your own minds, and you may be sure that every inch of your progress will open out to you brighter and brighter prospects.

"I have only to wish you success in your education, and that every good may be yours which God in His infinite wisdom and in His immeasurable mercy may vouchsafe to you.

(Signed) "RAMAH VURMAH, First Prince of Travancore."

Again; on the occasion of the visit of his Excellency Lord Napier (of Merchiston), Governor of Madras, to Nāgercoil, in Oct., 1868, his lordship thus spoke:—

"I need not assure you that I have been deeply gratified by my visit to this numerous and flourishing community of Protestants, living in security and prosperity under the tolerant sway of an enlightened native prince, and under the guidance of zealous and benevolent pastors, who have dedicated their lives and energies to the prosecution of a holy cause. I have heard the record of your past exertions in promoting the evangelization, education, and industrial development of this people with the sincerest interest. I trust that the future may not be less prosperous than the past, and that your labours may be abundantly rewarded in the increase and welfare of those who commit themselves to your spiritual charge. You may be assured of the sympathy, and, if it were ever necessary, of the protection of the Government of Madras.

(Signed) "NAPIER."

The question of *liberality* in the support of Christian ordinances is one which, from its practical bearing upon the support of missions by friends at home, demands some notice. Our work in India, it is well known, has demanded, and will yet, we fear, require, a larger proportion of expenditure on native agency than in other parts of the world. But it should be remembered that in the South Sea Islands and Madagascar, and most other fields of labour, the people are homogeneous; and kings and nobles and the wealthier classes, as well as the common people, have received the Gospel, so that the Christian community have been able to provide for the support of their own native teachers. But in India, where the fearful system of Hindu caste, isolating class from class, prevails, a very small proportion of the higher ranks have united themselves to the Christian Church; and the small farmers, farm labourers, trades-people, and slaves, who constitute the body of native Christians, are as yet unable to support the ordinances and ministry of the Christian religion as both we and they would desire. Hence the necessity for the support of native teachers in India in connection with all the missionary societies.

Still it is reasonable and necessary, as well as desirable, that the expenditure of European funds on the instruction of native Christian converts should be reduced to a minimum, by the latter contributing, according to their ability, for the incidental expenses of Christian worship and the support of native pastors and teachers. This is just what we have been teaching them to do. During the year 1869, over £20,000 were raised and expended at the mission stations of the London Missionary Society in various parts of the world, the larger portion of which was contributed by native converts. And in Travancore we have endeavoured continuously and steadily to train our native churches to independency of action and feeling, and to liberality in the support of Christian ordinances.

In estimating the contributions of native Christians, the relative value of money should be taken into account. The rate of pay of a labouring man in Travancore is now about 5 chuckrams = 4¼d. per day, about ten shillings per month—not a great sum with which to meet all demands,—

and many of our poorer Christians receive no larger income; yet they contribute readily in money and kind according to their ability—on the whole, perhaps, in larger proportion than most Christians in England.

Occasionally large contributions are made by the wealthier members of our congregations. In 1867 one of our native Christians, Nathaniel, a silk-weaver and deacon of Nāgercoil church—a very remarkable man, who speaks of the great salvation by Jesus Christ to every person, I believe, whom he meets—contributed 700 rupees for the erection of a single chapel. He bore the whole expense of its erection, and it stands in a position highly favourable for the preaching of the Gospel to thousands of pilgrims and visitors to Cape Comorin and Suchindram.

Others present plots of land as sites for mission chapels, or bring contributions of rice during harvest season, and of sugar, cotton, and other produce of their industry, or articles of property. Some of the women are accustomed to lay aside a handful of rice as a contribution to the Lord's work every time they cook a meal of food.

I have seen amongst these poor black Christians what I have never witnessed in England. I have known them take off rings, bracelets, and other ornaments of silver and gold, and place them in the plate when they were desirous to contribute more than they could afford in the form of money.

On one occasion, an account of the extraordinary liberality and zeal of the Nestorian Christians in the cause of the Gospel was read at the monthly missionary prayer meeting at Nāgercoil. "During the reading of the paper a very powerful impression seemed to be made upon the meeting. The person who conducted the meeting was himself also much moved by the intelligence then given, and proceeded to address the people on the necessity of greater self-denial and liberality, and called upon them to make special efforts to support their own catechist without delay. It was a word spoken in season. On finishing his speech he took from his finger a gold ring; and, placing it on the table before him with great emphasis, said, 'This is my contribution—those willing to consecrate of their substance to the Lord, let them come forward.' The silence that followed was broken by one and another moving towards the pulpit, some with donations of money, others with jewels taken from their persons, after the example set by the speaker. But the people generally did not come prepared for anything so unprecedented and sudden as this, and the scene that followed was a very remarkable one. The majority having nothing to offer in the way of money or other valuables just then, the entire congregation dispersed to their respective houses, and having gathered together jewels and ornaments of various descriptions, earrings, turbans, cloths kept for special occasions, brass cups, cocoa-nuts, lamps, umbrellas, a cow, and various other articles, the value of which amounted to 117 rupees, it was resolved by the people themselves that this sum should be appropriated towards the support of the catechist. Their example had a powerful influence for good upon the surrounding congregations."

The churches at Nāgercoil, Neyoor, Dennispuram, &c., are now either wholly or to a great extent self-supporting. The native contributions have been rising from year to year, and in 1869 amounted to no less than 12,047 rupees, or £1204 14s.; a sum practically equal in value to £7,000 or £8,000 contributed by English Christians.

Such are some of the results, very succinctly and certainly very imperfectly stated, of the preaching of the Gospel and of missionary operations in Travancore. Surely we have reason, in the review of the whole subject, to "thank God and take courage." But let it not be imagined that the country is now Christianized, and that little remains to be effected. We have tried throughout this work to present to our readers both sides of the question—a comprehensive though necessarily very condensed view of the entire field. On the one hand, we have, it is true, nearly 33,000 native professing Christians under instruction, besides some 13,000 in connection with the Church Missionary Society; but what are these amongst *a million* of idolaters and devil-worshippers, still unenlightened and unsaved? There is still a great work to be done for the conversion of the higher classes and the general enlightenment and reformation of the country. Moreover, the conversion of the Shānars, Pariahs, and Pulayars has rather tended to set the higher castes in opposition to the Gospel, and has placed additional difficulties in our way.

The mission, having had of late years to struggle with sudden and severe retrenchments, is in several respects rather going back than otherwise, as evidenced by recent reports of the missionaries. Drought, famine, and cholera have again appeared in the South of Travancore. More European labourers are required—additional native agents—special efforts for special classes of the population, and continuous, loving, patient care in the training of the native churches and congregations. "The harvest truly is plenteous, but the labourers are few; pray ye therefore the Lord of the harvest, that He will send forth labourers into His harvest." "Let us not be weary in well doing: for in due season we shall reap, if we faint not."

In conclusion, we who have personally engaged in the work, and are acquainted with its history and details, have no doubt as to the ultimate result of this blessed and glorious undertaking. We engage in this warfare certain of victory. We sow the seed of life, assured by the Divine promise of an abundant harvest. God is working by His Spirit and His word. Providence is on our side, overruling evil, and favouring the progress of good. We trust in the power of God's truth to save—of the blood of Jesus to cleanse the vilest and most polluted—of the Holy Spirit to convert and save the most hardened and obstinate sinners.

In Travancore we see fields white already to the harvest. The night is far spent—the long, dark, cheerless night of idol-worship, devil-worship, and serpent-worship, of Hindu philosophical speculation and unbelief—is far spent, and the day—the glad and joyful day of Gospel light and privileges—is at hand. We look forward with hope, confidence, and joy to the time when Travancore shall be wholly Christianized, and every blessing—material, intellectual, and social, as well as spiritual—shall follow in the train of religion.

We rejoice to picture to ourselves the period when the material resources of that rich and beautiful country shall be developed, when manufactures shall be introduced, and national commerce and intercourse with other countries be widened and extended—and all consecrated to Christ; when the talents and energies of the rulers and statesmen, the poets and historians, now devoted to the service of false gods, shall be imbued with revealed truth, and used to the glory of God and the highest good of man; when woman shall occupy her due position in society, and the marriage relationship be sanctified and honourable in every home; when caste feeling shall be qualified and turned into attachment to law and order—the rich kindly to the poor, and the poor affectionate and grateful towards the great and wealthy; when the various castes and peoples of India shall be fused into one great people, exemplifying as a whole the various excellences which even now glimmer forth in particular classes—the commanding intellect of the Brahmans, the shrewdness and business capacity of the Súdras, the humble laboriousness of the Shānars and

Pulayars, the self-denial and devotion of the ascetics, the simplicity and hospitality of the hill tribes, the indomitable vigour and courage of the Mohammedans; when the religiousness and liberality now evinced in the support of the temples and worship of false gods, and the punctual attendance on religious festivals, shall become true holiness and practical piety; when kings shall be nursing fathers and their queens nursing mothers to the church.

Then shall Travancore indeed be what she is now fancifully denominated by her people, *Tiru-vārung-kodu*—the Sacred, Prosperous Kingdom; *Vanji Bhúmi*—the Treasure Land; DHARMMA BHUMI—the Land of PIETY, CHARITY, and TRUTH.

THE END.